This publication has been supported by a subvention from the Gustave Reese Publication Endowment Fund of the American Musicological Society.

The publisher gratefully acknowledges the generous contribution to this book provided by the Music in America Endowment Fund of the University of California Press Associates, which is supported by a major gift from Sukey and Gil Garcetti, Michael Roth, and the Roth Family Foundation.

CAPTURING SOUND

CAPTURING SOUND

HOW TECHNOLOGY HAS CHANGED MUSIC

mark katz

UNIVERSITY OF CALIFORNIA PRESS   BERKELEY   LOS ANGELES   LONDON

University of California Press
Berkeley and Los Angeles, California

University of California Press, Ltd.
London, England

Library of Congress Cataloging-in-Publication Data

Katz, Mark, 1970–.
Capturing sound : how technology has changed music / Mark Katz.
p. cm.
Includes bibliographical references and index.
ISBN 0-520-24196-7 (cloth : alk. paper)—
ISBN 0-520-24380-3 (pbk. : alk. paper)
1. Sound recording industry.   2. Music and technology.   I. Title.

ML3790.K277 2005
781.49—dc22   2004011383

Manufactured in the United States of America
14 13 12 11 10 09 08 07 06
12 11 10 9 8 7 6 5 4

We must expect great innovations to transform the entire technique of the arts, thereby affecting artistic invention itself and perhaps even bringing about an amazing change in our very notion of art.

PAUL VALÉRY

A recording is one thing, a concert is another, and never the twain shall meet.

JOHN PFEIFFER

The machine is neither a god nor a devil.

H. H. STUCKENSCHMIDT

CONTENTS

ACKNOWLEDGMENTS

The author's spouse is traditionally acknowledged "last but not least." But in my book, Beth Jakub comes first, for there is no one to whom I am more indebted. For more than a decade she has read nearly every draft of everything I have written on this subject, and has never failed to give an honest and perceptive critique, even if I might have preferred otherwise. But Beth has been much more than an excellent editor. Her genuine interest in this topic, her faith in me, and her unflagging support quelled my doubts and buoyed my spirits throughout this long process. I cannot imagine getting to this point without her.

Like Beth, William DeFotis was with me at the beginning. Sadly, he could not see me through to the end. Bill, a composer, conductor, clarinetist, scholar, and professor at the College of William and Mary, supervised my undergraduate thesis, the project in which I first explored the ideas behind *Capturing Sound*. He was a generous and kind mentor, and it is absolutely clear that I would not have become a musicologist were it not for him. After a long struggle with multiple sclerosis, he died in February 2003. His last moments were spent listening to a recording of Mahler's Symphony no. 9; I consider this his last lesson to me about the power of music and recording.

Over the course of this project, three schools were home to me, first as a student and now as a professor; at each, my work benefited from many people. At the College of William and Mary, in addition to Bill DeFotis, Katherine Preston and George Harris advised me on my thesis and kept up the conversation long after I left Williamsburg. At the University of Michigan, my dissertation committee—James Borders, Andrew Mead,

Kendall Walton, Glenn Watkins, Roland John Wiley, and especially my advisor, Richard Crawford—shepherded me through the doctoral program, helping me become a better thinker, writer, and musician. I finished *Capturing Sound* while a member of the musicology faculty at the Peabody Conservatory of Johns Hopkins University. Special thanks go to my colleague John Spitzer, who read the entire manuscript and provided valuable feedback; Director Robert Sirota and Dean Wolfgang Justen, who helped fund my research and the production of the accompanying CD; Sean Finn, who mastered the CD; Aeja Killworth, my research assistant, and the staff of the Arthur Friedheim Library. And I really cannot say enough to thank the scores of students who, perhaps without realizing it, shaped, challenged, and enriched my work; I sometimes wonder who really teaches whom.

One of the real joys of this project is that I have gotten to meet many of the people I have written about, among them some truly gifted performers, composers, producers, and impresarios. They include Yehudi Menuhin, Camille Yarbrough, Norman Cook, Paul Lansky, A-Trak, I.Emerge, Sugarcuts, Supa Dave, Rob Swift, the members of Rotoglow, John Pfeiffer, and Christie Z-Pabon. It is after meeting and talking with these people that I often find it hard to believe that I actually get paid to do what I do.

A variety of scholars—many of whom I am pleased to call friends—have generously shared with me their time and expertise, and have acted as guinea pigs, sounding boards, advocates, and devil's advocates. I hope the following is not too incomplete a list: Tamar Barzel, Amy Beal, Hans-Joachim Braun, Mark Clague, Jennifer DeLapp, Martin Elste, Patrick Feaster, Judith Fiehler, Kyra Gaunt, David Gramit, Ellie Hisama, Susan Schmidt Horning, William Howland Kenney, Ralph Locke, Andre Millard, Felicia Miyakawa, Robert Osberg, Timothy Taylor, Mark Tucker, Paul Wiebe, and Amanda Winkler. Will Crutchfield, whom I met only recently, deserves special mention, for it was his 1990 *New York Times* article "Historical Playing Styles: Myth and Reality" that first sparked my thinking about what I later came to call phonograph effects.

It has been a great pleasure to work with the University of California Press over the past several years. Former music editor Lynne Withey, who has since become director of the Press, approached me when I was still a student, and encouraged me from the start. Mary Francis, Lynne's successor, has been a wonderful editor—attentive, sympathetic, and insightful. I am particularly fortunate that Mary is also a fine musicologist, and this book is all the better for it. Moreover, Mary was able to secure four thoughtful and sharp-eyed readers both inside and outside the Press—Christopher Burns, Scott Norton, Jack Talbott, and Philip Yampolsky—all of whom offered constructive feedback on the manuscript in its various stages. The final stages of this process were aided by the excellent editing, proofreading, and indexing of Kitty Allen, Anne Canright, Stephanie Fay, and Erin Marietta.

Some of the material in this book has been published in earlier versions. My thanks to the University of Illinois Press, Wolke, and Taylor and Francis for permission to adapt "Making America More Musical through the Phonograph, 1900–1930," *American Music* 16 (1998): 448–75; "Aesthetics out of Exigency: Violin Vibrato and the Phonograph," in *I Sing the Body Electric: Music and Technology in the Twentieth Century,* ed. Hans-Joachim Braun (Hofheim, Ger.: Wolke, 2000), 186–97; and "Hindemith, Toch, and *Grammophonmusik,*" *Journal of Musicological Research* 20 (2001): 161–80.

Finally, I gratefully acknowledge my family for their love, support, and tolerance. I mention tolerance because from an early age I tested the effects of recording on them, simultaneously testing the limits of their patience. On long car rides I often got to hold the family's little tape recorder, and because I liked classical music (a good thing, it was thought) I was allowed to play my favorite pieces over and over and over again. And I did so, not only because I liked the music, but because I knew full well that it drove my sister and brothers crazy. I just hope *Capturing Sound* shows them that my interest in music and recording was not born *completely* out of spite.

INTRODUCTION

Several years ago a friend asked me to explain the subject of this book, then in its early stages of development. Opting for a dramatic approach, I pulled a CD at random from a nearby shelf and brandished it in front of me. "This," I declared, "has changed the way we listen to, perform, and compose music." My friend squinted at the CD, gave me a quizzical look, and asked, "*That* did?" "Yes!" I answered with gusto. Seeming unconvinced, he clarified his question. "*Van Halen* changed the way we listen to, perform, and compose music?"

Maybe, but that was not my point. My claim was that the technology of sound recording, writ large, has profoundly transformed modern musical life. At its broadest, that is the thesis of *Capturing Sound*.

This thesis may at first seem counterintuitive. After all, the function of recording, or so it might seem, is to *record* music, not to change it. Indeed, for more than a century, what I would call a discourse of realism has reinforced the idea of recorded sound as the mirror of sonic reality, while at the same time obscuring the true impact of the technology. Consider the series of television and print ads from the 1970s and 1980s in which the voice of jazz great Ella Fitzgerald was shown shattering glass.

While a feat in itself, more remarkable was that it was Fitzgerald's *recorded* voice that had such awesome power. Though the purpose of the ad campaign was to sell cassettes, it also espoused the ideal of realism. "Is it live, or is it Memorex?" consumers were asked. The implicit answer was that the two were indistinguishable.

Memorex was not the first to make such a claim. Turn-of-the-century advertisements touted recordings as "lifelike," "a true mirror of sound," "natural," and "the real thing."[1] In the 1910s and 1920s the Victor Talking Machine Company ran ads that would make an ontologist's head spin: beneath illustrations of famous artists standing next to their records, captions proclaimed: "Both are Caruso," or "Heifetz is actually Heifetz."[2] Like Memorex, Victor and its competitors were in the business of selling sound, and it behooved the industry to convince consumers that the tiny grooves incised in the black discs could somehow capture the essence of their flesh-and-blood musical idols. As Oscar Wilde once remarked in a very different context, "What a fuss people make about fidelity!"[3]

The discourse of realism is not limited to marketing campaigns. Musicians and scholars, too, have long testified to the objectivity of recordings. Igor Stravinsky averred that "a recording is valuable chiefly as a mirror," one that allowed him to "walk away from subjective experience and look at it."[4] Jaap Kunst, one of the pioneers of ethnomusicology, argued that his discipline "could never have grown into an independent science if the gramophone had not been invented. . . . Only then," he claimed, "was it possible to record the musical expressions of foreign peoples objectively."[5] Similarly, Robert Philip, author of the important study *Early Recordings and Musical Style,* argued that "we do not have to conjecture about how Elgar or Rachmaninoff or Stravinsky or Bartók performed their own works," for through recordings "we *know* how they performed them."[6] Unlike in the advertising slogans, no ulterior motives seem to lurk behind these statements. Certainly, we cannot dismiss the documentary value of recordings, for they tell us a great deal about the musical practices of the past. But such language ignores a crucial point: that recorded sound is *mediated* sound. It is sound mediated through a technology that requires its users to adapt their musical practices and habits in a variety of ways.

I should say that I am hardly the first to realize that recording does more than record.[7] What I am offering here is to expand the discussion by focusing on *how* and *why* recording influences musical life. I do this through the concept of the phonograph effect.[8]

Simply put, phonograph effects are the manifestations of sound recording's influence. Consider a straightforward example. When Igor Stravinsky composed his Serenade for Piano in 1925, he wrote the work so that each of the four movements would fit the roughly three-minute limit of a ten-inch, 78-rpm record side. "In America I had arranged with a gramophone firm to make records of some of my music," he explained in his autobiography. "This suggested the idea that I should compose something whose length should be determined by the capacity of the record. And that is how my *Sérénade en LA pour Piano* came to be written."[9] Stravinsky was not alone. Many composers of classical and especially popular music followed a similar compositional approach. (Today's three-minute pop song is a remnant of this practice.) Stravinsky's decision to tailor his Serenade to the length of the record side is a clear manifestation of recording's influence. It is just one of countless phonograph effects, ranging from the obvious—jogging while listening to Wagner on a Walkman, a pop star harmonizing with herself on disc—to the more subtle changes in the way we speak and think about music in an age of recording technology.

Though I say that recording influences musical activity, I am not espousing technological determinism, particularly what some scholars refer to as hard determinism.[10] This is the idea that tools, machines, and other artifacts of human invention have unavoidable, irresistible consequences for users and for society in general. The idea pervades the way we talk about technology. In their book on the subject, Leo Marx and Merritt Roe Smith cite several common examples: "'The automobile created suburbia.' 'The robots put the riveters out of work.' 'The Pill produced a sexual revolution.'"[11] Further examples come quickly to mind: "TV has restructured the daily life of the family," "Photography has altered the way we look at the world," or more grandly, "The computer has changed everything."

I myself write of recording's *influence* on human activity and of phonograph *effects,* both of which impute causal powers to technology. Although we often respond to technology within a context of limited options not of our own making, we must remember that in the end, recording's influence manifests itself in *human* actions. Put another way, it is not simply the technology but the relationship between the technology and its users that determines the impact of recording. It is important to add, too, that the influence I describe does not flow in one direction only, from technology to user. As we will see throughout this book, users themselves transform recording to meet their needs, desires, and goals, and in doing so continually influence the technology that influences them.[12]

If the impact of recording manifests itself in the actions of its users, what exactly are they responding to? The answer leads to a central premise of this book: all phonograph effects are ultimately responses to differences between live and recorded music. It is not enough to compare the two solely in value-laden terms, as is often the case. While some say that CDs sound better or are more aesthetically satisfying than live concerts, and others insist exactly the opposite, such arguments tell us little about the impact of the technology. Instead of asking which is better, the more revealing question is this: How are live and recorded music *different?*

To answer this question we must realize that any broadly used technology is intimately connected to another existing technology, system, or activity. The automobile, for example, serves transportation—obviously, an existing human activity—and must be understood in relation to other means of transportation, such as the bicycle or the horse. Conversely, an utterly novel technology—one that does not relate to any existing way of doing things—would be useless. A device to prevent time-travel sickness would (at least at the moment) have little impact on human life. Essentially, then, the impact of any new technology, whether the "horseless carriage" or sound recording, arises from the differences between it and that which it supersedes, improves upon, or extends and—crucially—the way users respond to those differences. For example, one difference between the horse and the car is that the car (at least by a certain point in its development) could travel faster and farther than the horse. Particularly in the United States, this difference allowed car owners to work in cities while residing in the country. It would not be a stretch, therefore—however odd this may sound—to see the growth of American suburbia in the 1940s and 1950s in part as a large-scale response of the middle class to an attribute of the automobile not shared by the horse.[13]

This model of technological influence applies equally well to recording. We may thus understand the Stravinsky example as a response to an aspect of recording technology (the limited playing time of 78s) that distinguished it from traditional musical activity (live performance, in which there is no similar time limitation). Of course, when one recording technology coexists with or supersedes another, users may respond to differences between the two systems. The concept of the phonograph effect is equally applicable here, for we simply shift our focus to a comparison of the two technologies. Indeed, later in this book we will see how the impact of the cassette tape on the one hand, and MP3 on the other, can be traced to their respective differences from LPs and CDs.

Several key differences between live and recorded music come up over and again. When performed live, musical sound is fleeting, evanescent. Recordings, however, capture these fugitive sounds, tangibly preserving them on physical media, whether wax cylinders or plastic CDs. Once musical sound is reified—made into a thing—it becomes transportable, salable, collectable, and manipulable in ways that had never before been possible. And like Billy Pilgrim in Kurt Vonnegut's *Slaughterhouse-Five,* recorded sound comes unstuck in time. No longer temporally rooted, recorded music can be heard after it was originally performed and repeated more or less indefinitely. The dead can speak to the living; the march of time can be halted. As I will explain throughout the book, the distinctive aspects of recorded sound have encouraged new ways of listening to music, led performers to change their practices, and allowed entirely new musical genres to come into existence.

To define phonograph effects in terms of technological traits and users' actions, however, is not to dismiss the influence of other, less easily isolated factors. The way users respond to recording is also shaped by personal, aesthetic, economic, and cultural forces. To return to the Stravinsky example, we should see that his actions might also have been shaped by his penchant for self-imposed limitations. In the first of his Three Pieces for String Quartet (1914), for example, the first violin plays only four different pitches, yet the result is impressively complex; his piano piece *The Five Fingers* (1921) is comparably constrained. Stravinsky imposed a similar challenge when he decided to keep each movement of his Serenade under three minutes. Business considerations also helped shape the work. The even number of movements was in part dictated by the fact that record companies were loath to issue a set of 78s with a blank side, since they could not charge as much for such a set. Thus, while phonograph effects arise from the ways in which users interact with recording as a distinctive medium, this interaction is itself shaped by both broader and narrower considerations, whether social forces or personal concerns.

While Stravinsky's compositional approach to his Serenade is a clear and well-documented example of a phonograph effect, it can hardly communicate the full scope of recording's influence since the late nineteenth century. Thus this book has been conceived broadly, ranging across time, space, and genre. It also engages a broad spectrum of users. Although I have called on Stravinsky to introduce my thesis, I am no fan of the "great man" approach to history. For every Armstrong, Copland, and Heifetz in this book, there is a schoolteacher, amateur DJ, or teenaged MP3 junkie whose response to recording technology is just as interesting and just as important to our understanding of phonograph effects.

Capturing Sound is divided into eight chapters. Chapter 1 stands apart from the rest; focusing on *causes,* it explores the nature of sound recording and the distinctive qualities that make the phonographic experience unique. The remaining chapters investigate specific phonograph *effects,* comprising seven case studies that progress more or less chronologically from the early twentieth century to the early twenty-first. Chapter 2 tells of how the phonograph became a central figure in the movement to elevate American musical life (and improve life more generally) in the early 1900s through the dissemination of recorded classical music. We stay in the United States for chapter 3 as well, which explores how both the possibilities and limitations of early recording technology shaped nearly every aspect of jazz performance and composition. Jazz musicians were not the only ones who responded to the demands of recording, however; in chapter 4 I argue that classical violinists in the early twentieth century responded to similar technological demands by intensifying and expanding their use of vibrato. Classical composers are the focus of chapter 5, which revisits the avant-garde musical scene of the 1920s and 1930s in Europe to uncover a forgotten fascination with the phonograph as a compositional tool. The final three chapters bring us to the turn of the twenty-first century. Chapter 6 is the result of fieldwork in the world of hip-hop DJ battles, competitions in which musicians display their virtuosity not with traditional instruments but on turntables. Chapter 7 delves into a compositional practice that simply could not have existed without sound recording—digital sampling—and addresses some of the aesthetic and ethical issues that arise from this new form of musical borrowing. Finally, chapter 8 provides a modern counterpart to chapter 2 and examines another technology freighted with utopian hopes—the Internet—and its impact on the modern musical listener.

The study of sound recording and its influence does not converge on a single work, figure, or musical activity. Rather, the technology is a hub from which the varied manifestations of its influence radiate. What do Paul Hindemith's *Grammophonmusik* and Public Enemy's "Fight the Power" have in common? Fritz Kreisler's violin playing and Bix Beiderbecke's trumpet playing? The musical memory contests of the 1920s and the Napster phenomenon of the 1990s? Collectively, their only point of intersection is recording. The broad scope of this work, then, permits the idea of the phonograph effect to be applied as widely as possible. Yet this book does not aim to be exhaustive. Of necessity, I have been selective in my choice of case studies, and the fact that this book engages mostly (though by no means exclusively) Western popular and classical music reflects my expertise, not the idea that little else merits study. In fact, there is a whole world of phonograph effects waiting to be studied. My hope is that this book will encourage further exploration of the technology's impact on musical life and become part of a rich and continuing discussion.

CAUSES

Anytown, U.S.A., 1905: a family and several neighbors stand in the parlor of a modest home, staring with equal parts curiosity and skepticism at
one of the technological marvels of the day. Staring back at them is the
unblinking eye of a megaphone-shaped brass horn. It protrudes about two
feet from a small wooden cabinet with a crank on one side and a felt-cov-
ered metal plate on top. The marvel is a phonograph, or "talking machine,"
as it was commonly called.[1]

The gentleman of the house takes a heavy black disc, grooved on one
side and smooth on the other, and places it over the spindle with the label
facing up. He turns the crank several times, gingerly sets the needle on
the outermost groove, and hurries back to his chair. Everyone stares at
the phonograph in eager anticipation. The disc spins quickly, and above
the whooshing and crackling the machine begins to sing. It sounds to
them like actual voices and instruments, albeit in miniature. It is hard to
believe that little more than a needle and a record can bring the performers
to life, just as if they were right there in the parlor.

After three minutes of rapt attention, the small audience breaks into
spontaneous, unselfconscious applause and calls for more. Before the man

can replay the record, a small child runs to the machine, peering under the table and jumping up to look into the horn. Everyone laughs when it becomes clear that the boy is looking for the musicians! After each record is played several times, the crowd disperses, with everyone wondering if wonders will never cease.[2]

This quaint vignette may seem unremarkable, but it reveals a revolution in the making. Those gathered around the phonograph were experiencing music in ways unimaginable not so many years before. They were hearing performers they could not see and music they could not normally bring into their homes. They could listen to the same pieces over and again without change. And *they* ultimately decided what they were to hear, and when, where, and with whom. All of this was made possible by the distinctive characteristics of sound recording technology. This is a crucial point, for as I explained in the introduction, if we understand the nature of recording, we can understand how users have adapted to, compensated for, and exploited the technology. It is in these actions that we discover the influence of recording; it is here that we find phonograph effects.

Each of the following seven sections examines a distinctive and defining trait of sound recording technology. This chapter is intentionally broad, moving quickly and often between written and oral musical cultures, East and West, popular and classical, the late nineteenth century and the early twenty-first. Such breadth is imperative, for the impact of recording is strongly shaped by the time, place, and context in which the technology is used. As we will see, phonograph effects are not simply technological phenomena.

TANGIBILITY

Before even setting needle to groove, the operator of the phonograph in that Anytown parlor encountered one of the most remarkable characteristics of recorded sound: its tangibility. Taking the disc out of its paper sleeve, he held the frozen sound in his hands, felt the heft of the shellac, saw the play of light on the disc's lined, black surface. He was holding a radically new type of musical object, for whereas scores prescribe or describe music, and instruments generate music, recordings preserve actual sounds.

This tangibility has allowed extraordinary changes in the way music can be experienced. Prior to the invention of the phonograph, Karl Marx observed what must have seemed to be an unchangeable truth about music. "The service a singer performs for me," he noted, "satisfies my aesthetic need, but what I consume exists only in an action inseparable from the singer, and as soon as the singing is over, so too is my consumption."[3] When sound is recorded and preserved in a physical medium, however, the listener's consumption need not end when the singing is over, for the music can be separated from the performer and be replayed without the artist's consent. Indeed, the portability and repeatability of recorded sound—two of the technology's crucial attributes to be discussed in this chapter—derive from its tangibility. Yet tangibility is not simply a "meta-trait." In itself the material preservation of sound—"the stockpiling of music," in Jacques Attali's arresting phrase—deeply influences the consumption and production of music.[4] To illustrate this point I want to explore briefly the impact of recording's tangibility as revealed in, first, record collecting and, second, the physical characteristics of cassettes and compact discs.

As Evan Eisenberg has pointed out, "For the listening public at large, in every century but this one [now two], there was no such thing as collecting music."[5] Certainly, enthusiasts sought out instruments, manuscripts, program books, autographs, and the like. Record collecting, however, represents a new relationship with music, for these collectors seek neither the means to create sound nor mementos of it, but sound itself.

This new relationship is most vividly illuminated in its pathological extremes. Record collecting has long been described (affectionately, for the most part) as an illness or addiction. In 1924 the British magazine *Gramophone* playfully warned of "gramomania," alerting readers to its "insidious approach, its baneful effects, its ability to destroy human delights."[6] Two years later, on the other side of the Atlantic, the *Phonograph Monthly Review* asked readers to recount their most dire sacrifices in the name of grooved shellac. One contestant, with the self-deprecating pseudonym "Adam Pfuhl," spun a woeful tale of spending all the money for his family's Christmas presents on records; another told of literally selling his shirt to support his habit.[7] Appropriately—or perhaps not—the winning contestants received gift certificates for records. Nick Hornby's 1995 novel *High Fidelity* demonstrates that the disease is far from eradicated. Rob, the owner of a second-hand record shop and a passionate collector of pop music discs, sympathetically observes the habits of his more obsessive customers:

> You can spot the vinyl addicts because after a while they get fed up with the rack they are flicking through, march over to a completely different section of the shop, pull a sleeve out from the middle somewhere, and come over to the counter; this is because they . . . suddenly sicken themselves with the amount of time they have wasted looking for something they don't really want. I know that feeling well: . . . it is a prickly, clammy, panicky sensation, and you go out of the shop reeling. You walk much more quickly afterward, trying to recapture the part of the day that has escaped.[8]

In the world of hip-hop, hunting for LPs is known as "digging in the crates," a reference to the way in which discs are typically stored and displayed in second-hand stores and thrift shops. As we will see in chapter 6, digging is a way of life among hip-hop DJs, for their creativity is judged in part on their ability to find rare, unusual, and catchy tracks. The 1992 rap song "Diggin' in the Crates," by Showbiz and A.G., makes it clear that this activity is as addictive as any form of collecting: "Buying old records is a habit/You know I've got to have it."[9] The darker side of this addiction comes out in Pearl Jam's 1994 rocker "Spin the Black Circle," in which a phonograph stylus is like a hypodermic needle and the act of playing an LP parallels the ritual of shooting up heroin.[10]

Such addictions are directly connected to the materiality of recorded music, for it is often the physical artifacts themselves, more than the sound of the music, that collectors find meaningful. In speaking of his records, *High Fidelity*'s Rob explains: "This is my life, and it's nice to be able to wade in it, immerse your arms in it, touch it."[11] To be sure, record collecting involves more than music. Collecting is about the thrill of the hunt, the accumulation of expertise, the display of wealth, the synesthetic allure of touching and seeing sound, the creation and cataloging of memories, and the pleasures (and dangers) of ritual. Record collecting represents a relationship with music that helps us, in some part small or large, to articulate and, indeed, shape who we are.[12]

The relative affordability of these musical objects is also significant, and has affected all types of listeners, whether the sweaty-palmed disc junkie or the casual consumer. Recordings are often (though not always) cheaper than tickets for concerts of the same fare, and their affordability may affect listeners' access to music. As the next chapter will show, the inexpensive disc was hailed as one of the keys to helping America become a more "musical" nation in the first decades of the twentieth century, for cheap records of the classics meant that access to "good music" need not be the exclusive domain of the rich. And one of the crucial issues in the debate over file-sharing—which I explore in the book's final chapter—is that these sound files are being collected by the millions free of charge, much to the delight of many listeners and to the outrage of the recording industry. But as we will see, MP3s and the like are a special case, for they are not tangible in the way traditional media are.

To understand the full significance of the tangibility of recorded sound, we must know something about the specific physical characteristics of the various media, and the differences among them. Consider, for example, the cassette tape. Developed in 1963 by the Dutch company Philips, the small plastic cassette was markedly different from its predecessor, the long-playing record. Perhaps most important was that its physical characteristics made recording and duplication much easier and cheaper than had been possible in the LP era. As Peter Manuel asserts in his 1993 book *Cassette Culture,* these attributes have led to enormous changes in music and musical life. One compelling case in point, the focus of Manuel's research, is North Indian popular music. Before 1978 cassettes were rare in India (LPs being dominant), and a single entity, the Gramophone Company of India (GCI), controlled the nation's recorded music. GCI's monopoly led to an extreme concentration of performers and styles. Most of its releases were of a particular type of love song, an adaptation of the classical *ghazal* form, updated for use in films; moreover, nearly all of the tens of thousands of songs—which even to fans tended to sound similar—were recorded by just a handful of long-lived singers. The resulting homogenization of Indian popular music is hard to comprehend. Imagine that for the past fifty years popular music in the United States has consisted of several thousand slight variations on "I Will Always Love You" (featured in the movie *The Bodyguard*), all sung by Whitney Houston. (Now imagine that you don't like Whitney Houston.) When one critic quoted by Manuel complained of "the crushing power of the monotony of musical soundscape" in India, we should not take this to be hyperbole.[13]

In the 1980s, with relaxed government regulation on their importation, cassettes quickly came to account for 95 percent of all commercial recordings in India.[14] The arrival of the cassette utterly changed the pop scene. The less complex, cheaper medium allowed smaller labels and even individuals to create and distribute recordings, ending GCI's stranglehold on the market. This diversification brought new perspectives, giving rise to new stars, even new musical genres. And it was precisely the physical characteristics of the cassette, tangibly different from the LP, that helped prepare the ground for this revolution.

We may see a parallel phenomenon with the compact disc, though the early years of the CD suggested a return to the "one-way, monopolistic, homogenizing tendencies" of the LP that Manuel has pointed out.[15] Yet in the 1990s it became much easier and cheaper to create CDs, and today most personal computers come with CD burners, making any home with a PC a potential pressing plant. With the advancement of CD production technology, many performers have decided to go into business for themselves. When the San Francisco Symphony could not get a contract with one of the major labels, they created their own; alternative pop musician Ani DiFranco, never interested in working with one of the majors, established Righteous Babe Records; and cellist David Finckel and pianist Wu Han created ArtistLed, "Classical Music's first Internet recording company," in order to "produce recordings in an environment free from constraints."[16]

We must be careful, however, not to assume that ease of production necessarily leads to diversification. Remarkably, the cassette seems to have had very nearly the opposite effect on the gamelan tradition of Java. Traditionally, each gamelan is a unique and matched collection of largely brass and bronze percussion instruments, with each ensemble having its own distinctive tuning. Although gamelan recordings date to the early twentieth century, it was not until cassettes came ashore in the late 1960s that gamelan recordings circulated widely across the island, and this was precisely because they were so simple to produce and disseminate. One striking effect of the new medium was that it seemed to facilitate a certain standardization within the world of gamelan performance practice. In his fieldwork in Java, ethnomusicologist Anderson Sutton observed gamelan teachers changing the patterns and structures of certain pieces to match what they had heard on cassettes by prominent ensembles.[17] It has also been reported that when new gamelans are made nowadays they are often tuned to match a frequently recorded gamelan.[18]

Thus, whereas the advent of the cassette led to musical diversification in North India, it has encouraged musical homogenization in Java. One reason for this difference is fairly clear: where the Indian music industry was monopolized by a single, giant corporate entity, no such market concentration existed in Java. The contrast between these "cassette cultures" illustrates a point I have already made, but one that bears repeating: phonograph effects are not dictated solely by the traits of the technology, but arise out of broader contexts, whether economic, cultural, or aesthetic. Yet despite their differences, both cassette cultures illustrate how a very basic difference between recordings and live performance can have a profound impact on music and the way we interact with it.

PORTABILITY

When music becomes a thing it gains an unprecedented freedom to travel. Of course, live and recorded music are both portable, but in different ways. The portability of live music depends on the size of instruments and the number of musicians needed to perform a work. Minstrels and marching bands move easily; orchestras and anvil choruses less so. With recording, however, all music is more or less equally portable, from harmonica solos to the massive works of Mahler.

Furthermore, when music is recorded and replayed, it is removed from its original setting, losing its unique spatial and temporal identity. This loss was the subject of Walter Benjamin's famous 1936 essay "The Work of Art in the Age of Mechanical Reproduction." While the visual arts concerned Benjamin most, his ideas are relevant here. "Even the most perfect reproduction of a work of art," he maintained, "is lacking in one element: its presence in time and space, its unique existence at the place where it happens to be."[19] Reproductions, therefore, lack what Benjamin called the "aura" of the artwork. From Benjamin's standpoint this absence is to be lamented. He speaks of the *withering* of the aura, the *depreciation* of the artwork, the *loss* of authenticity, and the *shattering* of tradition. Benjamin, however, missed half of the equation. True, mass-reproduced art does lack temporal and physical uniqueness, yet reproductions, no longer bound to the circumstances of their creation, may encourage new experiences and generate new traditions, wherever they happen to be.

Consider the *picó* of modern-day Cartagena, Colombia.[20] A picó is a large, elaborately designed sound system used to supply music for dance parties. Owners take great pride in their fancifully adorned picós, which they often tote through their communities in the back of pick-up trucks, competing with one another for the loudest, most extravagant system. While the picó is native to Cartagena, the music they play is not. The records, having arrived with traveling sailors, are mostly of African and Afro-Caribbean genres whose sound and language are foreign to coastal Colombia. Listeners do not typically understand the lyrics, and any dances originally connected with those genres are severed from the music. Yet the music is deeply meaningful to Cartagenos, and is central to the pleasures and experiences of picó culture. As the picó demonstrates, while recorded music is often decoupled from its origins in space and time, this "loss" begets a contextual promiscuity that allows music to accrue new, rich, and unexpected meanings.

Globetrotting recordings have also been deeply meaningful to composers, and have changed, even started, many careers. For the bandleader and composer Alton Adams (1889–1987), hearing 78s of John Philip Sousa was a formative experience. As a young man living in the Virgin Islands, he had no other access to this music. "How well do I recall," he wrote late in his life, "the many hours spent in rhapsodic ecstasy, listening outside the residence of a devotee of the art to the recordings of beautiful music— orchestral and band selections, operatic arias, and so forth, but particularly . . . the marches of Sousa. . . . After each of these musical experiences, stretched on my bed, I would then imaginatively conduct a Sousa's band in one of my own compositions."[21] Adams, a black composer living in a black society, was influenced by the recordings of a white musician. Darius Milhaud, a white European, found great value in the discs of black jazz musicians. "Thanks to the phonograph," he wrote in 1924, "I will be able to play the discs of black music—recorded and published by blacks—that I brought back from the United States. It is truly very precious to be able to study the folklore of all the world thanks to this machine."[22] Records, and with them musical influence, traveled not only from north to south and west to east, but from east to west as well. Hearing discs of Balinese gamelan music in 1929 proved decisive to the career of Canadian Colin McPhee, leading to his move to Bali in 1931 and immersion in its music and culture.[23] Steve Reich's exposure to recordings of African music in the 1950s made a similar impression, and indirectly led to his visit to Ghana and to his 1971 work *Drumming*.[24]

Even when recordings aren't winging their way across continents, they can move easily within our daily lives, detaching music from its traditional times, venues, and rituals. While hardly noteworthy today, such possibilities were once considered radical. In 1923 British writer Orlo Williams made what would today seem an oddly superfluous argument: that it should be perfectly acceptable to listen to recorded music at any time of the day. He offered a scenario involving a wealthy bachelor, and intercut his description with the imagined responses of a hidebound reader.

> He comes down to breakfast at half-past nine: he skims the headlines of his paper over the kidneys and reads the feuilleton over his marmalade. Then, if I am right, he lights a large but mild cigar, sinks into an armchair, and rings for the butler to set the gramophone going. "My dear fellow . . ." you say in expostulation, "how absurd . . . how could anybody . . . I mean . . . can't you see?" I apologise. Imagination, yours at any rate, boggles at the thought: yet what I see in alluring clearness, is a gentleman tastefully attired, smoking in an easy but not too soft a chair, while at ten o'clock on a sunny morning, he listens to the voice of Caruso issuing from a little cupboard in a mahogany cabinet.

It seems hard to believe that anyone would be shocked by such a scene. Yet because it had never been customary, morning music—especially opera—must have disrupted the fabric of daily life. "Here," Williams explained, "we touch one of the ingrained superstitions of the Englishman, that music, except for the purpose of scales and exercises, is not decent at such an early part of the day." But its "indecency," he argued, was merely a function of its previous impracticality. There should be no reason, he concluded, to avoid listening to music in certain ways simply because they only recently became possible.[25] Today, of course, the morning listener raises no eyebrows; in fact, listening to the radio or recordings during breakfast is for some as ingrained a habit as breakfasting in silence must have been for people of earlier eras.

The portability of recordings has also allowed listeners to determine not only when and where they hear music, but with whom they listen. Solitary listening, widespread today, has been an important manifestation of this possibility. The practice, however, has not always been common. In the 1923 article just cited, Orlo Williams wondered how one might react upon walking in on a friend who is listening to recorded music . . . alone. His answer illustrates the puzzlement that may once have met solitary listening.

> You would think it odd, would you not? You would endeavour to dissemble your surprise: you would look twice to see whether some other person were not hidden in some corner of the room, and if you found no such one would painfully blush, as if you had discovered your friend sniffing cocaine, emptying a bottle of whisky, or plaiting straws in his hair. People, we think, should not do things "to themselves," however much they may enjoy doing them in company: they may not even talk to themselves without incurring grave suspicion. And I fear that if I were discovered listening to the Fifth Symphony without a chaperon to guarantee my sanity, my friends would fall away with grievous shaking of the head.[26]

Even if a bit melodramatic, Williams's remarks remind us that before the advent of recording, listening to music had always been a communal activity. In prephonographic times it had been for the most part neither practical nor possible to hear music alone. Listening was a culturally significant activity, for music accompanied central communal events, including birth or death rites, weddings, and religious festivals. Solitary listening, then, contradicted centuries of tradition. Nevertheless, the practice came to be accepted. In 1931, one writer touted its advantages: "Alone with the phonograph, all the unpleasant externals are removed: the interpreter has been disposed of; the audience has been disposed of; the uncomfortable concert hall has been disposed of. You are alone with the composer and his music. Surely no more ideal circumstances could be imagined."[27] Today, solitary listeners are everywhere, in living rooms, dorm rooms, bathrooms, offices, cars, and anywhere they might take a portable player. But there is still something strange about seeing people in public places, plugged into the earphones of the players they tote around as an emphysemic might carry an oxygen tank. (For many, in fact, music is as necessary as oxygen.) Journalist Paul Fahri wonderfully captured that strangeness, evoking images from the classic horror movie *Night of the Living Dead:* "It is so familiar now that we don't see or hear it anymore. It is the look and sound of the Walkman dead: the head cocked at a slight angle, the mouth gently lolling. From about the skull comes a tinny low buzzing sound, like metallic bees. The eyes flicker with consciousness, but they don't *see.* They're somewhere else."[28] Perhaps we should not wonder that solitary listening was once considered unusual, but rather that it should have come to be so widely, unremarkably practiced. The same is true for the act of listening to music far removed from one's home or culture or of experiencing music whenever and with whomever one wishes. In each case, the portability of recording has made the once unimaginable commonplace.

(IN)VISIBILITY

Imagine that it is 1916 and you are shopping for records. Upon entering a store you are invited to take what is called "The Edison Realism Test." You are led to a quiet spot where you find a phonograph, a chair, and a scrapbook, and are handed a sheet of paper with a set of six instructions. First, you are to choose the type of music you would like to hear. Next you are asked to sit facing *away* from the phonograph while looking at a scrapbook of concert reviews and photographs of musicians (all Edison recording artists, naturally). Then you are directed to remember the last time you witnessed a performance of the music you have chosen to hear. "Picture the scene," you are told, until "it is clearly . . . in mind." Once this mental image is firmly in place, you are to say, "I am ready," at which point the demonstrator plays your chosen record. The final instruction is wonderfully complicated: "About forty-five seconds after the music begins, close your eyes and keep them closed for a minute or more. Then open your eyes for fifteen seconds but do not gaze at your surroundings. After this, close your eyes again and keep them closed until the end of the selection." If you follow these directions exactly, you will supposedly get "the same emotional re-action experienced when you last heard the same kind of voice or instrument." If for some reason you do not, it is because "you have not wholly shaken off the influence of your surroundings," in which case you are to repeat the test until successful.[29] What is fascinating about the Edison Realism Test—essentially a set of instructions for how to listen to a phonograph—is the importance given to the visual dimension of the musical experience. Listeners must go to great lengths not only to conjure up the correct mental imagery, but also to avoid all possible conflicting stimuli. The assumption behind the test is clear: in order for recorded music to be comprehensible, listeners must visualize a performance. Seeing was indeed believing. In fact, this had always been true, as Richard Leppert makes clear in *The Sight of Sound:* "Precisely because musical sound is abstract, intangible, and ethereal—lost as soon as it is gained—the visual experience of its production is crucial . . . for locating and communicating the place of music and musical sound within society and culture."[30]

The Edison Realism Test reveals another little-appreciated fact about recorded music: that listeners and performers cannot see one another.[31] Although unremarkable today, this was once a source of great anxiety. As an English music critic explained in 1923, some listeners "cannot bear to hear a remarkably life-like human voice issuing from a box. They desire the physical presence. For want of it, the gramophone distresses them."[32] This anxiety is understandable, for voices are typically accompanied by bodies—in fact, "hearing voices" without seeing their source is a sure sign of an unwell mind.

Various strategies were employed in the attempt to restore the missing visual dimension to the phonographic experience. The Stereophone and the Illustrated Song Machine, both introduced in 1905, consisted of similar mechanisms that, when attached to cylinder-playing phonographs, rotated images in time with the music. As an article in a trade journal crowed, the Illustrated Song Machine "is just what the public has wanted since the first automatic machine [i.e., phonograph] was placed on the market, and the listener drew a mind's picture as the words and music were repeated to him."[33] In 1929 a British phonograph enthusiast reported on the miniature stages he had constructed to look at while listening to his favorite operas. He meticulously fashioned scaled-down sets and wooden cutouts of characters in various costumes, all of which he changed with every new scene.[34] In the United States, music educator Albert Wier devised what he called the "projecting phonograph" in 1936, for use in music classes. Wier created slide shows, in which main themes or motives, graphic analyses, translations of texts, and images of musicians or opera sets were projected in time with recordings. In the absence of these rather extravagant remedies, listeners simply stared at their phonographs—a practice that was, as one observer noted in 1923, "an unthinking inheritance from the days when we had no phonographs, and when we naturally had to look at the performer."[35]

When musicians record, their invisibility to listeners removes an important channel of communication, for performers express themselves not only through the sound of their voices or instruments but with their faces and bodies. In concert, these gestures color the audience's understanding of the music. As Igor Stravinsky rightly explained, "The sight of the gestures and movements of the various parts of the body producing the music is fundamentally necessary if it is to be grasped in all its fullness."[36] The violinist Itzhak Perlman, for example, is effective in concert in part because his face registers and reinforces every expressive nuance in the music. Perlman himself once remarked that "people only half listen to you when you play—the other half is watching."[37] The visual aspect of performance is especially important for pop musicians. What would pop be without the wriggling and jiggling, the leaping and strutting, the leather and skin, the smoke and fire? It would merely be sound, and so much the poorer for it.

The power of the visual is further demonstrated when the audio and visual channels are at odds with each other. Consider the violinist Jascha Heifetz, known for his rigid posture, skyward stare, and blank expression when performing. A 1925 article remarked on his deportment: "Cold, calm, dispassionate, he stands on the platform and performs miracles of dexterity, displays his beauties of tone; but do we not feel slightly chilled, anxious perhaps for less mastery and more humanity?" Yet the author also noted that Heifetz sounded rather different on disc: "These impressions are to some extent corrected by Heifetz's records. There is certainly a hint of passion, of tenderness."[38] In other words, with the visual channel off, Heifetz no longer seemed emotionless. Heifetz's playing provides a musical analogue to what is known as the McGurk Effect. In a 1976 experiment, psychologists Harry McGurk and John MacDonald showed subjects a video of a young woman speaking certain syllables, while what they heard were sounds of *different* syllables dubbed onto the tape. The results were striking: the subjects, who could readily identify the syllables being spoken when *not* looking at the video, consistently misidentified the sounds when the video presented conflicting information.[39] The psychologists' conclusion, which Heifetz had demonstrated long before, is that what we hear is deeply influenced by what we see.

For quite a different example, take the case of Milli Vanilli, a 1980s pop duo. Their popularity stemmed in large part from their good looks and provocative dancing. They fell from stardom, however, when it was revealed in 1990 that all along they had lip-synched to the recordings of two unknown performers.[40] That the real singers, a pair of middle-aged men, were not deemed glamorous enough to be put before the public suggests how crucial a group's look is to its success.

Yet as the Heifetz example reveals, the *absence* of the visual can have its own appeal. A 1912 article in the *Musical Courier* praised the recorded medium for stripping away all that the author considered unnecessary to the musical experience. "In listening to the Talking Machine," he explained, "the hearer must of necessity concentrate upon the tonal performance and does not have his attention diverted to extraneous matters, such as scenery, costumes, [and] acting . . . that keep him from directing his faculties to the music itself."[41] Theodor Adorno agreed, and argued that opera—the most visual of musical genres—is in fact best heard on recordings, that is, without seeing the costumes and sets. In his 1969 article "Opera and the Long-Playing Record," Adorno explained that contemporary stagings detracted from the musical experience, whereas, "shorn of phony hoopla, the LP simultaneously frees itself from the capriciousness of fake opera festivals. It allows for the optimal presentation of music, enabling it to recapture some of the force and intensity that had been worn threadbare in the opera houses."[42]

A musicology graduate student once told me that, for him, the experience of sacred music on disc was powerful precisely because he could not see the musicians; hearing such bodiless music made him feel closer to God. This effect is not new to recording; it is the same achieved by the age-old practice in Christian churches of placing the organist and sometimes the choir out of the sight of the congregation. The removal of visual cues, certainly no accident, separates body from sound, heightening the sense that the music comes not from humans but from heaven. In prephonographic times such unseen music was the exception, used for specific purposes. Today, however, given the ubiquity of recorded music, such sightless hearing is closer to the rule. However listeners have responded—whether by compensating for it or exploiting it—the invisibility of performance is a fundamental part of the modern musical experience.

Ironically, this invisibility can have observable consequences. Conductor Nikolaus Harnoncourt suggested that recording artists must somehow compensate for the missing visual dimension. "If you don't *see* the musician—and this is the case with all recordings—you have to add something which makes the process of music making somehow visible in the imagination of the listener."[43] As I will argue in chapter 4, it is precisely this missing dimension that encouraged classical violinists to "add something" to their playing—in their case, an intense vibrato that helped communicate a sense of physical and expressive immediacy. Sometimes, however, musicians have responded by taking something away. Because recordings provide no visual continuity during extended pauses or tempo changes, musicians may deemphasize temporal discontinuities when performing in the studio. This may be accomplished, as several performers have attested, by "tightening" the spaces between phrases and larger sections. Cellist Janos Starker has explained that "while in a concert hall, the performer is able to create tension with rests . . . he cannot do this with recording." On disc, then, "the presentation of a composition" must "become much tighter."[44] Eugene Drucker of the Emerson String Quartet has offered a specific example of this "tightening" response. Drucker recounted how, in recording the Schubert Quintet, guest cellist Mstislav Rostropovich encouraged the group to shorten pauses that, in concert, they might normally extend for dramatic effect. For example, "after the big chord in the coda of the first movement [m. 428] . . . we took no extra time for rhetorical effect. Rostropovich pointed out that in a recording, one cannot always afford to play quite as broadly as in a performance. The impact of the performer's presence, even visually, can flesh out the musical ideas and add interest to phrases that might sound dull on tape." In concert, the performers would have lifted their bows off the strings after playing the chord, paused for a moment, and slowly returned them for the following phrase. Such a gesture would have heightened the drama of the moment and visually linked the two chords. On a recording, however, an extended silence like this would simply have been "dead air," something to be avoided. "This streamlining of approach," Drucker explained, "is required by recording."[45]

Why, however, should a second here or there make any difference in the larger scheme? Over the course of the century, there has been a noticeable move in classical performance toward steadier tempos, with fewer and less marked tempo fluctuations.[46] What seems to be a common and almost instinctive "tightening" response has, in part, contributed to this general change in the rhetoric of modern performance.

Recording artists have also reacted to the fact that *they* cannot see their audiences. For many, the task of performing to unseen listeners, with recording equipment as their proxy, can be both daunting and depressing. In her memoirs, French soprano Régine Crespin registered her dismay at the artificiality of performing in the studio:

> Fear of an audience is healthy; it stimulates you. The people are there in front of you. With them there can be mutual lovefests. But how can you fall in love with a microphone? First of all, a microphone is ugly. It's a cold, steel, impersonal thing, suspended above your head or resting on a pole just in front of your nose. And it defies you, like HAL the computer in Stanley Kubrick's film *2001: A Space Odyssey*, although at least he talked. No, the microphone waits, unpitying, insensitive and ultrasensitive at the same time, and when it speaks, it's to repeat everything you've said word for word. The beast.[47]

Not only Western classical performers are affected by the absence of the audience. Before the era of the phonograph, Hindustani classical musicians not only took inspiration from their listeners, but also improvised directly in response to their reactions. The exact sound and shape of the performance, then, was determined in part by the interaction of artist and audience. For those who recorded, one way to compensate was to manufacture an audience, planting enthusiastic listeners in the studio. On an acoustic-era recording of Maujuddin Khan, for example, one can hear a few "plants" shouting "Wah! Wah! Maujuddin Khan! Subhanallah!," praising the divinity of the singing.[48] In a more recent example, I myself was an unwitting plant in a recording session for the rock group Rotoglow. After observing from the control room, I was invited to sit in the studio while the band was recording. During a break I asked if I had been a distraction (I was occupying the very small space between the lead guitarist and the drummer) and suggested that I should perhaps return to the other side of the glass. To my surprise, the group insisted that I stay. "You're a part of this, man!" one of them declared.[49] I hardly acted like a typical rock concert-goer—I sat still, remained silent, and took notes when not stuffing my ears with wadded toilet paper to protect my hearing. Nevertheless, my presence must have in some way met the band's need or desire for an audience.

For some, however, the absence of an audience may be welcome, providing respite from the stress and distractions of concert performance. In a classical concert, coughing, snoring, talking, program rustling, and candy-wrapper crinkling may fluster or irritate the performer; at a pop concert audiences may in fact be louder than the performers, and can distract the musicians in any number of other ways. Removing the audience may therefore permit a sharper focus on making music to the artist's own satisfaction. Violinist Yehudi Menuhin, for one, valued recording for allowing him a "monastic dedication which is oblivious of audience."[50] As with every aspect of recording, the mutual invisibility of performer and listener offers both drawbacks and benefits, though in all cases it presents challenges to which both parties must respond.

REPEATABILITY

Sing a single note. Now try to recreate that sound *exactly*—not simply its pitch, but its precise volume, length, intensity, timbre, attack, and decay. Now imagine trying to repeat an entire song in this way, down to the smallest detail. It simply cannot be done. The impossibility of such an exercise reveals what is perhaps the most unbridgeable difference between live and recorded music: live performances are unique, while recordings are repeatable.

This statement deserves further explanation. Live music is in fact repeatable, but in the form of works, not performances.[51] That is, any orchestra can play Beethoven's Fifth Symphony many times; each performance, however, will necessarily be different. Second, to say that a recorded performance is repeated without change is not to deny that a listener may experience a recording differently from one hearing to another, whether by adjusting the playback equipment or by focusing on different aspects of the music. I mean only that the actions that created the sound one hears on a recording are fixed, and do not change when the recording is replayed.

This difference between live and recorded music may not seem especially momentous, but in fact it may have the most complex and far-reaching consequences of any of the technology's attributes discussed in this chapter. Given this complexity, it would be helpful to approach the influence of repeatability from three different perspectives: that of listening, that of performing, and that of composing.

For listeners, repetition raises expectations. This is true in live performance; once we've heard Beethoven's Fifth in concert, we assume it will start with the same famous four notes the next time we hear it. But with recordings, we can also come to expect features that are unique to a particular performance—that a certain note will be out of tune, say. With sufficient repetition, listeners may normalize interpretive features of a performance or even mistakes, regarding them as integral not only to the performance but to the music. In other words, listeners may come to think of an interpretation as the work itself. When I was young, for example, I was particularly fond of Pablo de Sarasate's *Zigeunerweisen,* one of the flashier showpieces in the violin repertoire. I came to know the piece through Jascha Heifetz's 1951 recording, which I listened to obsessively until every nuance of the performance was ingrained in my musical memory.[52] One such nuance was actually an error: in m. 9 of the first movement (0:34 in the recording), the violinist accidentally plucks his open E string. Though I knew the plucked E to be a mistake, I came to expect it not only when listening to Heifetz's recording but whenever hearing the work, even in concert. In fact, I would be a bit surprised and even disappointed when I did *not* hear that E. Though I knew better, on a certain level I regarded that wayward note to be part of the piece.

Expectations can also be raised by sounds that originate not from a performance at all, but from defects in playback equipment or individual recordings. Anthropologist Thomas Porcello tells of the intense expectancy he experienced when listening to recordings afflicted with print-through— a defect in the recording process that results in a faint pre-echo:

When I was a teenager, I owned a couple of albums with extreme print-through at the beginning. . . . I'd put the needle down and faintly, but distinctly, hear a perfect, amplitudinally miniaturized replica of *what I was about to hear.* That tiny audio shadow always seemed to generate a visceral tension. I'd hold my breath, waiting for the release that came with the "real" beginning of the song, like smelling tequila as you bring it to your mouth, before it scalds your throat on the way down to your stomach.[53]

However arbitrary or incidental, such sonic artifacts can and do affect the listening experience, and do so by virtue of their repetition. If these two examples of raised expectations seem somewhat arbitrary, we can be sure that they stand in for countless experiences of listeners who may not even realize the power of repetition.

The repeatability of recorded sound has affected listeners' expectations on a much broader scope as well. When the phonograph was invented, the goal for any recording was to simulate a live performance, to approach reality as closely as possible. Over the decades, expectations have changed. For many—perhaps most—listeners, music is now primarily a techno-logically mediated experience. Concerts must therefore live up to record-ings. Given that live music had for millennia been the only type of music, it is amazing to see how quickly it has been supplanted as model and ideal.

The impact of recording's repeatability on performers is no less signifi-cant. In concert the artist is typically concerned with the first—and only—impression, but with recordings, "shelf life" must be considered. Profes-sional musicians have long been aware of these differences, and have often felt the need to minimize errors and even otherwise acceptable manner-isms when recording, for such "deviations" may become distracting with unchanging repetition. David Soyer, cellist for the Guarneri Quartet, has made this point: "Recordings have a tendency to iron out the eccentric, idiosyncratic, personal things that happen in a concert hall."[54] But what happens when listeners are repeatedly exposed to note-perfect recordings? Do they then expect and demand similar performances? And do performers then feel the need to meet such expectations? Undoubtedly, such feedback loops are created, with performers striving to recreate their recordings. Critic and historian Joseph Horowitz observed this in a concert perfor-mance of Brahms's Symphony no. 1, which he described as "machine-like" and "precision-tooled," concluding that the Chicago Symphony had perfectly imitated the sound of an orchestra "fed through giant speakers." In other words, "they sounded like a phonograph record."[55] At least they were actually playing. Many pop stars, and even some classical musicians, have been known to lip-synch to their own recordings. (The Milli Vanilli case was unusual only in that they were pretending to sing to someone *else's* recordings.) But such phonograph effects are certainly not a necessary consequence of recording. Witness what appears to be the increasing popularity of live recordings—the recent releases by classical violinist Anne-Sophie Mutter and rock group Pearl Jam being two very different examples—which preserve spontaneous, idiosyncratic, even messy performances. These offerings, which seem to represent a reaction against overproduced recordings, suggest that the unique qualities of the live performance are still highly valued.

Repeatability has also affected musicians in their capacity as *listeners*. With recordings, performers can study, emulate, or imitate performances in a way never before possible. In the early days of recording, this possibility was trumpeted as a gift to all musicians, who could learn from the world's great masters by studying their discs.[56] For performers of popular music, recordings have been especially valuable learning aids. The available scores do not always represent performances adequately, and they cannot easily indicate the timbres and sonic effects that musicians seek to develop. An aspiring rock guitarist once explained why he studied recordings instead of scores: "I want to hear what the thing *sounds* like, and there ain't no way a sheet of paper sounds like Jimi Hendrix."[57] As I will explain in chapter 3, the study of recordings is also crucial to the development of jazz musicianship, and has been for generations.

On the other hand, some have worried that repeatability may lead performers to mimic great artists without emulating their spirit, or to create bland patchwork interpretations based on their favorite recordings. The violinist Miha Pogacnik told of visiting a colleague who was preparing the Brahms Violin Concerto by listening to twenty different LPs of the work. "This was reflected in his playing," Pogacnik lamented: "two measures of poor Milstein here, four measures of second-rate Oistrakh and Szeryng there."[58]

Performers exploit repeatability by studying not only the recordings of other musicians, but their own as well. In 1905 soprano Adelina Patti was finally persuaded to commit her famous voice to wax. After singing a short selection, she heard her recorded voice for the first time. "My God!" she reportedly exclaimed, "now I understand why I am Patti! What a voice! What an artist!"[59] While most of those hearing themselves for the first time are probably less enchanted, surprise seems to be the universal reaction. Soprano Joan Morris, for example, "practically had a cow" upon hearing herself for the first time.[60] Once over this initial shock, however, performers often find recording quite useful in allowing them to assess their work at a temporal and spatial distance—an impossibility before the invention of the repeatable recording.[61] In listening to themselves musicians may hear mistakes—unnoticed during a performance—which can then be corrected. Sometimes, however, what performers notice is not errors, but aspects of style or interpretation. What may have felt right in the heat of performance may in retrospect sound overdone and contrived or, at the other extreme, flat and lifeless. Probably all recording artists modify their playing to a certain extent when a desired sound is not heard. Soprano Martina Arroyo has suggested how this process might work. "There are some . . . who say, 'Oh no, I do exactly the same thing in recording as in live performance.' But what happens is that . . . when you hear [yourself] you adjust without even knowing, because you say 'Ah, that's not exactly the way I want to sound.' And you adjust, perhaps without being aware that in a performance you wouldn't have made that adjustment."[62]

Consider also the testimony of French composer and pianist Camille Saint-Saëns, who made his first recording in 1900. "While the phonograph was repeating what I had played," he reported, "I listened with much curiosity and interest. I at once saw, or rather heard, two grave mistakes that I had made. In one part the music was more quick than I had intended, and in another the rhythm was faulty. These mistakes I subsequently corrected."[63] But what was Saint-Saëns really hearing? Perhaps what he described was not so much an error but the type of rhythmic inflection typical of early-twentieth-century performance as documented on countless recordings of the time. Such inflections probably passed unnoticed during the performance, but heard in retrospect may well have seemed objectionable, even wrong. I would speculate that as classical performers became accustomed to making and hearing repeatable performances, they gradually began to correct certain rhythmic "errors," by minimizing small-scale tempo fluctuations and curbing the once common habit of altering the length and placement of notes. I believe that this response to repeatability, in conjunction with the "tightening" of tempo I mentioned earlier, has led to a striking change in the way modern classical performers approach musical time.[64]

For performers, repeatability is thus a double-edged sword, equally capable of enriching and burdening their work. Its impact may also be more subtle and far-reaching, for if control and precision have become central values in classical performance due in part to this trait of the technology, then recording affects not only technique, but aesthetics.

Like performers, composers have also had an ambivalent relationship with the repeatability of recordings. Some have seen it as an advantage. Expressing an oft-repeated sentiment, George Gershwin wrote in 1933 that "the composer, in my estimation, has been helped a great deal by the mechanical reproduction of music. . . . Music is written to be heard, and any instrument that tends to help it be heard more frequently and by great numbers is advantageous to the person who writes it."[65] Yet repeatability can also have a negative side for composers. Second-rate concert performances fade away, but inferior recordings live on to distort or misrepresent a composer's music every time they are replayed. In a 1937 essay, Béla Bartók described the musical work as a living, evolving entity, suggesting that even composers' own recordings may ill serve their music. Aaron Copland agreed, writing that the "unpredictable element, so essential in keeping music truly alive . . . dies with the second playing of a record."[66]

Phonographic repetition has deeply affected the ways in which composers' works are circulated and received by listeners. Some have speculated that repeatability may have even greater power, influencing the compositional process itself. Jonathan Kramer has suggested that certain early-twentieth-century composers, particularly Arnold Schoenberg, responded to the nature of the medium by minimizing repetition in their works: "It seems as if composers realized subconsciously that their music would be recorded and thus available to listeners for repeated hearings."[67] The connection Kramer proposes is provocative, but unlikely. Schoenberg had only the barest interaction with the medium. None of his compositions appeared on disc until well into his career, and he did not make his first studio recording until he was in his sixties. Moreover, Schoenberg showed little enthusiasm for the phonograph. As he wrote in 1926, he saw "no advantage" in the mechanization of music.[68] Given his sparse recording activity and ambivalence toward the medium, it seems doubtful that he would have altered his compositional technique, even subconsciously, in response to the repeatability of recording.[69]

Nevertheless, I agree with Kramer that repeatability may influence the work of composers. Yet the effect is quite the opposite: recording has begotten whole genres whose identity is fundamentally connected to repetition. It is often forgotten that minimalism—whose most salient trait is the repetition and gradual development of brief musical cells—was indelibly shaped by recording technology. Steve Reich's early minimalist works came out of his experiments in the mid-1960s with tape loops. A tape loop is a length of recorded magnetic tape with its ends connected, so that when played on a reel-to-reel machine (the available technology at the time), the music repeats indefinitely. Purely by accident, Reich discovered that when trying to play two copies of the same loop simultaneously on different machines, the loops very slowly went in and out of synch, creating a type of musical process that he called phase shifting. Reich explored phase shifting in his tape works *It's Gonna Rain* (1965) and *Come Out* (1966), which he described as "realizations of an idea that was indigenous to machines."[70] He later applied the idea to non-tape works such as *Piano Phase* (1967) and *Clapping Music* (1972), demonstrating the deep influence of recording technology on his writing. It is interesting to note that minimalism is often derogated as "broken-record music." Flutist and conductor Ransom Wilson, who later came to perform the minimalist works of Philip Glass, initially had this reaction to Glass's five-hour opera *Einstein on the Beach:* "The music seemed to have no direction, almost giving the impression of a gigantic phonograph with a stuck needle."[71] Despite the dismissive tone of such statements, the link to recording technology is apt. And although it may just be coincidence, it is worth noting that the repeated motives heard in many minimalist works are often about two seconds long, the same time it takes an LP to complete a single rotation.

A decade after Steve Reich was experimenting with tape loops in San Francisco, hip-hop DJs in the Bronx found that a fragment of music could be repeated indefinitely by switching back and forth between two copies of the same LP, each on its own turntable. (See chapter 6 for a fuller account of what came to be known as turntablism.) These repeated musical fragments were also called loops, and became the basic structural unit in the instrumental accompaniment in rap. Even in the digital age, loops persist; listen to any rap song today and you are likely to hear an instrumental foundation of loops, though now the fragments are sampled and are no longer repeated manually. Although hip-hop and minimalism are rarely uttered in the same sentence—they share little by way of sound or audience—we find an unexpected kinship in their mutual reliance on mechanical repetition.

Repeatability is perhaps the most complex of recording's traits. It will arise in nearly every chapter of this book, and figures prominently in the discussion of jazz improvisation, classical violin playing, the computer music of Paul Lansky, and the hip-hop of Public Enemy. If nothing else, the diversity of responses to repeatability should dispel any notion of strict technological determinism, for such wildly disparate phonograph effects demonstrate that there can be no simple cause-effect relationship between recording technology and the activities of its users.

TEMPORALITY

With the advent of sound recording, a new rigidity was introduced into the world of music, one imposed not by performers or audiences, but by a machine. Although over the decades the time limitation has become less severe, for the seventy-one years between the invention of the phonograph and the introduction of the long-playing disc (1877 to 1948) recordings could play no more than about four and one-half minutes of music continuously.[72] Thus, for more than seven decades, listeners, performers, and composers had to live and work with a severe and arbitrary restriction, one that constantly impinged on their activities.

For listeners living in the pre-LP era, the brevity of recordings was, most superficially, a nuisance. Blues singer Son House recalled the trials of the phonograph owner in the 1920s: these included "gettin' up, settin' it back, turnin' it around, crankin' the crank, primin' it up, and lettin' the horn down," all to be repeated every few minutes.[73] Of greater consequence, however, was the fact that longer pieces had to be broken up over multiple discs. The discontinuity of the experience (caused by the need to change sides and records) could lead some to perceive works in units dictated not by the music itself but by the length of the discs. Composer and professor Andrew Mead has recounted how such listening affected his father's understanding of a Brahms symphony:

> My father has long held that Brahms wrote weak transitions, a position I simply couldn't fathom. One day, we were listening to the finale of the 1st symphony, just at the point of the syncopated climax preceding the continued recap [mm. 289–301] and Dad said, "Here comes one of those bad transitions." After the recap got under way, he allowed as how it was not a weak transition, but that he remembered it as such. I asked him how he had first gotten to know the work, and he said it was through a stack of 78 RPM discs. I asked if the passage in question marked one of the side breaks, and he said, somewhat surprised, that it did.[74]

The elder Mead's experience recalls Theodor Adorno's concept of "atomized listening." Atomized listening, which Adorno linked directly to both recording and radio, privileges the perception of works as collections of seemingly disconnected moments rather than unified compositions.[75] It is impossible to know how common this phonograph effect may have been—information on it can only be collected anecdotally—but given that generations of listeners grew up with cylinders and 78s, the phenomenon must have been pervasive. Moreover, I would speculate that the persistence of the three-minute pop song (more on which later) in an age when song lengths are no longer dictated by the capacity of 78s and 45s may well be a manifestation of atomized listening. The repetition of short pop songs over the decades almost certainly created a feedback loop in which listeners have come to expect works to be of a certain length and in which performers strive (or are pressured) to meet that expectation.

For performers, the impact of the technologically imposed time limitation is clearer. Most obviously, the four-minute limit affected repertoire. In theory, any piece, no matter how long, could have been recorded by breaking it into segments, and even whole operas were released in the era of the 78-rpm disc. Practically speaking, however, the time limitation encouraged performers to record shorter pieces. Any survey of record catalogs from the early part of the century will reveal the dominance of character pieces, arias, marches, and brief popular song and dance numbers, while a similar study of concert programs would show that longer works—sonatas, concertos, symphonies, musicals, and operas—were quite common. It was not long before the time limitation affected not only what musicians recorded but also what they performed in public. We see a striking example of this influence in violinist Maud Powell's Carnegie Hall "Record Recital" of 1917. Part publicity stunt, part serious venture, the concert consisted of seventeen works chosen by the public from her recorded catalog. While typical violin recitals of the time would have offered a combination of shorter and longer works of various genres, Powell's featured mostly character pieces, and all of them—by necessity—were brief.[76] In the 1950s, violin recital programs began to change, comprising fewer but longer works (mostly sonatas); not coincidentally, I believe, the new format arose only after the introduction of the long-playing record, an innovation that made it easier to commit such larger-scale works to disc.

The various characteristics of recording technology affect musicians of all types, and the same is true for the time limitation. Returning to the example of Hindustani music, Suman Ghosh has pointed out that while on disc whole pieces are compressed into just a few minutes, in a live setting "the performance of the *raaga,* the melodic structure of Hindustani music, has rarely taken less than an hour, and it often stretched well beyond two or three hours."[77] In Algerian *raï,* the length of performances is traditionally determined by the amount of money listeners are willing to pay to keep the musicians playing a favorite song, or alternatively, the amount of money competing audience members will pay to hear a different song. "In raï," scholar Marc Schade-Poulesen explains, "a song rarely had a 'full length,' [for] the music was embedded in a social relation which began and ended according to the money involved."[78] In the recording studio, however, the amount of tape available determines when raï begins and ends. And as I will explain further in chapter 3, the same was true with early jazz performers, who often stretched pieces out in concert well beyond three or four minutes, but had to plan their music making quite differently upon entering the studio. These examples should not surprise us, for much of the world's music exists in the oral tradition, with the length of performances fixed almost solely by the dictates of performers and listeners.

Before leaving the subject of performance length, I want to address a common misconception. It is often said that in the early 1900s Western classical musicians played faster in the studio than they would have in concert in order to stay within the time allotted by the 78-rpm disc. Although it may have happened on occasion, there is little evidence to suggest such a trend. If that had been the case, we would expect, for example, that the LP recordings Jascha Heifetz and Yehudi Menuhin made of the Beethoven Violin Concerto in the 1950s would be slower than their 78-rpm recordings of the work from the 1940s; yet both of their later recordings are *faster,* not slower, than the earlier ones.[79] More conclusively, José Bowen's study of tempo and duration in hundreds of twentieth-century orchestral recordings shows no decisive change in tempo over the course of the century. In fact, some works have gotten faster over the decades.[80]

Rather than rushing through a piece, performers were more inclined to accommodate the time limitation by cutting music. This was very common, as I have found in my own study of early-twentieth-century violin recordings.[81] Many of the concerto and sonata recordings from the 78 era had significant cuts. Even shorter pieces were sometimes truncated. For example, Mischa Elman's 1910 recording of the violin-piano transcription of Chopin's Nocturne in E-flat omits fully one-quarter of the piece.[82] While the nocturne can be played in its entirety on a ten-inch 78, Elman's redaction allowed him to take a quite leisurely pace. In fact, in comparing works recorded over the course of the century, I found the slowest tempos most frequently on the earlier recordings. For Elman, and the countless others who recorded abbreviated works, it would seem that playing at a desired tempo was more important than playing all the notes. Apparently, there are certain changes performers are not willing to make, regardless of the limitations of the technology.

Perhaps surprisingly, however, composers were often willing to cut their own music. Edward Elgar, for example, was merciless in editing his works for the studio. For a 1916 recording of his Violin Concerto he reduced the score so that the performance would take only four record sides. Modern recordings of the work usually fill fifty minutes or more; Elgar's lasts about twenty.[83] Fritz Kreisler's *Caprice viennois* shows another approach. The sketches for this violin showpiece reveal that the work originally ended with a varied repetition of an earlier section (the presto in 3/8).[84] Kreisler cut that section before recording it in 1910; had it remained, the work would have been too long for even a twelve-inch disc. (His several recordings of the piece average about 3:25.) Kreisler often recorded his works shortly after writing them, so he may have composed with the limitations of the medium in mind. Indeed, fellow violinist Carl Flesch noted that Kreisler's short pieces were "put together with a watch in the hand. They were intended first and foremost for the gramophone."[85]

A number of composers wrote works specifically for the length of the 78. In 1934, Roy Harris composed a four-minute-twenty-second-long work for flute and string quartet that he called, appropriately enough, *Four Minutes-20 Seconds*. The title and its duration are significant to the work's origins, for Harris composed it to accompany the set of discs on which his Symphony no. 1 was recorded.[86] The symphony took up seven record sides, leaving the last side of the fourth disc blank. Harris was asked to provide a piece to fill out the set. Harris was hardly alone in tailoring a work to fit on one side of a 78-rpm record: eminent composers such as Edward Elgar, Gabriel Fauré, Paul Hindemith, Vincent d'Indy, Fritz Kreisler, Ruggero Leoncavallo, Gabriel Pierné, Kurt Weill, and, as we know from the introduction, Igor Stravinsky, did the same, whether to accompany a composition that filled an odd number of sides, or on commission by a phonograph company.[87]

The time limitation affected popular music even more deeply. Martin Williams suggested that some early blues singers crafted the narrative structure of their songs specifically to fit the playing time of the 78, while Gunther Schuller has pointed out that Duke Ellington's mastery of the small form was born out of the same technologically imposed necessity.[88] The three-minute pop song itself may be considered a phonograph effect. In the late 1940s, RCA Victor introduced the 45-rpm record as an alternative to the 33⅓-rpm long-playing format that Columbia had developed. Because of its limited playing time—about the same as a 78—the 45 could not compete with the LP for recording classical music. Instead, it became the standard format for pop, and remained so for decades. Although popular music was sometimes released on LPs beginning in the 1950s, few musicians took advantage of the possibility to record longer works.[89] The reason was strictly commercial. Much of the revenue of pop music came from the sale of "singles" released on 45s, which filled the jukeboxes and received the most radio play. A longer song would have practically no chance to sell well. Billy Joel's 1974 song "The Entertainer" attests to the pressure to keep songs short:

> You've heard my latest record, it's been on the radio
> It took me years to write it, they were the best years of my life
> It was a beautiful song, but it ran too long
> If you're gonna get a hit you gotta make it fit
> So they cut it down to 3:05.[90]

Joel is making a bitter and thinly veiled reference to his 1973 song "Piano Man," which stands at 5:37 on the album but was cut nearly in half for radio play, much to his obvious displeasure.

Perhaps Joel is an exception, but there is reason to think otherwise. Rock musicians often extend their performances considerably in concert, where there is less concern about the salability or "radio friendliness" of the performances. To offer just a few examples, consider Eric Clapton's "Blues Power" and "Cocaine" — the studio recordings are 3:06 and 3:35, while the recorded concert performances are more than twice as long at 7:21 and 7:24.[91] Or compare Jimi Hendrix's live performances of "Killing Floor" and "Hey Joe" in 1967, which come in at 8:05 and 6:44, to the earlier studio versions, much briefer at 2:27 and 3:23.[92] Clearly, not all pop musicians are satisfied with the customary 180 seconds allotted them.

What determines the length of a live performance? Any of a thousand factors, whether the length of a written composition, the inspiration of a performer, the time it takes for a bride to march down the aisle, or the desire of dancers to keep shimmying. Yet of these countless possibilities, few of them fix with any great specificity or regularity the length of performances. Recording, however, parcels performances into fixed segments, regardless of the inclinations of artists or audiences. While this might seem solely a disservice to music, listeners, performers, and composers have, as we've seen, adapted in varied and remarkable ways to this fact of modern musical life.

The room was usually small, windowless, overheated, and empty, save for a large megaphone-shaped horn and a small red light or perhaps a buzzer attached to one wall. No vast stage, no ornate hall, no warm applause greeted the performer's entrance into this, a typical early-twentieth-century recording studio. A session began not with a performance, but with a series of tests. These tests established the type of recording horn and stylus to be used, the optimal distance between performer and horn, and the dynamic range allowed by the equipment. When all the tests were complete, the performance could start, but not at the artist's discretion. The red light would flash, the buzzer would sound, or an engineer would gesture, and the performer would begin. During the performance, musicians had to be careful not to make extraneous, recordable noises, not to gesture unduly (lest they knock the equipment over), and not to sing or play too loudly or too softly. After the performance was finished, total silence was necessary—any exclamation of relief, joy, or disappointment would ruin the recording. Thus ended the first take. (See Figure 1.)

Fast-forward nearly a century. A great deal has changed, and the performer entering a modern studio encounters not an oversized horn, but a multitude of microphones that can pick up any sound in the range of human hearing. Yet despite all the changes in recording technology, one constant remains: no recording equipment, from the simplest acoustic horn to the most sophisticated microphone, is sensitive to sound in the same way as the human ear. The earliest technology was far inferior to its biological model; the latest is in some ways more sensitive. Yet for more than a hundred years recording artists have had to adjust to the special nature of these devices, whether insensitive or hypersensitive.

Before the introduction of microphones in the mid-1920s, all recordings were made using the acoustic, or mechanical, process. Musicians sang or played into a recording horn, which funneled the sound to a narrow opening covered with a flexible membrane (often of mica or glass); the diaphragm, as it was called, transferred the vibrations to a stylus, which in turn engraved a cylinder or disc. No electricity was involved.

The demands this system placed on performers were tremendous. Soft

FIGURE 1 An early recording session using the acoustic process: Rosario Bourdon conducting the Victor Salon Orchestra. George H. Clark Radioana Collection, Archives Center, National Museum of American History, Behring Center, Smithsonian Institution. Used by permission.

and loud notes, for instance, demanded drastically different techniques. A vocalist might literally stick her head inside the horn to ensure that her pianissimo would be heard, but then, with the timing of a lion tamer, quickly withdraw for her fortissimo, so as to avoid "blasting" the engraving needle out of its groove. Alternatively, studio assistants would push the artists toward the horn or pull them away according to the changing dynamics of the music. German soprano Lotte Lehmann once quipped that in her early recording sessions she not only sang but danced as well, her partner being the "pusher," as this studio flunky was typically called.[93] Experienced recording musicians, however, could dispense with their dancing partners. In 1916 Yvonne De Treville, an American soprano, reported one musician's creative solution. At her first orchestral session she could hardly contain her laughter upon seeing the first violinist. He was, as she reported, "seated astride a little, low, rolling box, for all the world like the push cart of the beggar who has had his legs cut off and propels himself around Fifth Avenue, selling matches and shoelaces."[94]

Many performers learned to internalize the necessary adjustments by controlling their singing or playing to suit the limitations of the technology. In 1913 a British sound engineer stressed the importance of understanding the nature of recording equipment, particularly the diaphragm: "Much depends on the manner in which the musician sings or plays in intelligent rapport with the diaphragm before him, and by a little practice it is comparatively easy . . . to manipulate it for the production of first-class effects."[95] Sometimes adjustments in performance were simply not enough, and certain instruments were replaced or modified for studio use. Brass instruments often took the place of strings, for they could play louder and their sound was more easily directed toward the recording horn. In the case of the Stroh violin, string and brass merged. This contraption consisted of a violin fingerboard, bridge, and chin rest, but substituting for the traditional hollow wooden body was a conical aluminum horn with a flared bell. One Stroh could replace an entire section of fiddlers, and the sound was deemed sufficiently similar to the original.[96] (Notice the man playing the Stroh violin in the right foreground of Figure 1.)

It was not only the classical tradition that was affected in this regard. Consider the case of klezmer music. Before the twentieth century, one of the core instruments of any klezmer ensemble was the *tsimbl,* a gentle-sounding hammered dulcimer. Yet the tsimbl is rarely heard on early-twentieth-century recordings; it did not register strongly on acoustic machines, and its sound would have been lost in recordings of larger ensembles.[97] The tsimbl largely disappeared from the music, particularly in America where most klezmer discs were made. Its unsuitability in the studio was almost certainly a contributing factor. While the tsimbl recorded poorly, the piercing tone of the clarinet transferred well, and its growing prominence might also be linked to the phonograph. Jazz, too, saw similar changes in performance practice (as we will see more thoroughly in chapter 3). In early recordings, the double bass was often replaced by the tuba, and drummers were apt to eschew the skins for the more focused sound of woodblocks and cowbells. Some of the most distinctive aspects of klezmer and jazz sound, therefore, arose not within isolated musical worlds, but from their interaction with a recording technology.

An "intelligent rapport" was required not only with horns and dia-phragms. Microphones, used since the mid-1920s, are much more sensi-tive than their predecessors, but have their own demands. Because the microphone was generally placed only inches from the performer, the dynamic range appropriate in a hall or club was generally too great for the recording studio. Performing for the microphone, therefore, required moderating one's technique in a variety of ways. Martina Arroyo has de-scribed the restraint she exercised for the microphone: "There are certain sounds that you do on stage when, for example, in *Ritorna vincitor!* Aida says, 'affranto!' *(Rolls the* r *violently)* like that. You can do that on stage, but it can be picked up by the microphone in a rather ugly fashion. So you try to give the same intensity but with an amount of sound that will allow the machinery to record without distortion."[98] Like Arroyo, John Lennon was keenly aware of the need for special techniques, often singing into the side or back of the microphone to get a desired effect or waving his hand in front of his mouth to soften the sibilants that microphones tend to exaggerate and distort.[99]

Instrumentalists, too, must be aware of the sensitivity of microphones. In concert, the guitarist's left hand sliding up and down the strings or the clicking of the saxophonist's keys are rarely heard. Yet such incidental sounds are picked up in the studio, and although performers may not always want to eliminate the noises, they must be conscious of their pres-ence. In 1932 the Czech pianist Josef Jiránek noted that when recording he was instructed not to use the sustain pedal—a crucial expressive device in much of the repertoire—presumably because the noise of the mecha-nism itself would be picked up by the microphone.[100]

The sensitivity of the microphone also provided the means for new sounds and performance practices. Consider "crooning," the soft, re-strained vocal style popular from the 1920s to the 1950s, heard in the singing of Rudy Vallee, Bing Crosby, Perry Como, and Frank Sinatra. Crooning was only possible with the microphone, for without amplification such singing would be expressively flat and nearly inaudible. Yet the technique achieved a remarkable effect. Crooning is akin to whispering, which under normal circumstances can be heard only when one is physically very close to the speaker; crooning thus provides a sense of intimacy between artist and audience, collapsing the technologically imposed distance that would seem to preclude such a relationship. No wonder the only moderately pre-possessing Vallee was hailed as "God's gift to us girls."[101] As I hope is clear, although all recording machines require an "intelligent rapport," the ways in which the technology is accommodated may both limit and expand the possibilities of musical performance.

MANIPULABILITY

Listen to most early-twentieth-century recordings and you will hear a per-formance in the traditional sense. That is, you are hearing a single and complete take, in which the beginning, middle, and end of the piece were recorded in that order on the same day, in the same place, and by the same performer or group. This was hardly out of a desire for authenticity; it was a product of necessity. However, since the introduction of magnetic tape (in the late 1940s) and digital recording (in the late 1970s), it has been pos-sible to offer the illusion of a traditional performance as well as to create "performances" that could never have existed. With the ability to manip-ulate sound through such technology, musicians have been able to tran-scend time, space, and human limitations, and in the process have created wholly new sounds, works, genres, and performance traditions.

One of the most basic manipulations is splicing, in which passages re-corded at different times are joined together. The Beatles' "Strawberry Fields Forever" (1967) provides a famous example. The Beatles did over two dozen takes of the song, none of which completely satisfied John Lennon. But he did like the first half of Take 7 and the second half of Take 26. So he asked George Martin, their producer, to put the two together. Unfortunately, they were in different keys and tempos. The two takes, however, were related in such a way that when one was sped up and the other slowed down so that the tempos matched, the pitches also matched. Thus the two takes could be joined, the splice occurring at about 0:59 on the word *going* in "Let me take you down 'cause I'm going to Strawberry Fields."[102] Although the splice is nearly undetectable, the slightly altered speed of Lennon's voice helps give the song its distinctively dreamlike quality.

Pianist Glenn Gould, a passionate champion of splicing, recounted a similar experience, but with a very different repertoire. In recording the A minor fugue from the first book of Bach's *Well-Tempered Clavier*, he and his producer decided that the best of several takes were numbers 6 and 8. Neither, however, was acceptable on its own: "It was agreed that neither the Teutonic severity of Take 6 nor the unwarranted jubilation of Take 8 could be permitted to represent our best thoughts on the fugue." So they decided to combine them, opening and closing with Take 6 and splicing the middle of Take 8 in between. The result, Gould felt, was "far superior" to any single, real-time performance, and he declared that the technology had allowed him to "transcend the limitations that performance imposes upon the imagination."[103]

While the Beatles and Glenn Gould created "performances" that were theoretically possible but never actually took place, other performers have taken advantage of the technology to make recordings that could *never* have existed as performances. In 1946 Jascha Heifetz released a disc on which he is heard simultaneously playing both solo parts of Bach's Concerto in D Minor for two violins.[104] In 1991 Natalie Cole recorded the duet "Unforgettable" with her *late* father, Nat King Cole, whose contribution to the song had been made decades earlier and preserved on tape.[105] These documents could only have been created by overdubbing, in which recordings made at different times are combined, not sequentially, as in splicing, but synchronically.

Another crucial type of manipulation comes from the use of the stereo field—the sonic "stage" in which sounds occupy and move through space in a recording. Consider "Strawberry Fields Forever" once again. When listening through headphones, the song begins as if an organ or perhaps flute trio is playing softly into your left ear. (Actually, the sound comes from a Mellotron, an early synthesizer that played prerecorded tape loops.) A chord in the electric bass then sounds in your right ear, followed by John Lennon singing "Let me take you down," seemingly in the middle of your head. Ringo Starr joins the fray, playing the drums as if he were sitting on your left shoulder. A guitar slide, traveling *through* your head from left to right, rounds out the opening fifteen seconds. Clearly, the Beatles (in collaboration with their producer and engineer) created a musical space unique to the work, one with no possible physical counterpart.

Often the stereo field is used simply to enliven a song's texture or to provide added bounce or swing, but the way musical space is deployed can also enhance the meaning of a song. In "Strawberry Fields Forever," it is the fantastic disposition of sound that persuades us that "nothing is real." The guitar and drums moving slowly from left to right in the opening of Jimi Hendrix's "Crosstown Traffic" (1968) musicalize the song's title by imitating the sound of passing cars. Late in Led Zeppelin's "Whole Lotta Love" (1969), Robert Plant's voice travels from right to left to right with ever greater reverberation (c. 4:19–4:27), as if he is plunging into a cavernous space. Perhaps it is meant to illustrate the perceived emptiness of the woman he has just addressed with the single-entendre, "Way down inside, woman, you need it." Radiohead's "Creep" (1993) features the violent tearing sound of a distorted guitar each time Thom Yorke admits, "But I'm a creep" (c. 0:58, 2:01, and 3:28). The first two times it appears, the guitar erupts in the right channel, then moves front and center, filling the stage; the sound seems to depict the anger of the song's persona at the possibility that he is unworthy of the woman with the "face like an angel." The last appearance of the distorted guitar, however, is much different; it is distant and barely audible, having been pushed to the left rear corner of the stage. The sound is dulled and softened, suggesting the bitter resignation of someone who now believes the worst about himself. As careful listening and a good pair of headphones will reveal, the use of the stereo field can add depth to a recording, both physically and expressively.[106]

A more recent development in sound manipulation goes under the general heading of digital signal processing, or DSP. DSP far transcends the limitations and possibilities of magnetic tape. With rhythm quantization, for example, a performance with an unsteady tempo becomes metronomically precise as all notes are forced to fall on the closest beat. Pitch correction follows a similar principle, pushing pitches up or down to the nearest specified level. Moreover, both can be applied in real time. Thus I could go into a studio, belt out "Copacabana" in my wobbly pitch and uncertain rhythm, and have it come back at me through the monitor— *as I am singing*—sounding closer to Barry Manilow than nature or good sense should allow.

Digital processing, though widespread, is a controversial practice. As singer and producer Richard Marx puts it, "You have a guy or girl who literally can't sing one phrase in tune to save their lives, and I can make them sound like they can. It's misleading—but it's not overly uncommon."[107] In an episode from February 2001, the animated television show

The Simpsons skewered the prevalence of pop processing. Bart Simpson and three of his friends are brought together by a successful producer to form the next big "boy band." They have the right looks, the right moves, the right attitudes—everything except for musical ability. At first they can only croak out the lines to their song. The producer shudders, heads over to an oversized console labeled "Studio Magic," and turns the "voice enhancer" dial. The boys sing again, only this time we hear buttery voices, perfect intonation, and exquisite timing coming from the studio monitors.[108] This send-up only slightly exaggerates reality. The website for Auto-Tune pitch correction software and hardware made this triumphant claim: "Auto-Tune corrects 'intonation' problems of vocals and other solo recordings—in real time! In goes out-of-tune screeching, out comes bewdiful *[sic]* singing."[109]

But there is another side to the debate, and many feel that the benefits of processing are far from insidious. Producer Matt Serletic has pointed out that the technology allows performers to minimize the stress and strain of recording sessions. "You no longer have to beat an artist into submission by asking them to pound out a vocal 15 times to get that one magic performance—which can result in a recording that's technically accurate but passionately not convincing. With vocal processing, you can get the passion and then fix something."[110] Moreover, the technology allows singers to produce otherwise impossible sounds. Part of the appeal of Cher's 1999 hit "Believe" was certainly the slightly stuttered, mechanical sound of the title word, an effect created through digital processing.[111] Like splicing and overdubbing, DSP is a tool that can be, and has been, used in a variety of ways, both laudable and censurable.

It is important to realize that sound is manipulated in the studio not (or not typically) by performers, but by a variety of sound engineers and producers, sometimes referred to collectively as recordists. Recordists fall outside (or perhaps in between) the traditional triad of composer, performer, and listener. They might be thought of as sound shapers, artists in their own right who collaborate with performers and composers. Because their work is done mostly behind the scenes, their influence is not as widely or deeply appreciated as it should be, though a growing body of literature is starting to remedy the situation.[112]

Recording technology can be used to manipulate sound not only in the studio. In chapter 6 we will see how, beginning in the 1970s, hip-hop musicians transformed the phonograph into a performing instrument capable of generating complex compositions. Although turntablism, as their art came to be called, was new in its particulars, a long tradition of harnessing the technology for similar ends preceded it. As early as the 1920s, avant-garde classical composers treated the phonograph as a means to develop new sounds, and an influential school of thought developed around the possibility of what was sometimes called *Grammophonmusik* (the subject of chapter 5). Beginning in 1939, American experimental composer John Cage began using the phonograph in his music. The earliest example was *Imaginary Landscape No. 1,* scored for muted piano, cymbal, and two variable-speed turntables. It requires two musicians to "play" the machines by altering the speed of the discs and by rhythmically raising and lowering the styli. Although Cage was attracted to the possibilities of the phonograph, he had little interest in its intended use. "The only lively thing that will happen with a record," he once said, "is if somehow you would use it to make something which it isn't. If you could for instance make another piece of music with a record . . . that I would find interesting."[113]

Forty years after Cage's initial experiments, artist and composer Christian Marclay continued what might be called avant-garde turntablism. On one occasion, he created an art installation consisting of dozens of records arranged on a gallery floor, and instructed visitors to walk across them. Later, Marclay gave a concert in which he took the scuffed and scratched discs and, using several turntables, performed a musical collage of pops, clicks, and some heavily obscured tunes. "Instead of rejecting these residual sounds," Marclay explained in a 1998 interview, "I've tried to use them, bringing them to the foreground to make people aware that they're listening to a recording and not live music. We usually make abstractions of the [recorded] medium. For me it was important . . . to give it a voice."[114]

If recording could foster the work of composer-performers, it could also separate composers from performers. *Musique concrète* was an early manifestation of this radical change. The genre was the inspiration of Pierre Schaeffer, who in 1948 began composing musical works by mixing and arranging nonmusical sounds collected via microphone.[115] In the classical tradition, music is typically first conceived by the composer and then interpreted by performers. But musique concrète dispenses with performers by starting with sound rather than score; as the name suggests, it begins with the concrete rather than the abstract. Schaeffer's first such "concrete" piece was *Etude aux chemins de fer* (1948), a "railway etude" that, in the long history of train-inspired musical works, was the first to be derived solely from actual train sounds, which Schaeffer collected from a Paris station. In the United States beginning in the 1950s, a similar compositional approach arose known as tape music, which likewise treated recorded sound as raw material. Pioneer tape music composer Vladimir Ussachevsky, for example, kept dozens of individually boxed and labeled loops in his studio as a painter might keep jars of paint, ready for use in any future work.[116] John Cage used a library of six hundred different sounds to assemble (through chance means) thousands of minuscule bits of magnetic tape into *Williams Mix* (1952). Like Schaeffer, both worked directly with sound, leaving performers out of the loop, so to speak. Extending the possibilities of tape music is the more recent practice of digital sampling, a method in which sound is converted into highly manipulable data. The range of material from which composers draw is vast, including speech and environmental sounds, as well as live and recorded music; as we will discover in chapter 7, the practice raises difficult questions about every aspect of composition, from aesthetics to ethics. In fact, the very possibility of manipulating sound after its creation—from splicing to digital pitch correction—forces us to reformulate our ideas about composition, performance, and the relationship between the two.

ooo

Music and musical life have been transformed in the age of recording. However vast and complex, this transformation can be traced to ways in which users of the technology respond to the seven interdependent traits that define recording. Yet recording does more than influence the activities of composers, performers, and listeners. It affects the relationship among these actors and in fact challenges the stability, even the validity, of the triad. It is no longer necessary for listeners and performers, or for performers and composers, to work together in order to create music. Yet at the same time, listeners and composers have discovered a more intimate relationship, one that can bypass the mediation of performers, while performers can work in solitude, without the need to stand before listeners.

Performances and works are no longer clearly distinct, for recordings can take on the function and meaning of both. Just as recordings can be heard as spontaneous interpretive acts, their repetition can transform them into compositions, works that can be analyzed, historicized, canonized, politicized, and problematized. Nor are production and reproduction so easily separated when preexisting sounds can be manipulated in real time. With recording, listeners need not simply receive music, for they have an unprecedented control over the sounds they hear. While there have always been composer-performers—artists who interpret their own works—with recording we can conceive of listener-performers and listener-composers. Recording thus not only affects the practice of music, it shapes the very way in which we *think* about music: what it is, can, and should be.

CHAPTER TWO

MAKING AMERICA MORE MUSICAL

THE PHONOGRAPH AND "GOOD MUSIC"

Main Street was a musical wasteland. Parlor pianos gathered dust, violins moldered in their cases. Students joylessly rehearsed solfège, while inept organists left worshipers cringing in their pews. The town band was a disgrace. Then suddenly, after what came to be known as the Great Event, everything changed. Families organized string quartets, children eagerly studied music in school, and the community established an orchestra and revived caroling.

What was this Great Event? Simply this: one day the town barber, "Pa" Robinson, bought a phonograph for his wife and four children. This one purchase set Main Street's musical renaissance into motion. After tiring of their dance records, the Robinsons began listening to classical music—"good music," as it was called. Soon, however, simply listening no longer satisfied. The Robinsons, unearthing forgotten instruments, started making music themselves. Before long, Pa had the whole community involved, performing and enjoying the best music. A remarkable civic harmony ensued. Neighbors stopped feuding. Troubled children found discipline. Rowdyism and public drunkenness waned. Even Democrats and Republicans socialized.

Unfortunately for the future of bipartisan cooperation, this Main Street never existed. Robert Haven Schauffler created the fictional town in 1927 to illustrate the promise of a formidable force in American musical life: the phonograph.[1] While Schauffler's Main Street may seem far-fetched, it in fact reflected the widespread and seemingly boundless enthusiasm for the machine in early-twentieth-century America. While the phonograph had its detractors, its proponents were numerous, varied, and vocal, comprising teachers, critics, activists, patrons, performers, and "average" phonograph owners. All shared the belief that this technology would, as *Etude* magazine claimed in 1922, "help America become a truly musical nation."[2]

Sound recording, now ubiquitous, is no longer a symbol of American optimism, and the zeal for musical meliorism has faded. Yet this forgotten facet of American life deserves our attention, for it illuminates the social and cultural power of recording technology and provides a window into the ambitions and insecurities of a country struggling to find its musical identity.

AMERICAN ATTITUDES TOWARD MUSIC AND TECHNOLOGY

Why was the phonograph valued so highly as a means of musical progress? To answer this question we must recognize two perceptions widely held in early-twentieth-century America: that classical music was a powerful cultural and moral force to which Americans sadly lacked exposure, and that technology, perhaps more than any other agent, could foster positive social change. "In Germany, Italy, and, in fact, most foreign countries," noted an American journal in 1911, "the people's knowledge of good music is almost universal."[3] The same was not said of American musical life, however. As one schoolteacher complained in 1917, "In Germany, fat Gretchen scrubbing her kitchen pots keeps time to the heart-stirring passages of Wagner. Beggar boys in Rome trill with unction the tuneful melodies of Verdi. But our children, what shrills from their birdlike mouths? 'Everybody's doing it, doing it,' or 'Let me put my arms about you, I could never do without you,' and other syrupy masterpieces of mawkish sentimentality."[4] Whether Europe actually teemed with dishwashing Isoldes and panhandling Rigolettos mattered little; nor did it matter that the United States was hardly a musical backwater. Such common perceptions did not reflect reality as much as they did a distinctly American ideal: all members of a society should have equal access to the highest forms of culture.

Perception also held that only Europe produced what was known as "good music." (Its variants were similarly superlative: "the better class of music," "first-class music," "great music," and "the best music.") While typically denoting the Western European classical tradition, the term harbored complex connotations. Such music was valued in America as a civilizing influence and an agent of moral uplift. As a 1922 music appreciation text explained, "Where there is love of good music there is always promise of good morals, good citizenship, for love of the true and the beautiful makes for better men and women, and a better world in which to live."[5] A love of "good music" was also believed to steer young people clear of its presumed moral and aesthetic opposite: popular music, particularly ragtime and jazz. As one music teacher wrote, "If the children enjoy Schumann's *Träumerei,* Schubert's *Serenade,* and the *Pilgrim's Chorus* from *Tannhäuser,* they will not care to hear rag-time and cheap street music."[6] And when Anne Shaw Faulkner, one of the great champions of "good music" and the phonograph, asked in a 1921 article, "Does jazz put the sin in syncopation?," there was no doubt what her answer was.[7] Finally, "good music" was seen as a means to improve the cultural standing of the country as a whole. "If America is ever to become a great nation musically, as she has become commercially and politically," the influential educator Frances Elliott Clark claimed in 1920, "it must come through educating *everybody* to know and love good music."[8]

None of this rhetoric, however, removed the obstacles hindering "good music" from reaching the populace. Unlike many European nations, the United States did not subsidize its citizens' musical endeavors to any great extent, whether through a national conservatory or state concert halls or opera houses. Thus "good music" was beyond the means of many Americans, reducing its potential benefit to society. The country's vast size proved a handicap as well. Most of the population lived outside the musical centers, and although virtuosi and opera troupes toured the land, small-town America had limited access to European art music.

But why would a rather simple machine be seen as a way to remedy the country's presumed cultural deficiencies? Indeed, the phonograph might never have been put to the cause of "good music" were it not for an abiding technological utopianism in late-nineteenth- and early-twentieth-century American thought. As articulated in Edward Bellamy's influential and widely read novel *Looking Backward* (1888) and a host of utopian works following it, this philosophy held that technology was the solution to the ills plaguing modern life and the means to achieve a perfect society.[9] Any technological tool or system could be freighted with such potential, and the phonograph, too, had its place in utopian thought. From the time of its introduction, the machine was seen as a potential benefit to society. Not surprisingly, inventor Thomas Edison felt so, and in 1878 predicted that it would be a positive force in business, culture, and education.[10] Many others agreed, including Bellamy, who gave music technology an important place in the future society of *Looking Backward*.[11] Robert Schauffler's Main Street is obviously a phonographic-utopian construction, and much of the pro-recording rhetoric quoted throughout this chapter reveals the influence of this philosophy. Given such broad and deep sentiment, it is no surprise that the phonograph was seen as a way to remove the roadblocks preventing America's musical development. As we will see, three distinctive qualities of recorded music made this practicable, or at least possible: portability, affordability (as mentioned in the previous chapter, a consequence of its tangibility), and repeatability.

Portability meant that potentially every American could hear the classics, for phonographs and recordings could travel where professional musicians never ventured. "Good music" could therefore be heard at home more easily than ever, available to people of all classes and means. Speaking of the symphonic repertoire, one educator argued in 1916 that "today we common people make up the audience. And for all this the talking machine largely has been responsible."[12] The growing popularity of opera was also linked to sound recording. "Why has this great interest and enthusiasm for opera so suddenly developed?" asked the *National Music Monthly* in 1917. "Almost every layman will answer with the two words, 'the phonograph.' People have heard in their own homes beautiful excerpts from the greatest operas, and have come to know their meaning in connection with the stories of the operas."[13]

Recordings crossed boundaries not only of class but of race as well, providing African Americans increased access to "good music." For many blacks early in this century, classical music was seen as a tool for personal refinement. "We shall endeavor," wrote the editor of the *Negro Music Journal* in 1902, "to get the majority of our people interested in that class of music which will purify their minds, lighten their hearts, touch their souls and be a source of joy to them forever."[14] Thanks to the portability of the phonograph, African Americans were able to hear "that class of music" at home, bypassing public venues from which they were often barred. In 1916 the *Chicago Defender* noted the popularity of classical recordings among middle- and upper-class blacks: "During the Christmas holidays there were thousands of dollars spent by our people for Victrolas. They paid to hear Tetrazzini, Caruso, Paganini, Mme. Schumann-Heink, Geraldine Farrar, and other noted artists."[15] The Black Swan Phonograph Company went further, encouraging listeners to seek out "good music" as recorded by African Americans. A 1922 ad in the magazine the *Crisis* appealed directly to its black readership: "If you—the person reading this advertisement—earnestly want to Do Something for Negro Music, Go to your Record Dealer and ask for the Better Class of Records by Colored Artists."[16] The pursuit of classical music was not only considered a marker of culture and gentility among blacks, it was also seen as a means to achieve equality with whites. As musicologist Lawrence Schenbeck has explained, "The demonstrated existence of a 'better class' of African Americans could be used to refute racist views of them as biologically inferior and unassimilable."[17] Thus, black *and* white Americans cultivated "good music" as a way to deny their inferiority, though while whites were responding to a European prejudice as much perceived as real, blacks were reacting to undeniable discrimination.

While recorded music could cross boundaries of geography, class, and race more easily than live music, its portability would have meant little were it not affordable. Prices started dropping in the 1890s: the price of the Edison "Home" phonograph fell to $40 by the spring of 1896, and by 1900 anyone with a Sears, Roebuck catalog could order "The Wonderful Home Graphophone" for $5.[18] More expensive machines were available on installment. Records were also relatively inexpensive: in 1928, an opera lover in Manhattan could pay one dollar for a Victor Red Seal record— the top of the line—or ten dollars for a seat at the Met.[19]

Finally, the easy repeatability of recordings was seen as a further aid in promoting classical music in America. Repeatability was believed to serve two related functions: to differentiate good music from bad, and to help listeners appreciate the classics. In the age of the phonograph, repeatability became a criterion for evaluating music; it was frequently remarked that the best works rewarded numerous hearings, whereas lesser pieces palled upon repetition. Predictably, popular music was said to wear poorly, while "good music" continually paid aural dividends. As one writer claimed of popular music in 1931, "Repeated listening makes it recognizable for what it is and turns liking into loathing."[20] Psychologists even tested this commonly held belief. Two sets of experimenters concluded in 1924 and 1927 that while young people immediately enjoyed listening to popular selections like the "Kismet Fox Trot" or "Sultan One Step," their interest waned with repeated hearings; on the other hand, the subjects found the classical discs more appealing after each playing.[21]

Repeatability not only separated wheat from chaff (however defined), it was believed to be the key to understanding and developing a taste for "good music." As one writer noted in 1912, "practically every talking machine sold has made itself an educational force, for, by law of Nature, through constant listening we begin to tire of the trashy and desire something better."[22] These ideas were later put to the test by "S. K.," a New York City record dealer who wrote a series of letters to the *Phonograph Monthly Review* between 1927 and 1929. S. K.'s first letter demanded to know how anyone could enjoy classical music, singling out for derision the *Firebird* Suite by "Strangle-insky."[23] After heated epistolary exchanges with several partisans of classical music (one of whom challenged him to a duel), the writer agreed to give art music another try. Almost two years later, S. K. reported partial success. After repeated listening he had come to like Schubert's orchestral music, and while he never did warm to Stravinsky, he saw that the Russian master was perhaps worth the effort. The music still sounded to him "like dishes breaking and cats howling"; nevertheless, he admitted, "I only make a fool out of myself to come out and boast about it, for it's likely my own fault and not Strawinski's."[24]

At the turn of the century, unique problems faced the project of disseminating classical music throughout America: the country's size, the government's laissez-faire attitude toward the arts, and the limited possibility of repeated exposure to "good music." The phonograph seemingly brought a solution to the fore. Recordings, because of their portability, affordability, and repeatability, made classical music accessible to all Americans. The benefits of the phonograph seemed limitless, particularly in two spheres of American life, home and school—which the remainder of this chapter will explore.

THE PHONOGRAPH IN THE HOME

A vexing problem at the turn of the century was the challenge of bringing "good music" into the home. Dedicated amateurs might play piano reductions of operas or symphonies, sing arias with piano accompaniment, or perform chamber music. Nevertheless, this was no simple prospect, and it was impossible to hear much of the classical repertoire in its original form. Then too, the music that was performed in the parlor was not always considered of "the highest class." "The prevailing music in American homes is of a cheap and vulgar character," wrote one music teacher in 1912, arguing that "if we are to develop a truly musical nation the child must have a wider musical experience than he can cover in his own singing."[25] Furthermore, amateur music-making was not always considered an unalloyed pleasure. A 1912 editorial in the *Musical Courier* commented with no great fondness on "the agonies of Susie's and Jane's parlor concerts on the untuned piano"; a magazine columnist described home concerts as "a solemn formality, usually undertaken upon occasions of importance only and led up to by hours of trembling preparation on the part of the performer."[26]

With the phonograph, however, "good music" was easily domesticated. The first two decades of the twentieth century saw the American phonograph market blossom. Falling prices and an ever-growing selection of records allowed families to hear almost any kind of music. Moreover, the industry responded to the demand for phonographs that looked more like furniture than machines (often meaning that the horns disappeared, enclosed within cabinets), allowing them to blend into the home environment.[27] Americans increasingly welcomed the phonograph into their parlors, a development widely touted as the best means to help America become a "truly musical nation." Dozens of articles explaining and extolling the medium's contributions to the American home appeared in newspapers and journals of every sort.[28] One crucial constituency was especially vocal in its praise: American phonograph owners. Their testimony, found in a variety of forums from letters in magazines to questionnaire responses, reflected the view that the machine fostered the appreciation of "good music" and could do so for all Americans, regardless of ability, wealth, or location.

The phonograph was welcomed by Americans who considered themselves lovers of "good music" but felt they lacked the abilities to explore the repertoire as amateur performers. George Ruhlen of Tacoma, Washington, was one of them. In response to a 1921 questionnaire sent out by Thomas Edison's phonograph company, Ruhlen explained, "I am not a trained musician, never tried to sing correctly a single note and do not try to play any musical instrument of any kind, but am none the less fond of good music and for want of opportunities of hearing it have gone in for the phonograph."[29] Dorothy Fisher echoed Ruhlen's sentiments in a 1926 letter to the *Phonograph Monthly Review,* writing that "there are many others whose musical training, like my own, is completely nil, but . . . whose intellectual curiosity about great music . . . will receive great satisfaction in becoming familiar with music through the medium of the phonograph."[30]

The phonograph also offered poorer families the chance to hear classical music. In 1922, *Etude* reported the story of a New York City woman whose machine was threatened with repossession. She pleaded to the officer at the installment house that if her phonograph were taken away, "the children will never hear good music. . . . Poor folks like us," she explained, "can't afford tickets to shows and the best they ever see is nickel movies, which you know, sir, is bad for them. Now I know I ain't done what I should to pay for that machine, but if you will let me keep it a little longer, the children will come here every week with twenty-five cents, and they will make up the difference in gratitude."[31]

Phonograph owners furthermore praised their Edisons and Victors for allowing them to hear "good music" wherever home might be. A fire ranger stationed in an uninhabited forest explained in a 1927 letter to the *Phonograph Monthly Review* that "I should quickly face insanity if it were not for my music. Yet my tiny portable [phonograph] and every record has meant a thirty-mile round trip on foot, down the rock wall of the mountain, through the woods to the nearest settlement, and return, 'toting' everything on my back." (His favorite record? Wagner's "Magic Fire" music.)[32] Similar testimonials were made at the time by a trapper in the Pacific Northwest, an Alaskan music lover, and a Wyoming telegrapher living in a boxcar.[33] But one need not have been so confined to benefit similarly. Dorothy Fisher, who grew up in a small midwestern town, insisted that except through recordings "I don't know how else a girl from Kansas would be conscious of the Siegfried motif from the Ring or that there is a great thrill to the last movement of the Chopin B Minor Sonata or that DeBussy ever wrote a great quartette."[34] This Dorothy had no need to leave Kansas to be transported to a new and magical world.

A final testimonial shows Phillip Gibbons of Milton, Oregon, earnestly trying to appreciate "good music," but failing. He included this message with his response to Edison's 1921 questionnaire:

> What few we have of the so called higher class records have been played extensively, and we have done our darndest [to] learn to like them and sometimes some of our more highly advanced relatives drop in and go into spasms of joy on hearing them and discourse learnedly about them but we are afraid we will never properly appreciate them for instance whenever we hear Mr. Spalding [violinist Albert Spalding], it makes us feel uneasy, we feel as if he may bust something before he gets done, and the arias or whatever you call them that your higher class singers go into voice convolutions over make us think they are going in for an awful lot of agony. Christine Miller [contralto, known for her rendition of "Abide with Me"] is plenty good enough for us, but possibly after two or three thousand years our progeny may get far enough advanced to appreciate what we fail to understand.[35]

Despite Gibbons's pessimistic tone, his statement reveals attitudes toward music and the phonograph that were quite common. He felt a need (if not a desire) to cultivate an appreciation for "good music," he saw progress in musical taste as a path from popular music to classical music, and he believed the phonograph to be the vehicle for such progress.

The mention of "higher class records" reveals another commonly perceived advantage of the home phonograph. Western European art music was closely linked to elite culture, often described as "high-class music" or "the better class of music." It was believed that in bringing classical music, the phonograph also brought refinement and taste. As one writer suggested in 1930, the phonograph "should not be thought of as a mere entertainment device, but as a cultural adjunct to every home that would dare call itself civilized."[36] This notion manifested itself in the concerts of recorded classics that music lovers sometimes held in their homes. As at classical concerts, programs were often distributed and proper concert decorum was expected. In 1921, Robert Schauffler (who was later to write about Main Street's musical transformation) noted that some home impresarios would even "go to the length of . . . maintaining as rigid a discipline against talking . . . as if Caruso or Rachmaninoff were there in person."[37] Contemporary advertising both reflected and reinforced the idea of the phonograph as culture bearer. Consider the Victrola advertisement that graced the back cover of *Collier's* in 1913 (Figure 2).[38] The lavish ballroom and elegantly dressed couples suggest wealth and refinement, and the procession of opera characters greeting the hosts makes it clear that the highest musical culture is at the service of the phonograph owner. While the illustration taps into the fantasies and aspirations of *Collier's* middle-class readers, the text (not all of which is included here) recognizes the realities of these readers, noting that machines can be had for as little as $10. The ad masterfully articulates a classic American belief: that everyone can have the very best.

The power of ads such as these to shape popular opinion should not be underestimated. The phonograph companies touted the same virtues of the new technology that educators and activists advocated, but with a much higher profile. Anyone reading *American Magazine, Collier's, Ladies' Home Journal, Literary Digest, Saturday Evening Post, Vanity Fair,* or a host of other publications would have been bombarded with ads—sometimes covering two full pages in vivid color—courtesy of every company from Aeolian to Zonophone. Their pithy slogans appealed to the desires and sensibilities of consumers: "The music you want, when you want it," "The stage of the world in your home," "The ideal drawing-room entertainer," "The highest class talking machine," "Make your home more complete," and so on.

Much of the advertising specifically targeted women, and many of the writings on the domestic role of the phonograph were by and for women.

The best friend of a hostess is the Victrola

FIGURE 2 Victor Talking Machine Company advertisement, originally published in *Collier's*, 4 October 1913.

For good reason: music in the home had traditionally been the province of women, and the advent of recording did nothing to change this. A 1919 study of stores in sixty-seven American cities, for example, found that women bought phonographs more than twice as often as men and, in general, were the primary decision makers when it came to phonograph purchases.[39] But the phonograph had a significant impact on the male of the species as well. It offered something new to the average American man: a way to enjoy music without risk of being unmanly or, in the parlance of the day, "sissy" or "soft."[40] The phonograph also mitigated the supposed "feminizing" influence of music (particularly classical music), for as a machine it opened opportunities for tinkering and shop talk, traditional men's activities. As one writer explained in 1931, "That men are notoriously fascinated by small mechanical details is a securely established fact. Well, then, is it any wonder that . . . men suddenly became profoundly interested in the phonograph?"[41]

The fact that the phonograph allowed men to listen to "good music" at home was significant. Men could therefore experience the classics without the self-consciousness that might follow them into public forums such as concert halls and opera houses. The phonograph also gave nonmusical men the possibility of self-expression through music, permitting them to do in private what they could not or would not otherwise do. Conducting was perhaps the most common manifestation of this possibility. The Minneapolis Phonograph Society reported that some of their members "have taken to 'shadow conducting,' that most exhilarating phonographic indoor sport."[42] (Note how music is incorporated into the masculine sphere by invoking athletics.) A personal recollection on this subject has come from musicologist Richard Crawford, who remembers his father's double life as a foundry supervisor and phonograph conductor:

> Fairly early in my life, I became aware that my father would go into a room of our house that was glassed in, with opaque glass, and I would hear music coming out of that room. If I stood outside, I could see shadows moving inside the room. Now, my father . . . was not a musician in any sense at all. But I eventually put together what he was doing in that room when I saw him walk into the house one day with a baton. He was going into that room, turning on the record player and conducting. I imagine it must have been a very important experience for him.[43]

Another illustration of the phonograph as an aid to self-expression comes from a 1916 advertisement. The ad includes a testimonial from a man who describes how he became a "musician" after playing an Aeolian phonograph at a friend's house. Playing the phonograph, in this case, meant using the new Aeolian accessory called the Graduola. The Graduola was simply a volume control mechanism attached to the phonograph by a cable.

Nevertheless, Aeolian rhapsodized that in using it one could feel the music, live the music, and give to it "a part of your own soul."[44] While this is a fictional account, the idea behind it was widely accepted: the phonograph offered even the most hardened man a way to express deeply felt emotions and explore his latent musicality.

The following story also features a distinctively erotic (if unintended) subtext; the talk of pushing, pulling, trembling, swelling forth, and dying away (not to mention the rather phallic Graduola) imbues the musical transformation it chronicles with all the ecstatic power of a sexual awakening:

> To my friends and associates and indeed to myself, I've appeared until recently, simply a plain, middle-aged, unemotional businessman. And now I find that I'm a *musician*. How did I find this out? I'll tell you! Last Tuesday night, my wife and I were at the Jones's. Jones had a new purchase—a phonograph. Personally, I'm prejudiced against musical machines. But this phonograph was *different*. With the first notes I sat upright in my chair. It was *beautiful*. "Come over here and sing this yourself!" said Jones. I went to see what the slender tube terminating in a handle [the Graduola] could be. It looked interesting. "Hold this in your hands!" said Jones. "Move the handle in to make the music louder; draw it out to make it softer." Then he started the record again. At first I hardly dared to move the little device in my hands. Presently, however, I gained confidence. As the notes swelled forth and softly died away in answer to my will, I became bolder. I began to *feel* the music. It was wonderful! I . . . fairly trembled with the depth of emotion. The fact that I was—must be—a natural musician dawned upon me. And with it came a glimpse of the glorious possibilities opened to me by this great new phonograph.[45]

This last sentence captures the significance of the phonograph for the American man of the early twentieth century. It opened up the possibility of interacting socially through music and of experiencing music on an intimate, personal level. Thus the phonograph essentially allowed men to engage in activities that had long been construed as feminine pursuits, but in ways that encouraged mastery and exploration rather than uplift and education. I would argue that the interaction of men and phonographs helped bring about a reevaluation of music as a gendered activity in America. If today the love of music, especially Western art music, is no longer so widely derided as unmasculine, it may well be due to the mediation of a machine: the phonograph.[46]

THE PHONOGRAPH IN THE SCHOOL

The first decades of the 1900s witnessed a revolution in American music education. In the nineteenth century the primary goal was to teach students how to *make* music, particularly through singing. In the twentieth century, however, the focus began shifting from the practical to the aesthetic. The ideal became known as appreciation—generally understood as the intelligent enjoyment of music, typically classical music, as a *listener*.[47]

With the emphasis on appreciation came a change in the conception of musicality. To be musical, it had generally been assumed, one had to perform or compose. But many began to argue that careful and intelligent listening could also be a sign of a musical person. "Now what does it in reality mean, this 'being musical'?" asked a writer in a 1912 issue of *Musician*. The author's answer could be taken for a definition of music appreciation: "In the first place it ought to mean that we are *receptive* for music, that is, for *good music;* that we feel its uplifting, soul-liberating power. . . . Finally . . . it means that we recognize the kind or type or class of work to which we are listening; to estimate, approximately at least, its merits; to distinguish the dross from the gold, the trash from a work of art, in short, to have and to exercise good judgment in musical matters."[48] Many educators agreed. One offered these rather more succinct guidelines in 1917: "If one loves to listen to good music, one *is* musical."[49]

In teaching children to become musical listeners, educators faced difficulties that their predecessors did not. In a singing class, the instructor and pupils made the music themselves. The goal of appreciation, however, was to develop in students an understanding of music "beyond their own ability to perform."[50] Appreciation therefore required that either music be imported into the classroom or the children be transported to the concert hall. Neither option was easy. What was considered "good music" was often beyond the ability of teachers to perform, and it was all but impossible to bring large instrumental or vocal ensembles into the classroom; and for most schools, field trips to the concert hall were just too expensive.

In 1912 Frances Elliott Clark called for all children to have the opportunity to "hear music, good music, the best music, almost from birth—hear it over and over again and again."[51] The phonograph allowed this widely shared dream to be realized. With it, the type of music and level of performance heard in the classroom were not limited by the talents of teachers, students, or available musicians. Nor did a school's ability to bring classical music to its students depend on its wealth or location. "A talking machine and a few records," suggested *Musician* magazine in 1919, could turn any classroom into a "world-laboratory and Musical History Museum at small cost, no matter how remote . . . from the acknowledged centres of music."[52] Furthermore, the repeatability of recording allowed students to absorb the classics, hearing them "over and over again and again." In addition, as the recorded repertoire expanded, it came to include works rarely heard in public concerts; discs of early Western music as well as Asian and African music began to be issued in the first decades of the twentieth century.[53] Finally, by disseminating "good music," the phonograph, so it was believed, could guide students' moral development. As one educator claimed in 1917, "It is impossible to appreciate good music without hearing it; it is impossible to hear it and not love it, and to love it without knowing high yearning that make[s] for character."[54]

The phonograph affected all types of music study at every level of American education. Three brief case studies—of rural music education, the music memory contest, and the college-level appreciation course—will demonstrate the range of the technology's impact.

In 1913 Annie Pike Greenwood, fresh from college, arrived in Milner, Idaho, as the town's new teacher. She was appalled at what she saw on her first day of school: a one-room shanty overcrowded with unruly and, as she soon discovered, unmusical students. "The pupils could neither sing nor march," she later noted, "and the enthusiasm of youth found vent in most objectionable ways."[55] In 1918, Henry Tovey left the Chicago public school system to become a music supervisor in Arkansas. On his first visit to a country school he asked the children to sing. "They sang the first two lines of 'Columbia the Gem of the Ocean' and hummed the rest. Then they sang a verse of some horrible thing called 'I'm Getting More Like Jesus Every Day.' This was the extent of their repertoire."[56] What Greenwood and Tovey encountered was typical, for in the underfunded, understaffed, and isolated American rural school, "good music" was not a luxury, it was an impossibility.

Once again, recording was embraced as a means to overcome obstacles facing American musical progress. The phonograph provided for the first time a reliable source of classical music for children in rural schools. Its compact size and portability were also advantages. The machine occupied little space in crowded schools and could easily be moved inside or out, or from school to school.

After procuring a Victor phonograph for her school, Annie Greenwood saw an immediate change in her charges. The students were entranced with the music of Mendelssohn and Verdi emanating from their new machine. Discipline improved, and the children even became interested in making music themselves. (Notice the real-life parallels to Schauffler's Main Street.) "We have only had our Victor a week," Greenwood reported, "but have already used it to march by, to play games by, and to sing by. We are learning new songs from the records and the boys are trying to become excellent whistlers. . . . If ever a Victor was needed anywhere," she concluded, "it is in the tiny, crowded, starved, ugly rural school. You would appreciate all it means if, on a dark and stormy day at recess or at noon, you could see the light in my pupils' eyes as they gather around the Victor to hear the records."[57]

Henry Tovey found similar results in Arkansas, but on a much larger scale. Tovey compiled a library of forty records and had them circulated to schools across the state. The discs illustrated all the voice types and orchestral instruments, and included operatic excerpts, folk music, sacred music, and one record of "strange music" from Syria, Japan, China, and Arabia. The demand for the records was overwhelming, and the effects of his program were soon evident. "The result thus far," he boasted, "is that the majority of schools throughout the state have talking machines. There is a growing interest in the better class of Music. Several schools have credit for Music in High Schools. There are more Supervisors and a bill will be presented to the Legislature . . . asking that Public School Music be compulsory in every school."[58]

Perhaps the only problem phonographs posed for rural education was their cost. In 1917 a sturdy educational machine like the Victrola XXV cost

$67.50, and even the modest model VI was $25.[59] Yet the lack of money did not stop schools from acquiring a phonograph. One possibility, pursued by Annie Greenwood, was to raise funds outside the school budget. Greenwood and her students held a Halloween entertainment that raised $20; they also took over the school's janitorial work for $5 a month, until they had enough for a player and records. Henry Tovey found another option: having the state buy and circulate the records so that schools paid only for phonographs.

Recorded music—portable, repeatable, and relatively affordable—proved a godsend to rural schoolteachers. Indeed, A. E. Winship, the editor of the *Journal of Education,* invoked the Almighty in praising the machine in 1916: "I yield to no one in my appreciation of the rural mail service, and of the rural telephone, but I place above either and both of them in the service for God and humanity the possibilities of the instrument which will evermore thrill country life with the richest music of the greatest masters."[60]

At about the same time Winship was praising the phonograph for its impact on rural life, Charles Tremaine, a New Jersey music teacher, devised a novel use for the phonograph that captured the imagination of schoolchildren throughout America. It began when he challenged his children to identify the music on the family's piano roll collection, offering a prize to whomever performed best. The children pursued this "game" eagerly, listening to the music intently and memorizing the relevant facts. Tremaine was astounded at the effect of this exercise on his son, who won the contest. The boy joined a mandolin club, started picking out tunes on the family piano, and even expressed a desire to attend concerts of classical music. "Without question his life has been enriched," Tremaine gushed.[61]

Thus inspired, Tremaine planned a similar competition for the children of his community—now using phonographs instead of player pianos—and the music memory contest was born. The first was held in Westfield, New Jersey, in October 1916, and within a few years contests were being organized throughout the country. By 1926, more than 1,400 cities were participating.[62] It is not clear how long the phenomenon endured, but events were reported as late as 1929.[63] These contests quickly assumed a common format. A committee of prominent local musicians selected between fifty and one hundred works of "good music" which the children—typically middle-school students—were to study. Local newspapers were enlisted to advertise the contest and post the list of works, with accompanying descriptions and analyses. After a study period of several weeks the contest proper was held in a local auditorium. Contestants, either alone or in teams, noted the composer and composition as they heard works selected from the master list. The student or team that scored highest, and often several runners-up, received prizes, usually donated by area businesses. The purpose of these contests was clear: "to cultivate among school children an appreciation of good music, to turn children away from a fondness for the coarser and more meaningless forms of musical composition to a genuine love for the classical productions of the great masters."[64]

The phonograph played a crucial role at every stage of the music memory contest.[65] Organizers chose works from record catalogs, music magazines printed lists of recommended discs, and Victor even published a guide specifically for use in these contests.[66] Children typically prepared by studying the works in recorded form at school or at home. Local phonograph shops made sure to stock every record on the list; sometimes they loaned records to contest organizers in exchange for free advertising in contest notices and programs. While the availability of works on record often dictated what appeared on contest lists, influence could flow either way. The industry often responded to the demand for certain works by recording them for the first time or by reissuing records that had gone out of print. Finally, at the contest itself the works were generally played to the children on the phonograph, rather than by live musicians. The importance of the machine was not lost on contest organizers. "As a rule," one teacher observed, "all that is required is a phonograph and access to a group of records"; another writer simply defined a music memory contest as "a way of teaching the people of a locality—especially the children—something about music, and using talking machine records largely to do it."[67] The phonograph provided an inexpensive, reliable source of music that students and organizers could draw upon as often as necessary. Simply put, the music memory contest could not have existed and thrived as a national phenomenon without it.

The educational influence of the phonograph was not limited to the primary schools, for the technology played an equally important role in the musical life of American colleges and universities. Seeking to implement the ideals of music appreciation, educators at the turn of the twentieth century began insisting that music education serve not solely musicians, but everyone. "In the college," the prominent professor Waldo Selden Pratt wrote in 1900, "musical effort should address itself explicitly and largely to the needs of those who felt shut out from the experiences of musicians." But for many years this wish remained largely unfulfilled. As Pratt recognized, "The most serious obstacle to scholarly musical work is that of providing the student with materials of study."[68] The usual problems of expense and the dearth of available performances plagued universities just as they did rural primary schools.

With the phonograph, however, such difficulties were rendered moot and the new goals of higher music education suddenly became attainable. The phonograph debuted in the university classroom at least as early as 1913, when Mount Holyoke College purchased a phonograph and a number of records for use in music courses; that same year, Professor L. A. Coerne of the University of Wisconsin used a phonograph in his lectures on Wagner's *Ring*.[69] New York University was using a Columbia Grafonola in its music courses in 1916, and many other schools followed suit.[70] Textbooks began appearing in the 1910s and early 1920s; unlike modern music textbooks, almost always written by scholars with academic affiliations, these first texts were produced by the phonograph industry—such as Victor's *What We Hear in Music* (1st ed., 1913)—and typically served as teachers' manuals.[71] Textbooks independent of the industry were first published in the mid-1920s, many of which were written specifically for students rather than teachers. One of the earliest was *Music Appreciation in the Schoolroom,* from 1926; a remarkable aspect of the project was that members of the New York Philharmonic Orchestra and other noted performers were hired to make records expressly to accompany the text.[72] In 1928, Agnes Winslow's *An Appreciation and History of Music* established a model still followed today: its introduction focused on musical rudiments, followed by a main section devoted to a chronological narrative of Western music.[73]

Today, music history and appreciation classes are firmly established in the liberal arts programs of most American colleges and universities. Such classes are now taken for granted, but less than a century ago neither the scholarly nor avocational pursuits of music were officially sanctioned by most schools. While the push for reform preceded the phonograph's appearance on the educational scene, it was the phonograph that made the study of music as a liberal art a reality on a nationwide scope.

THE END OF AN ERA

In 1917 Anne Faulkner, an educator and patron of music, described her vision of America's musical future in an impassioned credo:

> I believe that there will not be a home in the land that does not realize the importance of music. I believe that at least three quarters of the youth of this country will be studying the technic of some instrument. I believe that musical education will be considered of such importance in our general educational scheme that all schools and colleges will give full credit for music study. I believe that before the next generation the American School of composers will hold equal rank with the greatest schools of the past. I believe that long before twenty years have passed America will be considered the most musical nation on the earth. And I believe these things will come to our country because of the vital importance of mechanical music.[74]

While Faulkner proved prescient on some matters, she could not have foreseen the circumstances of a dozen years hence. By 1930, attitudes toward music and the phonograph had changed considerably. The journals no longer teemed with claims about the civilizing effect of music. Though "good music" had never accounted for more than a small fraction of record sales (perhaps no more than 10 percent), its power as a rallying point among musical activists diminished as opposition to jazz cooled.[75] Given the dystopian realities of depression-era America, technological utopianism no longer held so much influence. Meanwhile, enthusiasm for mechanical music was waning, particularly among professional performers. As sound film technology steadily improved, the orchestras that had accompanied silent films were being disbanded across the country. Seeing their livelihood imperiled, musicians and their unions took a very public stance against all forms of "canned music," including the phonograph.[76] Moreover, another new technology—radio—threatened to render recordings obsolete. The advantages of radio during the depression were clear, for it brought

Americans a steady source of free music when few could afford anything more.[77] The fortunes of the phonograph industry suffered in consequence. In 1927, 104 million discs and 987,000 machines were sold; by 1932, the numbers had plummeted to 6 million and 40,000.[78] Many believed that "the story of the phonograph . . . was done," as one premature eulogy remarked.[79] Although the book had not closed on the phonograph, this particular chapter had indeed come to an end. America was no longer the set of problems to which the phonograph was the solution.

MAKING AMERICA *UNMUSICAL*?

Although the rhetoric of the day was predominantly pro-phonograph, a sizable minority was troubled by the technology, worried that it would deter amateur performance and turn Americans into passive musical consumers. Such concern prompts us to wonder whether so much phonographic enthusiasm promoted appreciation at the expense of live music-making. I will consider this difficult question by way of conclusion, offering some final musings on the impact of recording on musical life in the United States.

A number of early commentators saw the phonograph as a troubling influence. In "The Menace of Mechanical Music" of 1906, John Philip Sousa predicted that "when music can be heard in the homes without the labor of study . . . it will be simply a question of time when the amateur disappears entirely."[80] Some music teachers agreed, afraid that the availability of the phonograph might discourage their students. In 1916 an organ teacher reported in *Etude* that he had "several pupils who . . . gave up study when they secured a mechanical machine, as it enabled them to enjoy correct performances of music which they could never be able to execute."[81] The phonograph was sometimes even lauded as a way to weed out incompetent amateurs, typically (and tellingly) girls or women. In 1893 one writer expressed the hope that in the future "cheap phonographs . . . might make superfluous the painful attempts—painful to others as well as to herself— of the unmusical young woman to master impossibilities."[82] The 1912 editorial cited earlier that snidely referred to "Susie's and Jane's parlor concerts" suggested that the earlier author's hopes had been realized, for the apparent demise of such "agonies" was touted as "another achievement for which Victor Records are in no small way responsible."[83]

Pointed commentary also came from the literary sphere. In 1906 Ella Wheeler Wilcox versified her worries about the mechanization of music in her poem "Wail of an Old-Timer":

The risin' generation is bent so on creation,
Folks haven't time to talk or sing or cry or even laugh.
But if you take the notion to want some such emotion,
They've got it all on tap fur you, right in the phonograph.[84]

Sinclair Lewis's 1922 novel *Babbitt* provides another literary response to "canned music." In a speech to the Zenith Real Estate Board, George F. Babbitt expatiates on "Our Ideal Citizen," whom he describes in part as

the canniest man on earth; and in the arts he invariably has a natural taste which makes him pick out the best, every time. In no other country in the world will you find so many reproductions of the old masters and of well-known paintings on parlor walls as in these United States. No country has anything like our number of phonographs, with not only dance records and comic but also the best operas, such as Verdi, rendered by the world's highest-paid singers.[85]

With Babbitt as his mouthpiece, Lewis exposes what he sees as the superficiality of the American bourgeoisie, who regard culture as a commodity and whose engagement with art aspires only to the level of owning reproductions of imported masterpieces.

Finally, the available statistics are also suggestive (though far from conclusive). A 1914 government study reported that the production of phonographs had surpassed that of pianos, and a 1925 survey of thirty-six cities in the Midwest found that more families owned phonographs than pianos.[86]

Nevertheless, the phonograph was often considered a *positive* influence on the amateur musician, and was regularly used as an adjunct to live music-making. Until 1912 many phonographs, specifically cylinder-playing machines, were equipped to allow users to make recordings themselves. Home recording was widely popular, discussed at length in the phonograph journals and even promoted by the industry. The 1899 pamphlet "How We Gave a Phonograph Party," for example, tells of two sisters who invite their friends and neighbors over to make recordings. All the party-goers, regardless of ability, play for the phonograph, and then listen with great amusement to their performances as they enjoy phonograph-shaped gingersnaps baked by the sisters.[87] Evidence of such private entertainments is preserved in the thousands of homemade cylinders that still survive. All of them are unique (they could not be duplicated at home) and provide a fascinating window into domestic musical life. Consider the undated phonographic "letter" sent by A. H. Mendenhall to Guy Willebrand, in-cluded on the accompanying CD as Track 1. "Friend Guy," he begins, "I am making you a record." After asking Guy to send his regards to family and friends, he clears his throat and belts out a comic song about Casey and O'Brien, two Irish bricklayers. With the briefest pause, he clears his throat again and proceeds with a harmonica solo. (Neither of the selec-tions would have qualified as "good music," however.) "And now," he signs off, "wishing you a Merry Christmas and a Happy New Year, I will bid you good-bye for the present. Yours truly, A. H. Mendenhall of Pomeroy, Washington."[88]

The demise of home recording came only with the standardization of the disc-playing machine, which did not easily allow home recording. (It was not until tape recorders became available in the 1950s that home record-ing became popular again.) Yet live and recorded music continued to remain partners. Books such as *Grand Opera with a Victrola* provided piano reductions of works commonly available on disc so that music lovers could perform their favorite recorded music themselves.[89] Furthermore, phono-graph owners could and did play along with recordings. As Marie Chaffee, an amateur violinist, explained in 1921, "I often learn how to interpret a piece by listening to Mr. Spalding play it on the Edison—then I play it along with him."[90] Many teachers argued that recordings would in fact encourage children to take up music. In a 1916 *Etude* forum, several promi-nent pedagogues came out in favor of the phonograph. J. Lawrence Erb, for one, argued that "the total effect of mechanical players has been to increase interest in music and stimulate a desire to make music on one's own account."[91] Some teachers even employed the phonograph as a ped-agogical tool. Oscar Saenger published a course of vocal study in which the student listened to and then imitated various exercises on several spe-cially made discs; Hazel Kinscella and Gustave Langenus published similar methods for piano and clarinet.[92] For many Americans, whether teachers, students, or music lovers, the phonograph clearly did not deaden the urge to perform. For them there was nothing mutually exclusive about music appreciation and musical activity.

ooo

Was recording, then, a menace or a blessing? This turns out not to be a very good question. To assert an exclusively affirmative or negative answer is to fall into a naive form of technological determinism, one that excludes the role of human agency by asserting that machines directly and solely dictate how they are used. To be sure, design circumscribes use, and users often alter their actions to best accommodate a technology's limitations or exploit its possibilities. Yet no design is completely deterministic. The phonograph is a perfect example. Music was neither its first nor its only application. Originally built as a dictation device for business executives, the phonograph was also employed to calm surgical patients, to teach foreign languages, as an exercise aid, and even as a purported cure for deafness.[93] There was nothing inherent in the machine that led logically or inevitably down any one avenue; more to the point, neither did the technology dictate its role as an agent of either musical activity or passivity. The fact that the phonograph was once at the center of efforts to enrich American musical life reveals less about the machine itself than it reflects contemporary attitudes about music, technology, morality, culture, education, class, race, and gender. Thus the phonograph is a mirror, not simply of music, but of society.

CHAPTER THREE

CAPTURING JAZZ

The Original Dixieland Jazz Band was in the right place at the right time. It was early 1917, and while engaged at Reisenweber's Restaurant in New York City, the group attracted the attention of the two leading phonograph companies of the day. Columbia auditioned the ODJB first, but did not immediately hire the New Orleans quintet. Much to Columbia's later regret, rival Victor hired the band in late February to record two numbers, "Livery Stable Blues" and "Dixie Jass Band One-Step." In stores by March, this double-sided disc—the first jazz recording—eventually sold more than a million copies.[1]

It has often been said that this recording was hardly representative of contemporary jazz playing.[2] It was performed by white musicians, while most of the seminal jazz performers were black. And the music was lighter on improvisation, heavier on novelty sounds than was usual (evidenced by the barnyard imitations on "Livery Stable Blues"). Yet this music was atypical for a reason having nothing to do with race or sound. It was uncharacteristic simply because it was recorded. Up until this point, jazz was most at home in nightclubs and dance halls, and was an art known for its freedom and spontaneity. Once on record, however, the music left its traditional venues and became fixed, replayable not by performers, but only by listeners. If jazz musicians wanted to record in those early years, they had to come to terms with the peculiar traits of the technology. The ways in which these performers exploited and accommodated sound recording—whether its portability or its time constraints, its repeatability or its insensitivity—were to change jazz indelibly.

PORTABILITY

In the 1910s and 1920s, jazz musicians fanned out from New Orleans, traveling north to Kansas City and Chicago, west to Los Angeles, and east (often via Chicago) to New York City. While this "Great Migration" carried jazz throughout the country, the music tended to reach only relatively small audiences within the larger cities. Recordings, however, were able to bring jazz to a much larger audience, and to listeners far removed geographically and culturally from the urban centers in which the music flourished.[3]

Phonographic dissemination made jazz accessible not only to the listening public, but to aspiring jazz performer-composers as well. The career of cornetist Bix Beiderbecke is nearly inconceivable without the phonograph. Growing up in Davenport, Iowa, Beiderbecke had little chance to hear live jazz. His first encounter with the music was in fact courtesy of his family's wind-up talking machine. In late 1918, the teenaged Beiderbecke heard the ODJB on discs his older brother had brought home. Fascinated with the music, he first tried to imitate it on the piano; he soon acquired a cornet and, much to his family's relief, a mute.[4]

Trumpeter Jimmy Maxwell, living in the San Joaquin Valley during the depression, was similarly isolated, and his early knowledge of jazz also came through records. "There wasn't that much jazz coming out to California," he said in a 1979 interview. "But about once a month one Armstrong record would come out and one Duke Ellington record would come out. And some way I would beg, borrow or even steal, truthfully, for one of those records."[5]

It was not only the musicians living far from the big cities that benefited from the phonograph, however. Trumpeter Henry "Red" Allen, for example, lived in New Orleans at the same time as Louis Armstrong, but came to know Armstrong's playing chiefly through his recordings. "Louis wasn't an influence to us until he started making records," Allen explained. "We got Louis from records, like all the other jazz musicians in the country, I suppose."[6]

Even musicians who frequented jazz clubs sometimes preferred listening at home. As tenor saxophonist Bud Freeman recalled of his youth, "I was learning more about jazz just through listening to records than I was occasioned to learn by going to the clubs, because in the nightclub atmosphere, your attention was not always on the music [but on] a lot of interesting things we had never seen before."[7]

Phonographs and records, small and easily transportable, gave budding musicians unprecedented access to jazz. Without this feature of recording technology, some jazz artists might never have pursued their careers.[8]

TEMPORALITY

Until the introduction of the long-playing record in 1948, jazz was recorded for the most part on ten-inch discs limited to about three minutes of music per side. Although we have little direct knowledge of how long live jazz performances typically lasted, the testimony of musicians suggests that works were not consistently so short. Consider bassist Al Morgan's account of a 1932 performance of "The Reefer Man" with Cab Calloway's band: "Cab let it go on. Me, alone, chorus after chorus. And the guys kept encouraging him, yelling, 'Go, go, let him go!' . . . I played alone for . . . five or six minutes."[9] On the contemporaneous recording of "The Reefer Man," Morgan's solo lasts only a few bars; in fact, the whole of the record could have been played twice during his live performance. Drummer Baby Dodds remarked that when recording with his brother Johnny's band, "we could never play as many choruses as we used in dances, and if there were solos they had to fit into the exact time, too."[10] Early jazz was typically dance music, and bands were unlikely to cut a performance short if they sensed the audience would keep dancing, even if that meant playing for unusually long stretches. According to Ralph Berton, Bix Beiderbecke also had to curtail his performances in the studio. "No wonder Bix didn't like record dates. For one thing, a 10-inch 78-speed record had a maximum of three and one-quarter minutes playing time on it; for a musician with a lot to say it was like telling Dostoevsky to do *The Brothers Karamazov* as a short story. Bix on a bandstand, if he was going good, would really stretch out—ten choruses were nothing."[11] For a later example, tenor saxophonist Paul Gonsalves famously took a twenty-seven-chorus solo at the 1956 Newport Festival performance of Ellington's "Diminuendo and Crescendo in Blue."[12]

When works were recorded, then, the performers had to accommodate the time limitation. The easiest solution was to reduce the number of ensemble choruses. But solos also had to be reined in, for in the studio the musicians often had merely eight (and usually no more than thirty-two) measures in which to make an impression.[13]

The limited playing time of the 78 forced musicians to trim their performances, but even more, it discouraged improvisation as well. It turns out that early jazz musicians did not improvise in the studio as much as is commonly thought. In recent years, the release of previously unpublished jazz recordings has made it possible to compare multiple versions (whether consecutive takes or separate releases) of a piece by a particular band. A consistent finding is that solos often changed very little from one recording to another. In several early Ellington works, for example, the solos are nearly unaltered from take to take, evidently having been plotted out ahead of time. In "The Creeper" (1926), for instance, Otto Hardwick changes few if any notes in his alto sax solo (the second of the piece) over the two takes.[14] Gunther Schuller pointed out another Ellington example: three recordings of "Black and Tan Fantasy" made over a seven-month span in 1927 reveal almost no change in the trumpet solos, even when Jabbo Smith substituted for Bubber Miley on the Okeh version.[15] In his study of Fletcher Henderson's band in the 1920s, Jeffrey Magee noted that "of more than a dozen alternate takes with [Louis] Armstrong . . . most reveal that the hot trumpet player had 'set' his solos to a large degree."[16]

Jazz musicians also followed written sources more closely than previously realized. David Chevan found that in the 1920s many bands followed published stock arrangements in their recordings, with little embellishment or change. Chevan also discovered that in 1924, Louis Armstrong sent a manuscript of his famous "Cornet Chop Suey" to the Copyright Office at the Library of Congress—two years *before* he recorded the work. The recording, long hailed as a masterpiece of improvisation, is in fact remarkably similar to the copyright deposit. For the most part, only the phrase endings differ; nearly everything else had long been set down on paper. Several other Armstrong recordings reveal similar parallels with their copyright deposits.[17] Of course, even if the solos were more or less set when he arrived in the studio, he may well have developed the final version through improvisation, having it transcribed (probably by his wife, Lil Hardin Armstrong) only once he was satisfied. Still, the fact that these solos remained nearly unaltered for years challenges traditional assumptions about the role of improvisation in jazz.

But was the tendency to plan solos for the studio attributable to the influence of recording? This is a difficult question, for we do not know to what extent musicians were improvising when playing live. One thing, however, is clear: live performances tended to be longer than recorded ones, with the extra time usually going toward additional solos. If a musician were to play several solo choruses in a live performance, it is unlikely that *all* the solos would have been fixed. In other words, the longer the performance and the more solos played, the more the performers were apt to improvise. The corollary is that a shorter performance with fewer solos made improvisation *less* likely. Knowing that time was short and aware of the permanence of recordings, performers and their bandleaders would want not only to choose their best work to commit to shellac but also to ensure that all solos stayed within a prescribed time. To do either would require careful planning and thus militate against extensive improvisation.

Occasionally, early jazz transcended the technologically imposed time limitation, resulting in a small number of works displaying what Richard Crawford has called "two-side form."[18] Duke Ellington was foremost among those who recorded extended jazz pieces, notable examples being "Creole Rhapsody" (1931), "Reminiscing in Tempo" (1935), and "Diminuendo and Crescendo in Blue" (1937).[19] His first was an arrangement of the jazz standard "Tiger Rag" (1929). Structurally, the work does not seem to demand both sides of a record. The purpose of extending the performance was most likely, as Gunther Schuller remarked, "to give the musicians a chance at some uninhibited freewheeling improvisations."[20] In fact, it is one of the few occasions among Ellington's early recordings in which the solos change significantly between the first and second takes—suggesting, by implication, that when the band recorded single-sided works the performers did *not* feel free to improvise so extensively. Ellington's

"Diminuendo and Crescendo in Blue" was conceived for an entirely different purpose. The original version (but *not* the extended 1956 live performance) is, as Schuller observed, "a full-fledged written *composition* with virtually no improvisation."[21] This work fades toward a cadence on the first side (Diminuendo in Blue) and fades back in at the beginning of the second (Crescendo in Blue). The cessation of sound in turning the record over, then, is not a break in the music but its continuation, for the diminuendo ends and the crescendo begins at the same point: silence.[22]

With few exceptions, the length of recordings and the brevity of solos remained constant for the thirty-one years between the first jazz recording and the introduction of the long-playing record in 1948. This was hardly a temporary situation, and it affected jazz performance and composition alike. Concision became a virtue, if not a defining trait, of the music. How early jazz is understood, therefore, is often a function of its phonographic preservation, which in turn was for more than three decades subject to a severe and arbitrary time limitation.

REPEATABILITY

If the limited playing time of the 78 was a liability of the medium, its repeatability could be an asset, making the phonograph an important aid to jazz musicians learning their craft. Bix Beiderbecke played the ODJB's discs of "Tiger Rag" and "Skeleton Jangle" innumerable times until he could pick out every note of Nick LaRocca's cornet solos. As Jimmy McPartland—another cornetist—explained, he and his friends learned from the New Orleans Rhythm Kings by repeating and imitating their records:

> What we used to do was play the record on . . . play a few bars, and then get all our notes. We'd have to tune our instruments up to the record machine, to the pitch, and go ahead with a few notes. Then stop! A few more bars of the record, each guy would pick out his notes and boom! We would go on and play it. It was a funny way to learn, but in three or four weeks we could finally play one tune all the way through.[23]

Such examples could be multiplied almost indefinitely. Jimmy Maxwell spent four to five hours a day during his high school summers listening to Armstrong and Ellington discs until he could play along with them. Bud Freeman studied Beiderbecke's records, while Beiderbecke himself endlessly played LaRocca. Saxophonist Charlie Parker learned from Lester Young's discs; Young, in turn, was a devotee of Frankie Trumbauer's recordings. Trumpeter Wynton Marsalis, and probably countless others, memorized John Coltrane's famous saxophone solo on "Giant Steps." On it goes: these unusual student-teacher relationships and lineages, in which the parties may never meet, continue to form. Right now, budding jazz musicians are no doubt listening to or playing along with their favorite recordings for the hundredth time.[24]

In jazz, the study of recordings is considered essential. Much more than classical music, jazz is considered "ear music," in which learning from listening is privileged over the study of the printed note. Classically trained pianists and violinists have Czerny and Kreutzer; tenor players have Hawkins ("Body and Soul") and Coltrane ("Giant Steps"). All may be treated as etudes, practiced daily to sharpen the performer's skills; the difference is in the medium in which they are preserved. To be sure, today's jazz performers have access to a variety of published scores. Yet in jazz the printed page is often treated with some suspicion. Scholar and performer Paul Berliner has suggested why:

> Although experienced improvisers regard the published materials as valuable learning aids, they caution youngsters about becoming too dependent upon them. Without comparing transcriptions to the original recordings, students cannot determine the accuracy of the transcription work or its reproduction. Moreover, however useful they may be for accomplished musicians who can interpret them, all transcriptions are reductive or skeletal representations of performances and provide learners with little information about fundamental stylistic features of jazz. Finally, if students rely upon publications rather than recordings as sources, they deprive themselves of the rigorous ear-training that traditionally has been integral to the improviser's development.[25]

In jazz, the values of the classical world are inverted: the performance is the primary text, while the score is merely an interpretation.

To emphasize the oral transmission of jazz, however, is not to dismiss the role of the visual in the study of the music. Seeing the hands, mouths, postures, and gestures of established performers and their interaction with other musicians can be crucial to the development of less experienced players. The *lack* of the visual can be a handicap for those who learn solely by studying recordings. Keith Copeland has observed that "it's hard for drummers to learn from records because you can't see what the drummer's doing with his hands and feet, what sticks he's using and exactly what part of the drum he's hitting."[26] The missing visual dimension occasionally has unexpected consequences. Paul Berliner cites an example of a bass player who tried to master a rhythmically complex solo from a recording. He encountered tremendous difficulties, but was able to play most of the solo after devising special fingerings. Only when he went to a performance of the band whose record he had studied did he see what he had failed to hear: that the bass solo was in fact a duet![27]

Repeatability has influenced not only jazz education but the very nature of jazz improvisation. While hardly independent of models or rules, improvised music assumes its exact shape and sound only when executed. An improvised work or solo is, by definition, unique, belonging to a specific time and place. A recorded improvisation is therefore a paradox: it is music of the moment made timeless, the one-of-a-kind rendered reproducible, the spontaneous turned inevitable. How is jazz improvisation, then, affected when musical performance can be mechanically preserved and reproduced? I would point out three possible consequences, that is, phonograph effects: first, as I have already noted, improvisations may come to be treated as fixed compositions, and studied as such; second, mistakes or accidents may be preserved and later normalized by listeners and performers; and third, musicians may repeat their own recorded improvisations.

In jazz performances there is always a possibility that players will create novel harmonies, melodies, rhythms, and textures, which the musicians may or may not choose to recreate in the future. When jazz is recorded, however, any fortuity—happy or otherwise—is preserved, reproduced every time the recording is played. King Oliver's 1923 "Dippermouth Blues," for example, reportedly immortalized a memory lapse. As the culprit, drummer Baby Dodds, later recalled,

> I was to play a solo and I forgot my part. But the band was very alert and [banjoist] Bill Johnson hollered "Play that thing!" [c. 2:12; Track 2 on the

accompanying CD] That was an on-the-spot substitution for the solo part which I forgot. The technician asked us if that was supposed to be there and we said no. However, he wanted to keep it in anyway and ever since then the outfit uses that same trick, all because I forgot my part.[28]

Thus, although Johnson's vocal break originally served merely to cover Dodds's lapse, it came to be integral to the work. Bix Beiderbecke considered the mistakes preserved on his 1928 recording of "Goosepimples" less serendipitous. Beiderbecke was said to be furious when a band mate complimented his playing. "Jesus, kid, you must be deaf," Beiderbecke retorted. "Didn't you hear all the idiotic mistakes on that? How about where I spoiled the whole take by blowing sharp on purpose? And listen to this piece of corn, where I stuck in that phoney Charleston lick, as a gag; I was so upset about spoiling Frankie's [saxophonist Frankie Trumbauer's] chorus, I thought the take was n.g. [no good—to be discarded] anyhow."[29]

The Dodds and Beiderbecke examples illustrate how recording preserves the unintended in improvised jazz. When these are repeated, they can become set and normalized in the minds of listeners. Unique, spontaneous acts, then, may come to be regarded as fixed. This phenomenon is related to a third phonograph effect: the feedback loop. A particular recording can become so well known and admired that listeners will want or expect to hear the piece performed in concert in exactly the same way. Performers may feel pressure to meet those expectations. In other words, familiarity may breed repetition. Yet when a performer reproduces an improvised solo exactly (or perhaps even mostly) as it had been executed the first time, it is no longer an improvisation. It becomes a composition—unnotated, but a composition nonetheless. Even if there was little improvisation on a particular recording, its widespread popularity may discourage subsequent performances from departing from the original. For example, when Duke Ellington performed his well-known works for the radio he hewed closely to the versions recorded on 78, even though he was not constrained by the temporal limitation of the disc. As Mark Tucker pointed out, "The late '30s and '40s air checks [recorded broadcasts] reveal that Ellington was not significantly changing pieces for live performance, i.e. extending them. The fall 1940 air check of 'Concerto for Cootie' from Chicago is very close to the studio recording from the spring. Some details in Cootie's [trumpeter Cootie Williams's] soloing are different, but the piece is virtually identical in structure and length."[30] Similarly, when Ellington was asked by Victor to try out its experimental long-playing format in 1933, he did not write an extended piece or allow the musicians room for expanded solos; instead, he recorded two medleys of three works per side.

In jazz, the repeatability of sound recording has had many and varied consequences. For one, it has aided the close study of the repertoire. It has also had a complex effect on jazz improvisation. While recording may foster improvisatory skills by allowing musicians to analyze and extrapolate from solos, it can also inhibit experimentation and encourage the reproduction of once-improvised solos in live performance.

RECEPTIVITY

In 1923 the French critic Roland-Manuel declared that all jazz instruments were "phonogenic."[31] His observation, though understandable, is quite wrong. While some instruments recorded well, the range of sounds that acoustic and early electrical equipment could capture was much narrower than the range of sound that jazz bands produced. Consequently, the instrumentation heard on disc was in part shaped by the limitations of the technology. The piano, particularly when part of a larger ensemble, was difficult to record in the acoustic era. Banjos often substituted for keyboards, and many ragtime and early jazz pianists chose to make piano rolls instead.[32] Drums also fared poorly. Baby Dodds explained that in the acoustic era "the drumming didn't come out so well," and noted that he even played a washboard instead of drums on a few records.[33] Trombonist Eddie Edwards of the Original Dixieland Jazz Band pointed out that in the studio "you couldn't use a bass drum, which vibrated too much, or a snare drum, which came out blurred." He recalled that ODJB drummer Tony Sbarbaro "had to beat only on the cow bells, wood blocks, and sides of drums. . . . As a result, a great many drummers were influenced who heard only the record and didn't realize that the bass and snares were integral parts of Dixieland drumming."[34] The early microphones were hardly an improvement in this area. In a 1930 article, composer R. Raven-Hart advised against bringing the bass drum into the studio and called the snare "quite unusable."[35] The bass drum was a troublemaker even into the 1950s.

When Sam Woodyard went to record in a Columbia studio for the first time, "a guy came out of control with a blanket. 'Put it over your bass drum,' he said. 'For what?' 'We do it for all the drummers who come in here. If you don't cover the bass drum the needle starts jumping.'"[36]

The double bass, too, played at the edge of recordability. Raven-Hart noted that in the studio, "certain instruments are 'undesirables,' above all, the double bass."[37] Interestingly, the difficulty lay not in the reproduction of low frequencies. The problem, he explained, was that the high frequencies created by the attack of the bow were suppressed. Without a clear attack, the sound is muddied and not even clearly identifiable as coming from a bass. (While Raven-Hart addressed the challenges of electrical recording, we may assume that the same was true for the acoustic process, since recording horns were even more limited in their high-frequency response.) Perhaps this limitation led to the predominance of the "slap" style of early jazz bass performance. Instead of using the bow, the player plucks the string with great force so that the sound of the string hitting against the wooden fingerboard is heard as much as or even more than the pitch itself. This technique gives the bass a percussive, more intense and concentrated sound better suited to recording horns and microphones. Jazz musicians had to be resourceful in the studio, and bassists who did not want to be replaced by tuba players or simply left off recordings had good reason to develop a more "phonogenic" technique—which the slap style certainly was. This is not to say, of course, that performers and listeners alike did not also find the sound of slap bass appealing. Still, it is revealing that by the mid-1940s and the rise of bebop, slap bass went out of style. Perhaps performers were reacting to what seemed an old-fashioned sound, but they might also have been responding to the possibility that, with improvements in recording technology, they could finally use their instruments to their fullest effect.[38]

Ensemble placement in the studio was also affected by the limitations of early recording equipment. Depending on the instrument, some performers had to play right into the horn, some were put up on risers, and others had to face away from the machine or even play in an adjoining room. Rudi Blesh described a 1923 session in which Johnny Dodds stuck his clarinet practically down the throat of the recording horn, while trumpeter King Oliver stood a few paces behind, and Louis Armstrong—who had the most powerful sound in the group—played his horn about fifteen feet from the studio's horn.[39] Sometimes, however, the recording rooms were so small that the musicians were crowded against one another.[40] (Pity the poor musician who had to sit in front of the trombonist!) Whether jostling for space or standing barely within shouting distance, performers were thus often forced to work in unnatural arrangements that hindered the interaction among musicians so important to jazz performance.

The development of electrical recording made it possible to reproduce a much larger spectrum of sound; pianists, drummers, and bassists could finally be heard without undue modification. Nevertheless, the microphone had its own quirks, and may have also affected jazz performance. Duke Ellington stated a number of times that the sound of "Mood Indigo" (1930) was influenced by the nature of electrical recording. In 1933 he remarked that it was "the first tune I ever wrote specifically for microphone transmission."[41] He explained further in 1935 that when he first tried to record the piece, the playing created an unpleasant resonance with the microphone. "There was a funny sound in the first record we made, and we busted eight more recordings before we found the trouble. There was a loose plunger in the 'mike,' and we couldn't get rid of it nohow, so what did we do but transpose the piece to another key so the goofy mike sound fitted and it made a swell effect."[42] Quite a bit later, in 1962, Ellington called the resonance a "mike tone," and told an interviewer that he had sought to "employ these instruments [trumpet, trombone, and clarinet] in such a way, at such a distance, that the mike tone would set itself in definite pitch—so that it wouldn't spoil the record."[43] Ellington elaborated no further, so it is difficult to know the exact cause-effect relationship that shaped the sound of "Mood Indigo."[44] Yet he was certainly savvy in the ways of recording musical instruments. Perhaps, therefore, the unique timbral qualities achieved in "Mood Indigo" and in so many of his later works—what has been called the Ellington Effect—may also be a phonograph effect.

Roland-Manuel's claim that all jazz instruments are phonogenic, while inaccurate, is revealing. Whether in France, the United States, or anywhere in the world, most listeners who knew jazz knew it through recordings; the jazz they heard, therefore, was something of a distortion, having been adapted in response to the nature of the medium. The peculiar strengths and limitations of the technology thus not only influenced jazz performance practice, it also shaped how listeners—some of whom were also performers or composers—understood jazz and expected it to sound.

○○○

Jazz was the first major musical style whose early development was preserved on record. The technology did not, however, simply document the music. The portability of records allowed jazz to travel where the musicians did not, and in fact introduced a number of notable performers to their craft. The time limitation of the 78-rpm disc made it necessary for composers and performers to compress formal structures and limit improvisation. Because jazz was learned primarily by ear rather than through scores, the repeatable record became a crucial pedagogical tool for jazz musicians; this quality of repeatability also changed the way in which improvisation was conceived, heard, and studied. The mechanical limitations of early recording technology required bands to alter their instrumentation and seating placement, and impelled musicians to modify their playing styles. Jazz did not, however, collapse under the weight of these strictures; it in fact thrived in response to the demands and challenges of the technology. Although recording may have captured the music, jazz never lost its freedom.

CHAPTER FOUR

AESTHETICS OUT OF EXIGENCY

VIOLIN VIBRATO AND THE PHONOGRAPH

It has been described as a plague, compared to canine tail-wagging, and derided as vulgar; others have called it life-giving, a charming grace, or an emotional thrill. The subject of such equally passionate ridicule and praise is vibrato, perhaps the most hotly debated aspect of violin technique in the history of the instrument. Although violinists have been using vibrato for centuries, for more than three hundred years this pulsing effect, created by the rapid quiver of the left hand, was treated as an embellishment, considered artistic only in its subtle and sparing use. The first decades of the twentieth century, however, saw a transformation in the practice: concert violinists began using vibrato more conspicuously and nearly continuously, starting a trend still followed in the twenty-first century. What was once a special effect had become an integral element of violin sound.[1]

This dramatic change has long been something of a mystery. For decades writers have commented on the matter, but as yet no fully convincing explanation has been put forward. I propose that this shift in performance practice is in fact a phonograph effect. This is an argument some will find unpalatable, for I am claiming that such a crucial aspect of modern violin playing arose as a practical and largely unconscious response to the limitations of a machine. Yet I in no way want to deny violinists their agency or to devalue modern vibrato practice. Rather, my purpose is to reveal the intimate relationship between aesthetics and technology and question whether in this case, and perhaps in all cases, the practical and the artistic can truly be separated.

THE RISE OF THE "NEW" VIBRATO

Before the twentieth century it was not vibrato that violinists considered the most important agent of musical expression, but the bow—often called the "soul" of the violin.[2] Treatises rarely mentioned vibrato, and when they did it was usually to warn readers against its overuse. Typical was Louis Spohr's 1832 *Violinschule,* which counsels that vibrato "should hardly be perceptible to the ear."[3] Some writers were more specific, noting their recommended use of vibrato in musical examples (usually with wavy lines under the notes). Exercises in methods by Pierre Baillot and Charles de Bériot in 1834 and 1858 are positively frugal, indicating vibrato on only a very few of the highest notes.[4] In later decades violinists continued this cautionary approach. For instance, Joseph Joachim, one of the most famous and well-respected violinists of his age, admonished the readers of his 1905 treatise always to "recognize the steady tone as the ruling one."[5] Even one of the earliest tutorials devoted solely to violin vibrato, written by the Englishman Archibald Saunders, concurred with the prevailing view. Saunders advised that the violinist "should avoid its use altogether in rapid runs [and] bear in mind that good violin tone is possible without the employment of this fascinating embellishment."[6]

It is hard to pinpoint when vibrato first began to change. We can find isolated complaints about "constant" vibrato in the late nineteenth century, but not enough to suggest a trend.[7] Moreover, what these observers branded as overpowering might seem rather delicate when compared to later practice. The widespread use of vibrato really seems to have been noticed around 1910. In 1908 two British writers observed an increasing use of the "everlasting vibrato" among violinists, and both regarded the trend ambivalently. One compared the shaking left hand of vibrating violinists to "jelly on a plate of a nervous waiter."[8] The other could muster only enough enthusiasm to suggest that the practice "surely must have *some* virtue."[9]

Despite such complaints, vibrato was becoming more widely accepted. A 1910 German treatise proclaimed that "artistic finish is *impossible* without a correctly made vibrato," and in 1916 an English critic declared vibrato "indispensable."[10] In 1924 the eminent teacher Carl Flesch wrote that "if we consider the celebrated violinists of our day it must be admitted that in nearly every case they employ an uninterrupted vibrato."[11] By 1929 the practice had become so entrenched that one American teacher could write what would have been heretical nearly thirty years before: "Violin playing without vibrato," he claimed, "is like a day without the sun—dismal and gray."[12]

THE RECORDED EVIDENCE

Early-twentieth-century recordings of solo violinists corroborate the shift from the old to the new vibrato.[13] Generally speaking, on recordings made before 1910 vibrato is slight, used only to decorate melodically important notes. The 1910s are in retrospect a transitional period, with some discs demonstrating the ornamental approach and others revealing a conscious cultivation of a stronger, more frequent vibrato. After 1920 the new vibrato is apparent in the recordings of most violinists.

A few examples will illuminate this trend. A useful starting point is with the discs left by the two most renowned violinists of the later nineteenth century, Joseph Joachim and Pablo de Sarasate. Stylistic opposites, Flesch called them "the two poles of the axis around which the world of the violin had turned."[14] The Hungarian-German was considered serious, intellectual, and one for whom technical matters were merely a means to artistic ennoblement; the Spaniard was admired for his elegance, his "silken" or "silvery" tone, and his perfection of technique. Yet for all their differences, they shared a conservative approach toward vibrato.

As we know, Joachim militated against the overuse of vibrato, and he clearly followed his own advice. In his 1903 recording of the Adagio from

Bach's Sonata in G Minor he vibrates slightly on some of the sustained tones and applies a few quick shakes to a few of the highest notes in each phrase, but most of even the longer notes are played straight.[15] While a livelier vibrato might be expected from his performances of Romantic music, the old style prevails on his 1903 disc of Brahms's Hungarian Dance no. 1 (Track 3 on the accompanying CD).[16] In the first twenty-four measures, for example (0:00–0:24), he vibrates infrequently and often for only a fraction of the note's duration. Vibrato does not define Joachim's sound; rather, it is a means to various ends, whether distinguishing repeated pitches, intensifying the high point of a melody, or signaling upcoming cadences.[17]

Today, most violinists perform Sarasate's often intensely expressive works with a generous vibrato. Surprisingly, this approach is not in keeping with the composer's own practice. On the 1904 recording of his *Zigeunerweisen* he plays the dramatic opening phrase with almost no vibrato, something no modern violinist would do.[18] Over the whole of the work he adds a few quick bursts to relatively short notes, applying a slower, wavering vibration to some of the longer ones. And although he vibrates more often than Joachim, he too plays whole phrases straight. Interestingly, Sarasate often plays long notes without a hint of vibrato, even when contemporary taste would have allowed it. Perhaps he cultivated this practice to highlight the purity of his famed tone.

A transitional phase in the use of vibrato may be discerned in recordings from the 1910s. During this period two violinists entered the recording scene who are often cited as pioneers in the use of vibrato, Eugène Ysaÿe and Fritz Kreisler. Ysaÿe's vibrato was, according to Carl Flesch, "a whole world away from what had been customary until then: the incidental, thin-flowing quiver 'only on *espressivo* notes.'"[19] In Ysaÿe's 1912 recording of Henri Vieuxtemps's *Rondino,* the vibrato is faster and wider than Joachim's or Sarasate's.[20] Yet while the vibrato is strong at times, it is often entirely absent. In the beginning of the work he vibrates conspicuously only on the long notes of alternate phrases, and the difference between the vibrated and nonvibrated notes is clear.

If Ysaÿe hinted at the possibility of a new vibrato, Kreisler fully realized its potential. According to Flesch, Kreisler "started a revolutionary change . . . by vibrating not only continuously in cantilenas [lyrical, song-like melodies] like Ysaÿe, but even in technical passages."[21] When listening to Kreisler's 1911 recording of his *Liebesleid,* for example, one gets the sense that the vibrato is not merely added to individual pitches, but that it is a vital, underlying force that connects all the notes in a legato phrase.[22]

The shift was not yet complete, however. Whereas many recordings during this period point toward the new vibrato, others continue to exemplify the old school. Recordings made around 1910 by Marie Hall or Jan Kubelik provide perfect examples of the "thin-flowing quiver" Flesch described.[23]

The transformation of vibrato from the old to the new is nicely illustrated by comparing turn-of-the-century recordings by Joachim and Sarasate to those of the same works made in later decades. There is a world of difference, for example, between Joachim's 1903 recording of the Adagio from Bach's G minor sonata and the 1931 and 1935 recordings of the work by Joseph Szigeti and Jascha Heifetz. On the later discs vibrato is evident on most of the sustained pitches and many of the faster ones, even some of the thirty-second notes; furthermore, both artists (especially Heifetz) vibrate faster and wider than Joachim.[24] A marked difference is also clear in later recordings of the Hungarian Dance. The 1920 and 1940 recordings by Heifetz and Toscha Seidel (Tracks 4 and 5 on the accompanying CD) display a greater use and intensity of the vibrato; in the opening section we hear it on eighteen notes in Heifetz's recording (0:00–0:20) and twenty-five in Seidel's (0:00–0:23)—twice and nearly thrice as often as Joachim (Figure 3).[25] Heifetz's and Seidel's discs certainly confirm the worry of their teacher, Leopold Auer, that his students would not resist the lure of vibrato. As Auer wrote in 1921, "The excessive use of vibrato is a habit for which I have no tolerance, and I always fight against it when I observe it in my pupils—though often, I must admit, without success."[26]

Similar patterns in the use of vibrato may be observed in comparisons of Sarasate's recordings with later ones. Zino Francescatti, for example, introduces a rich, broad vibrato from the beginning of his 1922 *Zigeunerweisen.*[27] Francescatti's vibrato is much more an organic part of his sound than Sarasate's, and is actually less variable because of its constant intensity. Interestingly, the younger violinist takes the opening much slower than Sarasate, a decision that may have been necessitated in part by a desire to vibrate on nearly every note.

FIGURE 3 Brahms, Hungarian Dance no. 1 (arr. Joachim), mm. 1–24.
a. Joseph Joachim (rec. 1903)
b. Jascha Heifetz (rec. 1920)
c. Toscha Seidel (rec. 1940)

Many similar examples could be chosen from the hundreds of violin recordings released early in this century.[28] A broader survey, however, would only underscore what should be clear from the written and aural evidence presented here: the first decades of the twentieth century witnessed a fundamental transformation in the use of vibrato on the violin.

Although scholars widely agree that early in this century violinists began to use vibrato more often and conspicuously, there has been little serious discussion of *why* this happened. A few possibilities have been suggested, however, and these are worth considering.

One possibility is that the new vibrato arose as a reflection of changing artistic ideals. We must remember, however, that the practice met with strong critical disapproval. It is not surprising that violinists from the old school, such as Joachim and Auer, fought against the trend, but resistance continued well after the new vibrato became standard practice.[29] As late as 1950 violinist Adila Fachiri complained of the "unremitting, nauseating vibrato used by present-day violinists," and even more recently, Hans Keller decried the "mania for vibrato" in modern violin playing.[30] In *Vibrato on the Violin,* Werner Hauck sees the new vibrato as part of a much broader trend. "About 1900," Hauck notes, "concepts of the Universe changed," giving rise to a variety of phenomena, from impressionism and expressionism to quantum theory and psychoanalysis. "Is it surprising," he wonders, pointing to the new vibrato, "that violin playing, like a highly sensitive seismograph, was influenced by all this and also reacted?"[31] This conclusion is unverifiable and, indeed, counterintuitive. Considering the sharp edges, distinct lines, and hard, polished surfaces common in the art and architecture of the time (e.g., Art Deco, Bauhaus, Cubism, Precisionism), one might reasonably conclude that a clean, spare violin sound with *less,* not more, vibrato would have been embraced. The strong and continued critical opposition to the new vibrato, as well as its incongruence with broader trends, suggests that its development was not—or at least not solely or at first—tied to aesthetic considerations.

Robin Stowell has suggested that the introduction of the chin rest in the early nineteenth century contributed to the rise of the new vibrato. The chin rest, which transferred the weight of the violin to the neck and shoulder, liberated the left hand, which had previously helped keep the violin firm against the chest. According to Stowell, the "gradual adoption of the more stable chin-braced grip . . . freed the left hand to cultivate a more fluid vibrato movement."[32] Perhaps the full range of motion of the left hand was necessary for the new vibrato, but this explanation does not tell us why it developed in the early twentieth century and not decades earlier with the widespread use of the chin rest. Clearly, it was not simply the *possibility* of a prominent vibrato that led to its realization.

Another argument links the trend in vibrato to a later change in the instrument: the adoption of metal strings. After World War I, violinists began to replace their gut strings with steel ones. The latter have a harsher tone, and violinists may have felt the need to soften the sound with a generous vibrato. But the change in strings could not have been the main impetus behind the new vibrato, which arose well before most violinists were using metal strings. The widespread switch to metal began around 1920 but was not complete until nearly World War II. What's more, violinists can be heard on record playing with a generous vibrato on *gut* strings, while others, known to have used steel, vibrated infrequently. Such counterexamples include Fritz Kreisler's prominent vibrato on his earliest recordings, made at a time when all violinists were using gut, especially on the lower strings, and Maud Powell's selective vibrato on a steel E-string in her recordings from the 1910s.[33] Thus the change to metal, while it may have contributed to the new use of vibrato, could not have caused it.

The most commonly cited force behind the rise of the new vibrato is the influence of Fritz Kreisler. Ever since 1924, when Carl Flesch claimed that Kreisler "started a revolutionary change" in the use of violin vibrato, critics have pointed to him as the prime mover in this aspect of performance practice.[34] The suggestion is plausible, for Kreisler was immensely popular in the early twentieth century, widely heard both in concert and on his recordings, which exhibited a robust and almost constant vibrato. I question, however, whether the origins of this trend really lay with Kreisler. There was a significant delay—at least fifteen years—between Kreisler's "revolutionary change" and the broader adoption of the new vibrato. A throbbing, nearly uninterrupted vibrato is evident on Kreisler's earliest recordings, from 1904, yet although he had already been heard and admired throughout Europe and in the United States since the turn of the century, the majority of violinists did not adopt a comparable practice until the 1920s. Rather than having initiated the new practice, it is more likely that Kreisler was simply held up as a model when other violinists began to use a prominent vibrato.

Although a number of explanations for the transformation in violin playing have been put forward, none of them sufficiently tells us why vibrato
changed and why it changed when it did. I want to explore what is perhaps a radical possibility: that recording was largely responsible. Specifically,
I would suggest that a constant and strong vibrato became increasingly
useful for concert violinists who regularly made recordings, and it did so
in three ways. First, it helped accommodate the distinctive and often limited receptivity of early recording equipment. Second, it could obscure
imperfect intonation, which is more noticeable on record than in a live
setting. And third, it could offer a greater sense of the performer's presence on record, conveying to unseeing listeners what body language and
facial expressions would have communicated in concert.

When recording for the megaphone-shaped acoustic horn, the violinist faced a set of unwelcome alternatives: play as close as possible to the
horn and risk hitting it—thus ruining the take—or play at a comfortable
distance and risk being inaudible. Violinist Arcadie Birkenholtz remarked
on the former alternative, when he recalled that in the days of acoustic
recording "you had to get very close to the horn for the tone to register.
And when you did that, sometimes your bow or arm hit the horn and that
ended it—you had to make the record over."[35] A different but equally
unwelcome problem faced violinists recording with microphones. The
problem was that microphones picked up the frictional sounds of the moving bow, sounds seldom heard in the concert hall because of the distance
between violinist and audience. Veteran recording artist Louis Kaufman
noted that in the studio, "you must be a little more careful with the bow
pressure. You dare not press and get the extremes of *forte* that you could
get in a hall in which the airspace swallows up a lot of the surface noise."[36]

The violinist recording acoustically, then, needed a way to project sound
to the horn, and not simply by playing louder. And the violinist recording electrically—with microphones, that is—needed a way to avoid projecting normally inaudible scratchiness, but without sacrificing tone or
dynamic range.

Vibrato helped violinists resolve both dilemmas. For those recording
acoustically, a strong vibrato helped project their playing to the none-too-

sensitive machines, thanks to the periodic fluctuations in intensity—variations in pressure resulting from the contraction and expansion of air—that mark the technique.[37] By using more vibrato, the recording artist could increase the effective loudness of a note without overplaying and without coming into contact with the horn. A comparison of two acoustic recordings of Chopin's Nocturne in E-flat (arranged for violin) illustrates this point. The last note is a high E-flat, so high that acoustic machines were normally incapable of capturing it. Indeed, it is almost inaudible on Mischa Elman's 1910 recording (Track 6, 4:01ff.), where the artist uses no vibrato. On Jascha Heifetz's 1918 cut (Track 7, 4:22ff.), in contrast, the high note is much more easily heard—thanks to the vibrato, which gives it a pulsing quality.[38]

While an increased use of vibrato helped compensate for the insensitivity of acoustic horns, it also allowed violinists to project their sound to microphones while minimizing bowing noise. Louis Kaufman recognized vibrato's usefulness in this way. "This is something of a trick, you know—getting around the surface [noise] and yet getting the intensity at the same time. *The vibrato has to be somewhat heightened: it has to be somewhat faster than you really need for a public hall.*"[39] Kaufman thus knowingly increased his vibrato to meet the special needs of recording. Undoubtedly others, too, found that a heightened vibrato met the demands of the new process. In fact, many of the violinists whose recording careers spanned the acoustic and electrical eras, including Bronislaw Huberman, Mischa Elman, Joseph Szigeti, and Jascha Heifetz, can be heard using a stronger vibrato in their electrical recordings.

In addition to aiding in the projection of sound, an increased use of vibrato helped recording violinists hide imperfect intonation. Of course, it has always been important to play in tune, but with recording it became crucial. The repeatability of recordings renders bad intonation permanent, and the lack of the visual dimension means that the performer's gestures or expressions cannot draw the listener's focus from the sound, as may happen in concert.

When violinists do *not* use vibrato their finger placement must be absolutely precise; the slightest inaccuracies will immediately be heard as out of tune. Vibrato, however, gives the violinist some wiggle room—literally—to find the center of the pitch. Paradoxically, with vibrato, one need not *be* precise in order to *sound* precise. A note played with vibrato—if it is not too slow or wide—is perceived as a single pitch, even though one is hearing rapidly changing frequencies. Thus, as long as the violinist vibrates immediately, the initial finger placement need not be exact. Scientific experimentation has, in fact, proved this. As a 1998 study concluded, "Vibrato allows performers more time to adjust their intonation before an audience can detect the mean pitch."[40] Significantly, it was not until the advent of the phonograph that violinists widely started to recognize the use of vibrato to avoid bad intonation. In 1919 Edmund Severn described vibrato as "camouflage"; Auer complained in 1921 that too many artists employed vibrato "in an ostrich-like endeavor to conceal bad tone production and intonation"; and in 1924 Flesch wryly noted that violinists using vibrato may "create the impression of playing in tune."[41] Given the heightened perceptibility of poor intonation on recordings, the recognition that vibrato could compensate for errant finger placement, and the concurrence of vibrato's rise with the increased recording activity among violinists, it seems reasonable to conclude that professional concert violinists began to use more vibrato in part to conceal imperfect intonation from the unforgiving phonograph.

I say "in part" because there is yet a third way in which vibrato may be understood as a response to the exigencies of recording: the technique could also help compensate for the loss of the visual element in recordings. In concert settings, unlike in recordings, performers communicate to audiences and audiences react to performers through sight as well as sound. Consider Robert Schumann's remark about Franz Liszt in performance: "Within a few seconds tenderness, boldness, exquisiteness, wildness succeed one another; the instrument glows and flashes under the master's hands. He must be heard and seen; for if Liszt played behind a screen a great deal of poetry would be lost."[42] In 1993 music psychologist Jane Davidson reported some remarkable findings that confirmed Schumann's conclusion. In an experiment Davidson presented subjects with videotaped musical performances. She did so in three different ways: with the video on but the sound off, with the sound on but the video off, and with both sound *and* video on. Subjects were then asked to describe the performers' level of expressivity, choosing between deadpan, exaggerated, and projected, which is somewhere in between the two extremes. Davidson found that subjects were most accurate in describing the performers' intended level of expressivity simply by watching the performance. That is, subjects scored highest when they could not even hear the music. From these results, Davidson concluded that "vision can be far more informative than sound in the perceiver's understanding of the performer's expressive intentions."[43] (Notice the parallel to the McGurk Effect, mentioned in chapter 1.) One implication of this study is inescapable: listeners lose a good deal of information about the expressive manner of performances they hear on recordings.

I suggest that the more frequent and prominent use of vibrato helped violinists communicate to unseeing listeners what their gestures and expressions could not. It is no coincidence that in the age of recording violinists began to recognize that vibrato could help convey emotion. Early in this century vibrato was variously described as reflecting the violinist's "innermost soul," as an "inner, psychic vibration," or as "the barometer of our emotions and inspirations."[44] Before violinists began to record in significant numbers, such comments would have been made about the bow, not vibrato.

Violinists saw another important function for the vibrato as well: the individuation of tone. Siegfried Eberhardt wrote in 1910 that "the individual characteristics of different artists are . . . recognizable only . . . when the vibrato is employed."[45] In 1924 Carl Flesch remarked that vibrato could even be used to identify an unseen violinist. "If two violinists, whose tonal qualities differ most widely, play the same sequence of tones on the same instrument behind a curtain, each using his own vibrato, the individual player may be easily and surely distinguished, while without the participation of the left hand . . . the identity of the player can only be determined by chance."[46]

I believe that the new focus on vibrato as a means both for conveying emotion and for distinguishing among violinists is connected to recording's missing visual dimension. When seeing always accompanied hearing in musical performance, there was no question as to the identity of the performer, and the expressiveness of a performance was strongly a function of the visual—and visceral—impact of the artist's physical presence. It was purely hypothetical for Schumann to consider Liszt (or any other performer) playing out of sight—it just was not done. But when Carl

Flesch spoke of listening to two unseen violinists, he was not being fanciful, for every recording artist plays and is heard as if "behind a curtain."

Although there was no way for recording violinists to replace the visual dimension of live performance, it was possible to put a clearly individual stamp on one's playing and even to restore some of the "lost poetry" through the use of vibrato. A survey of early recordings supports this conclusion. Mischa Elman's "throbbing" could be easily distinguished from Jascha Heifetz's "nervous" vibrato; and no one would confuse Fritz Kreisler's omnipresent shake for Marie Hall's essentially decorative use of the technique. And within a single work, any of these artists might choose to emphasize certain notes or phrases with added vibrato, or to communicate increasing or relaxing emotional intensity through changes in the speed or width of vibrations. Yet while every variety, shade, and speed of vibrato may be heard, the study of historical violin recordings clearly reveals the transformation of vibrato from an accessory to expressive violin tone to a constituent of it.

ooo

I hope to have made a compelling case linking recording and the rise of the new vibrato. First, the timing is right: we hear the beginnings of the new vibrato just at the time recording became an important professional activity for violinists. Second, by using vibrato violinists were able to meet recording's distinctive challenges: the insensitivity of acoustic horns and the problematic sensitivity of microphones, the enhanced perception of poor intonation, and the lack of the visual element.

I should make clear, however, that by focusing on the influence of recording I do not intend to preclude other possibilities. Changing tastes, the technique of particular artists, and developments in the physical aspects of the violin surely had some role in shaping the practice of vibrato. Yet singly or taken together, these cannot fully account for the change in performance practice. I maintain that sound recording was the most direct cause, and perhaps the only *necessary* condition, for the rise of the new vibrato.

What, then, does this conclusion tell us? Most specifically, we may now better understand the forces behind an important change in violin performance practice. From this shift arose a new, distinct sound, one that remains with us today. Practically speaking, historically minded violinists may be inspired by the early Beethoven and Brahms recordings to use a more selective vibrato in the Romantic repertoire, and not solely in Baroque and Classical works. Violinists who record, whether commercially or for their own use, might also reflect on how they themselves respond to the demands of the technology. Such self-knowledge could perhaps lead to a fruitful reevaluation of technique or style.

There are broader implications as well, for I am questioning our preconceptions about the nature of sound recording. As I point out throughout this book, recording is not simply a preservational tool, but a catalyst as well. In order to best exploit the possibilities of this technology violinists made a small adjustment in their playing, but one that brought about a profound transformation in the way musical beauty is judged. As we have seen, the new vibrato arose as an accommodation to practical circumstances, but later came to be valued for its expressive potential. Necessity, it seems, may sometimes be the mother of aesthetics.

CHAPTER FIVE

THE RISE AND FALL OF
GRAMMOPHONMUSIK

In the mid-1980s, three seemingly unremarkable 78-rpm records arrived at Berlin's State Institute for Music Research. With their cryptic hand-written labels, the privately pressed discs gave little clue as to their contents or significance. It was soon discovered, however, that they contained works by German composer Paul Hindemith, music long believed to have been lost. Recorded in 1930 by the composer himself, these discs preserved works that existed in no other form. They were Hindemith's *grammophonplatten-eigene Stücke*—pieces written specifically, and solely, for phonograph records.

The institute, apparently, was not interested in the 78s. The discs were returned to the donor, who in turn sold them to a junk dealer. Their location, if they still exist, is now unknown. Fortunately, a musicologist at the institute, Martin Elste, recognized the importance of the records and taped them before they were returned.[1] This tape became perhaps the only existing aural evidence of *Grammophonmusik,* the first musical genre to use recording technology as a compositional tool. Though long forgotten, the brief life of *Grammophonmusik* deserves renewed attention, for it anticipated by decades now thriving musical practices, and marked a crucial transformation in a technology once thought capable only of reproducing sound.

Neue Musik Berlin 1930 was the tenth in a series of annual modern music festivals in Germany known for adventurous programming; previous festivals in Donaueschingen and Baden-Baden, for example, featured works written for player piano, mechanical organ, even radio.[2] The program for 18 June 1930, however, premiered a type of work new to the series and new, in fact, to most of the musical world. The final pieces that evening were several *Originalwerke für Schallplatten* (original works for disc), specifically two *Trickaufnahmen* (trick recordings) by Paul Hindemith and three works collectively titled *Gesprochene Musik* (spoken music) by his contemporary Ernst Toch.[3]

One of Hindemith's *Trickaufnahmen* was labeled *Gesang über 4 Oktaven* (four-octave song) and contained two similar studies, each lasting a little over one minute. Both consist of a brief melody and its variations, almost certainly sung by Hindemith himself. The other "trick recording" was an untitled instrumental work lasting just over two minutes. These short, simple pieces may be thought of as etudes, but not in the traditional sense, for they explore the technical abilities not of the performer but of the instrument. The vocal work clearly exploits a property of the technology that all phonograph owners at some point discover: when a record accelerates, the pitch rises; when slowed, it falls. In this work, phrases sung at normal speed alternate with double- and half-speed versions, creating passages that leap or drop an octave from the original. The end of the piece briefly explores another technological possibility: the ability to record sounds produced at different times "on top" of each other to produce harmony and counterpoint. (Only later, in the era of magnetic tape, did the technique come to be called overdubbing.) The studies end with a two- and three-voice chord, respectively, with Hindemith singing all the parts. The instrumental study (an excerpt of which is given as Track 8 on the accompanying CD) explores the two techniques equally. The piece seems to be scored for three instruments, xylophone, violin, and cello. Most likely, however, Hindemith used only a xylophone and viola (his own instrument) and changed the speed of the recording to create higher and lower string sounds. The viola, sometimes as violin and sometimes as cello, plays pizzicato throughout, combining with the xylophone (itself heard at different speeds) to create a lively study in timbre and polyphony.

It must have been tremendously difficult for Hindemith to create these works. Had magnetic tape been available, the pieces could have been easily created through simple splicing and overdubbing, but these techniques became feasible only after World War II. Although he had access to the latest equipment at the Hochschule für Musik, the conservatory that employed him at the time, Hindemith likely had nothing more than disc-cutting phonographs and microphones at his disposal. For the instrumental work, he probably recorded the viola part on one phonograph and the xylophone on another and then used a third to combine the different parts onto a single record. We can imagine the complex choreography of the process, with Hindemith moving from viola to xylophone to play each part, and then from phonograph to phonograph to start, stop, and change speeds. Poor timing or clumsy movements would have ruined the work.

When Hindemith presented these works (incidentally, only eight days after he created them), what exactly did the public hear? Perhaps the composer simply set the records going and sat down, but the evidence suggests that the performances were more involved. Hindemith actually made two discs of the xylophone-viola piece, raising the possibility that he had two phonographs on stage. He thus could have performed a phonograph duet, starting the records at different times to create a canon.[4] It is also likely that there was more to the performance of the vocal piece than mere playback. One critic noted that Hindemith had written an "aria with piano accompaniment, in which the human voice extends to a range of approximately 3½ octaves."[5] This could only describe the *Gesang über 4 Oktaven,* but since there is no accompaniment on the disc, Hindemith must have played the piano alongside the phonograph. Unfortunately, we will never know what he played, for the piano part was not preserved.

On the same night in Berlin, Ernst Toch presented his *Gesprochene Musik.* In an article published at the time of the festival, the composer explained his interest in *Grammophonmusik:*

Concerning my contribution to original gramophone music I would say this: the concept arose from the attempt to extend the function of the machine—which up to now has been intended for the most faithful possible reproduction of live music—by exploiting the peculiarities of its function and by analyzing its formerly unrealized possibilities (which are worthless for the machine's real purpose of faithful reproduction), thereby changing the machine's function and creating a characteristic music of its own.[6]

Gesprochene Musik consisted of three movements: two unnamed, the third called "Fuge aus der Geographie." The "Geographical Fugue" has since become Toch's most popular piece, and is now performed without phonographic manipulation. A charming work for spoken chorus, the performers declaim tongue-twisting place names in complex polyphony (e.g., in the English version, "The Popocatepetl is not in Canada rather in Mexico Mexico Mexico"). Few people know, however, that the piece began life as an experiment in *Grammophonmusik*.

Although the disc version of *Gesprochene Musik* has not survived, Toch himself offered some insights into its creation and sound:

I chose for this the spoken word and had a four-voice mixed chamber choir speak exactly indicated rhythms, vowels, consonants, syllables, and words, so that in exploiting the mechanical possibilities of recording (such as increasing tempo and therefore pitch), a kind of instrumental music came about, so that it may perhaps nearly be forgotten that its creation is based solely upon speech. (Only on one point did the machine unfortunately deceive me: it changed the vowels in a way I did not intend.) I attempted to tackle the problem from several perspectives in two little movements and a "Geographical Fugue."[7]

Like Hindemith, Toch created his works in the Hochschule für Musik. However, where Hindemith explored the contrapuntal possibilities of the phonograph, Toch's interest lay in timbre. As he discovered, it is not simply pitch that changes with the speed of a recording, but the quality of the sound as well. Anyone who has heard the Munchkins sing in *The Wizard of Oz* or a Chipmunks record knows the jittery effect of speeding up the voice. Before the advent of recording, however, such timbral effects simply were not possible, and in 1930 this was relatively unexplored territory. Toch's transformation of the human voice must have stunned the Berlin audience. One listener, Georg Schünemann, then the director of the Hochschule für Musik, was impressed and mystified:

> If vowels are sung and are raised in pitch, curiously strange sounds ring out; and if they are combined with consonants in the manner of solfège syllables, a nearly instrumental sound arises. How these amazing pieces worked hardly a musician could say, and how these unusual sounds came into being no one knew, whether through combining musical instruments, voices, or even noises. And yet every compositional, logical, and tonal aspect was precisely planned.[8]

(Incidentally, it was Schünemann who later came to own Hindemith's experimental discs and his family, apparently unaware of their significance, that disposed of the discs when the Institute for Music Research refused them.) The results impressed the other festival participants as well. In 1978 Lilly Toch, the composer's widow, recalled that some of the other musicians present were intrigued with Toch's work and tried manipulating records themselves. "Musicians found it an enormously interesting experiment," she reported, "and they went further in that experiment: they made records at the normal spoken speed, and afterwards they played the records twice as quickly and three times as quickly."[9]

Hindemith and Toch clearly saw great musical potential in sound recording, and in their phonograph etudes took a creative leap that led to a reconceptualization of the technology. But what compositional problems could be solved, what needs met, by exploiting what Toch called "the peculiarities of [the phonograph's] function"? Unfortunately, the 1930 concert in Berlin marked the end of their engagement with *Grammophonmusik*. Neither composer seems to have conducted further experiments, and they did not raise the topic in later writings. Yet *Grammophonmusik* did not die with them; nor, in fact, was the idea born with them. A number of composers, critics, and scholars in Europe and the United States had been theorizing and, to a lesser extent, experimenting with this new type of mechanical music. In surveying *Grammophonmusik* in the period leading up to Neue Musik Berlin 1930, we will see two interconnected currents that can help explain what might otherwise seem to be a sudden and unexpected innovation. These were, first, a drive to radically expand the sonic palette available to composers and, second, a desire on the part of composers to become less dependent on performers for the presentation and dissemination of their work.

GRAMMOPHONMUSIK IN THEORY (AND OCCASIONALLY PRACTICE)

An early hint of the possibilities of *Grammophonmusik* came in a 1910 article in the Berlin journal *Die Stimme.* Contemplating the grooves of a record, Alexander Dillmann wondered if it would be possible to create music with a phonograph not by recording sound but by engraving discs manually.

> There is, however, something strange about this puzzling engraving on the black disc before us. Engraving: yes, that's what it is, though an engraver could never imitate this soundwave-engraving. Really never? A crazy thought: why couldn't we go backward just as we go forward? Through the impressions of the soundwaves, the warm wax is given a form that is translated through the [reproducing] apparatus, and its form comes into tonal life. The voice has become "materialized." With a microscope, we can see its image, as good as anything that human art has created. What until now floated intangibly in space has gained form. What if we, without soundwaves, could create the same or similar form through purely mechanical means? Wouldn't this open the possibility of designing on such a disc a singer of an unlimited range and timbre?[10]

Dillmann reasoned that if a skillful engraver could etch a blank record so that the grooves exactly matched those of, say, a disc of arias, the disc with the imitation grooves should, when played, *exactly* reproduce those arias, even though no human voice was used to create the disc. Furthermore, if the grooves on a prerecorded disc could be manually replicated, it should then be possible to create entirely new performances, ones that would exist only on record. And if the human voice could be imitated in this way, the voice could also be extended beyond human capabilities. In essence, Dillmann was suggesting a pre-electronic form of musical synthesis in which the sound of a voice or instrument is created through artificial means.

A rather different approach was proposed by the German poet Rainer Maria Rilke in a 1919 article, "Ur-Geräusch." The idea of a "primal sound" arose from his comparison of the sutures of the skull with the wavy lines incised into phonographic cylinders. "What if," he gruesomely speculated, "one changed the needle and directed it on its return journey along a tracing which was not derived from the graphic translation of sound but existed of itself naturally—well, to put it plainly, along the coronal suture, for example?"[11] New sounds—primal sounds—and thus new music would arise from the sonic realization of once-silent grooves. Like Hamlet, who remarked in the graveyard, "That skull had a tongue in it, and could once sing," Rilke, too, contemplated the human skull (one sat on his desk while he was a student in Paris) and imagined music coming from it, though in quite a different way.

In 1922 and 1923 the Hungarian artist László Moholy-Nagy—who later heard the *Grammophonmusik* of Hindemith and Toch in Berlin—expanded on Dillmann's idea in two articles on the advantages of phonographic composition. In the first Moholy-Nagy spoke of disc inscription as a serious possibility for composers. "Grooves are incised by human agency into the wax plate, without any external mechanical means, which then produce sound effects that would signify—without new instruments and without an orchestra—a fundamental innovation in sound production (of new, hitherto unknown sounds and tonal relations) both in composition and in musical performance."[12]

In the second essay, Moholy-Nagy explained the advantages of phonographic composition. One was the possibility of establishing a "groove-script alphabet," a fundamentally new type of music notation. In traditional Western notation, the various characters stand in arbitrary relation to the sounds they represent; that the symbols for notes, rests, and so on look as they do is purely a matter of convention. Moholy-Nagy's characters, on the other hand, would be indexical. In philosophical terms, an index is a sign that has a nonarbitrary relationship with what it represents. To say that "clouds mean rain" or "where there's smoke, there's fire" is to refer to indexical signs, for clouds and smoke are causally connected (at least in certain circumstances) to the phenomena they indicate (rain and fire). In the groove-script alphabet, then, a wax-inscribed character would not only represent a specific sound, it would *cause* that sound if "read" by a phonograph needle. Perhaps *alphabet* is a misnomer, for such a set of characters is better considered a palette. Like the painter selecting and mixing pigments, the composer would choose and combine the various incised squiggles and curlicues to create a piece. No score, in the traditional sense, would be necessary. Moholy-Nagy deemed this a great advantage, for composers could communicate directly with listeners rather than relying on performers, who might not render a work according to the creator's wishes. "The composer," he argued, "would be able to create his composition for immediate reproduction on the disc itself, thus he will not be dependent on the absolute knowledge of the interpretive artist. Instead of the numerous 'reproductive talents,' who have actually nothing to do with *real* sound-creation (in either an active or a passive sense), the people will be educated to the *real* reception or creation of music."[13]

In subsequent years a new and passionate advocate of *Grammophonmusik* pursued the matter even further in a series of articles. The first essay by the young musicologist H. H. Stuckenschmidt, written in 1925, was especially bold. The twenty-three-year-old claimed that "the diversity of the sounds [possible with *Grammophonmusik*] will leave the traditional orchestra looking quite primitive," and insisted that "the role of the interpreter belongs to the past."[14] Stuckenschmidt's dismissal of the musical interpreter was sure to upset his readers, for his article was published in, of all places, a journal for conductors. The editor prefaced the essay by noting dryly, "The essay at hand will cause general head-shaking. Particularly among conductors."[15]

Stuckenschmidt further explored the possibilities of phonographic composition in a 1927 essay for the American journal *Modern Music,* in which he expanded on two ideas first proposed by Moholy-Nagy: the use of *Grammophonmusik* as a way to bypass traditional performance and the idea of a "groove-script" system of notation. For Stuckenschmidt, circumventing the interpreter meant that composers could avoid depending on possibly unreliable second parties. More important, it gave the composer the freedom to create music that would be impossible by ordinary means. "The artist is no longer content merely to express what is instrumentally feasible," he proclaimed. Instead "the composer can make use of any tone-color he chooses, even those non-existent in our modern orchestras. He can call for fantastic tempi and dynamics as well as the most complicated combinations of rhythm and not fear a poor performance. The composer becomes his own interpreter."[16]

To achieve this goal, a phonographically conceived system of notation was needed. Whereas Moholy-Nagy had offered a purely theoretical sketch of the possibilities of disc inscription, Stuckenschmidt contemplated the practical aspects of the idea. "The problem now is to find as adequate a system for instruments of the phonograph type," he wrote.

> Here the tone is not transformed into graphic signs easily recognizable, but into short, wavy lines so minute as to be extremely difficult to study. This obstacle, however, might be overcome with a microscope; the lines could be divided into definite rubrics and a fixed scheme established embracing all shades of tone-color, pitch and dynamic intensity. With this new script definite sounds could be transcribed. Sound waves would be shown in highly magnified form; in order to be transferred to the record they would need to be reduced by a photo-mechanical process.[17]

Such a process was never developed. In theory, such a system could work, but that was where the idea was destined to dwell—in theory. As the composer Ernst Křenek later wrote, "The notion of composing on a gramophone record seems preposterous. For who could so engrave the microscopic grooves and notches that a complex tone picture would emerge?"[18] No experiments are known to have been carried out, and few critics or composers raised the idea in later years.[19]

Other commentators at the time had similarly novel, but perhaps less ambitious suggestions for *Grammophonmusik*. In 1926 Hansjörg Dammert issued a call for a new type of concert music: "the concerto for phonograph with the accompaniment of 'real' instruments."[20] The idea was to treat the phonograph as a performing instrument—specifically a solo instrument that would play prerecorded discs with orchestral accompaniment. Like most proponents of *Grammophonmusik*, Dammert expounded on the possibilities of using the machine to enlarge the realm of musical sound:

> What possibilities a composer has to nuance the sound and color of the solo part! One can shape the conversation between both sound-groups [i.e., the phonograph and the traditional instruments] in strange and varied ways, as

contrary motion and even as a sequence of solo and tutti. (Think of, for example, matte colors for the accompanying ensembles: say, a flute, muted violins, the piano in its high range, and the sonorous sound of brass, all supported by a string orchestra in the phonograph.) The means of this type of music making are thus nearly limitless, from its simplest to its most refined.[21]

Dammert also claimed that this type of music making could turn a work on its head. For example, an enormous Wagnerian orchestra may perform the solo part while a much smaller ensemble accompanies.

Although much of the theoretical discussion of *Grammophonmusik* centered on the possibilities of inscribing records, the first actual experiments were quite different and involved the manipulation of prerecorded discs. One of the earliest was probably a 1920 Dada performance that featured eight phonograph operators simultaneously playing classical and popular discs backward and forward and at differing speeds; the effect was apparently an intentionally complex and absurd polyphony.[22] Various sources also indicate that in Paris during the early and mid-1920s composers such as Arthur Hoérée, George Antheil, and Darius Milhaud were independently testing the compositional possibilities of the record player by reversing recorded sounds and manipulating recording and playback speed.[23] None of these forays into phonograph music has been preserved, however, whether in score or recorded form, and little is known about them beyond the fact that they once existed.

More along the lines of Dammert's idea of the phonograph concerto were two works by Ottorino Respighi and Kurt Weill. Respighi's *Pines of Rome* (1925) has a small part for "Grammofono," the operator of which is to play a recording of nightingale song (without modification) at a point marked in the third movement.[24] Similarly, the score of Kurt Weill's comic opera *Der Zar lässt sich photographieren* (1927) calls for a "Grammophon-Solo." At the climax of the opera, the orchestra falls silent and a tango for big band, composed by Weill, plays on a phonograph.[25]

Over the next several years the subject of *Grammophonmusik* was broached in several music journals, not only in Germany, but also in France, England, and the United States. In the 1929 volume of *Modern Music,* the French composer Carol-Bérard suggested that his colleagues use recorded noises and sounds as source material for new works. "No longer at the mercy of interpreters, [the phonographic composer] may first listen to the sounds he wishes to combine, choosing what he wants from numberless possibilities at his disposal."[26] In 1930 the French writer Raymond Lyon proposed the new genre of the phonograph duet. (He recommended, for example, the unlikely combination of Schubert's "Unfinished" Symphony and the Al Jolson hit "There's a Rainbow Round My Shoulder.") Lyon moreover contemplated recording and manipulating noise. He imagined combining the revving of a car's engine, the slamming of a door, the whistling of a delivery boy, and a thousand other sounds into a recorded work called *Paysage* (Landscape).[27]

Also in 1930, Igor Stravinsky penned a brief position paper that encouraged composers to write music conceived idiomatically for recording technology. "It would be of the greatest interest to create music specifically for the phonograph," he noted in the German journal *Kultur und Schallplatte*, "music whose true image—its original sound—could only be preserved through mechanical reproduction. This would indeed be the ultimate goal for the phonographic composers of the future."[28] This article reveals an intriguing connection between the renowned composer and the little-known concept of *Grammophonmusik*. Unfortunately, Stravinsky did not explain how a composer might write such music, nor did he lead the way with phonographic works of his own. He may have known about some of the experiments taking place in Paris, but he seems not to have commented publicly on them. At the time, he was certainly unaware of the *Grammophonmusik* of Hindemith and Toch, for the article was published before the works were first heard; if he later learned of the music, he left no account of it. Yet knowingly or not, Stravinsky shared a sentiment held by many proponents of *Grammophonmusik*. Like Stuckenschmidt and others, Stravinsky saw in the phonograph a means to prevent what he saw as the willful distortion of his music by performers. As he wrote in his 1936 autobiography, "I had always been anxious to find a means of imposing some restriction on the notorious liberty, especially widespread today, which prevents the public from obtaining a correct idea of the author's intentions. The possibility was now afforded by the rolls of the mechanical piano, and, a little later, by gramophone records."[29] Stravinsky's solution, to conduct (and occasionally perform) his works for recording, could not, however, eliminate the performer altogether.

Grammophonmusik was also touted as a means for rhythmic experimentation. In one of the last articles on the subject from this era, Georg Schünemann suggested in 1932 that the phonograph could be an aid in counterpoint exercises, particularly in constructing what are known as crab canons, a work for two voices or instruments in which one part plays the reverse of the other. All that is necessary, he explained, is to play two recordings of a theme at the same time, with one running forward and the other backward.[30] Schünemann did not consider, however, that when a recording is played backward, not only is the order of the pitches reversed, but the attack and decay of the individual notes are as well. The effect would have muddied the counterpoint, rendering the experiment impracticable. Once again, we see that the reality of *Grammophonmusik* did not quite live up to its promise.

THE DEMISE AND LEGACY OF *GRAMMOPHONMUSIK*

After 1932 the subject of *Grammophonmusik* virtually disappeared from the music journals. Ironically, while the concert at Neue Musik Berlin 1930 produced the first true compositions created by phonographic means, it also signaled the end of an era. The timing of *Grammophonmusik*'s demise may have had some connection with the rise to power of the Nazis in 1933. Experimental music was labeled degenerate and discouraged under the new regime. Ernst Toch, a Jew, fled Berlin in 1933; Paul Hindemith remained until 1940, but his career suffered. Thus, two of the central figures in this story had little chance to pursue the compositional possibilities of the phonograph. Moreover, scholars and critics no longer wrote on the subject. While various aspects of recording were discussed in the German music journals after 1933, *Grammophonmusik* was never mentioned.

The change in Germany's political climate, however, cannot be solely responsible for the demise of *Grammophonmusik*. After all, composers and writers outside Germany had taken a great interest in the topic; surely no sinister force silenced them. The available technology was simply incapable of realizing the theoretical possibilities of *Grammophonmusik*, from discinscription to the phonograph concerto. And when experiments were conducted, the results may have been deemed unworthy. From today's perspective, Hindemith's *grammophonplatten-eigene Stücke* may sound crude, one-dimensional. That Hindemith had complete control over the creative and re-creative process may not have compensated for the limited interest of the final product. Toch apparently did not take his own *Grammophonmusik* too seriously, calling it "an interesting acoustical experiment... perhaps a musical joke."[31] Some critics agreed: One spoke of the "burlesque records by Hindemith and Toch" that "bordered closely on practical joking"; another called the performances "a poor joke."[32]

The decline of *Grammophonmusik* was further hastened by competition with newer technologies. Sound film, only recently developed, could be treated as a musical medium and had important advantages for the recording and manipulation of music. There was no four-minute limit on film as there was on the 78, and film could be cut, rearranged, and spliced, allowing previously recorded sounds to be changed and wholly new ones created. This latter possibility removed the obstacles presented by disc inscription. Comparing disc with film, Ernst Křenek noted that "the sound track of moving pictures appears to offer more hope. In this case, the indentations of the disk are represented by a curve in the oscillations of which all the elements of music played into a microphone are fixed. The prospect looks adventurous, but not impossible."[33] Indeed, beginning in the early 1930s composers and filmmakers in Europe and North America were exploring the musical prospects of film.[34] Radio, too, soon captured the imagination of the avant-garde. In Germany in particular, composers were writing works specifically for broadcast, and although radio did not offer the same possibilities as recording, it did draw attention away from the latter. Moreover, it was widely believed that the phonograph was a fad soon to be replaced by the radio, and few put much stock in the older technology as the depression settled in. Whether because of the changing political climate, the practical difficulties of *Grammophonmusik,* or the lure of newer technologies, the prospect of creating a vital new repertoire with the phonograph came to seem increasingly unlikely.

Grammophonmusik, however, was neither historical anomaly nor dead end. It was an expression of the musical zeitgeist and reflected the priorities and values of the avant-garde. The beginnings of *Grammophonmusik* coincided with a growing interest in what was called "mechanical music." In the 1920s, the player piano became a popular instrument with composers, notably Stravinsky.[35] Toch and Hindemith also wrote for player-less keyboard instruments, and both presented *Originalkompositionen für mechanische Instrumente* at the 1926 Donaueschingen festival.[36] Electronic instruments, such as the Sphaerophon (1921), Theremin (1924), Ondes Martenot (1928), and Trautonium (1930), were coming into vogue as well. Hindemith wrote for the Trautonium at about the same time he was working with *Grammophonmusik,* while Arthur Honegger, Edgard Varèse, and Darius Milhaud composed for the Ondes Martenot. The Theremin (its eerie glissando now best known from 1950s science-fiction film scores) was even a popular concert instrument for a time.[37]

Although Hindemith and Toch said little about their *Grammophonmusik,* each explained his general interest in *mechanische Musik.* In 1926 Toch praised its precision and objectivity: "Nothing occurs that is not fixed in the notes in terms of pitch, meter, rhythm, tempo, dynamics; every trace of spontaneity, of sentiment, of impulse is expelled."[38] (It may be hard to believe that Toch saw this as a good thing—we must remember, however, that many composers felt that performers inevitably distorted their music with this uncalled-for spontaneity and impulse.) A year later, Hindemith wrote that the advantages of mechanical music included "the possibility to define absolutely the will of the composer" and the "extension of technical and timbral possibilities."[39] For these composers the phonograph had the same appeal as electronic and automatic musical instruments. Like the electronic instruments, the phonograph could be used to create unusual and unfamiliar timbres, and like the automatic players, it gave the composers direct control over the sound and execution of their works.

If *Grammophonmusik* was of its time, it was also remarkably ahead of its time. In fact, if we consider nearly any major development in later twentieth-century electronic music we can see its germination and anticipation in the music and thinking of Hindemith, Toch, Moholy-Nagy, Stuckenschmidt, and others. The idea behind electronic synthesis—the creation of music independent of traditional instruments and performance—was prefigured by disc inscription. Hansjörg Dammert's proposed *Grammophonkonzert* and Hindemith's *Gesang über 4 Oktaven,* both of which combined live and recorded music, anticipated what came to be known in the 1960s as live electronics, in which performers interacted with taped or computer-generated sound (as well as a variety of electronic equipment). Magnetic tape also made commonplace the alteration of pitch and tempo and the layering of recorded melodies that Hindemith and Toch explored in their *Originalwerke für Schallplatten*. Raymond Lyon, in his 1930 proposal for a work using recorded human and environmental sounds, preceded *musique concrète* by nearly twenty years. His hypothetical *Paysage* might well have sounded like the early landmark of the genre, *Symphonie pour un homme seul* (1950) by Pierre Schaeffer and Pierre Henry, which coincidentally incorporates recordings of slamming doors and whistling, two of Lyon's suggested motifs. Even hip-hop turntablism (the subject of the next chapter) can trace its roots to *Grammophonmusik*. Nearly sixty years before the first DJs were manipulating records in live performance, like-minded experimentalists were doing the same in the musical capitals of Europe. As the story of *Grammophonmusik* makes clear, the ambitions a technology inspires in its users can far surpass the capabilities of the technology itself, ambitions that may only be fulfilled long after their originators are gone.

∘∘∘

Despite the gap between *Grammophonmusik* and the postwar developments that realized its goals, one person may be linked to both. Attending the concert of new music that night of 18 June 1930 was a teenaged art student from the United States who, while spending the summer in Paris, decided to visit Berlin. Several years later the young man created a phonographic composition of his own, the first of several that, in fact, have influenced modern composition more than the *Grammophonmusik* that inspired them. The teenager was John Cage. The work was *Imaginary Landscape No. 1* (1939), for muted piano, large Chinese cymbal, and two variable-speed turntables.[40] Although Cage said little about the impact of Hindemith's and Toch's *Originalwerke für Schallplatten,* he did acknowledge his interest in their experiments. As he told the grandson of one of those two pioneering composers, "Toch—boy was he onto some good stuff back there in Berlin. And then he went and squandered it all on more string quartets!"[41]

CHAPTER SIX

THE TURNTABLE AS WEAPON

UNDERSTANDING THE DJ BATTLE

The room is dark and crowded. At the front, two young men stand at opposite sides of a stage, making last-minute adjustments to the machines before them. They stop as a voice booms over a set of enormous loudspeakers, introducing one of them as the first contestant. He is spotlighted, and for the next few minutes he operates the machinery with dizzying virtuosity. His hands are a blur—darting, snaking, twisting, disappearing, reappearing. A barrage of sound emanates from the speakers: fragments of speech, snatches of song, and every timbre, pitch, and rhythm from high syncopated scraping to throbbing, chest-filling bass. In response, the crowd cheers, jeers, laughs, shouts, and applauds. The first contestant then yields the floor, and the second tries to vanquish his rival with superior skill and showmanship. Once his routine is complete, a panel of judges confers while the crowd mills and the contestants fidget. Then, to the audience's acclaim, outrage, or both, a winner is announced. With his arm raised boxing style by the MC, a new champion is crowned.

I have just described the final head-to-head round in what is known as a DJ battle. Such a scene might strike a newcomer as strange. For one, the musicians seem to be communicating with their audience and each other, but without ever speaking. At various points the crowd will guffaw or snicker, reacting to an outrageous boast or nasty insult. Moreover, nothing in the room looks like a traditional instrument. In fact, the machinery on stage was never intended to produce music, but to *reproduce* it: the musicians perform using turntables, records, and a mixer. But instead of merely letting the machines play, these DJs—also known as turntablists—bend the equipment to their will, altering existing sounds and producing a wide range of wholly new ones.

I am keenly aware of the strangeness I just described. When I attended my first battle I was enthralled, but also bewildered, for there seemed to be a great deal that I was missing. After spending the next few years attending battles, talking with DJs, and taking lessons on the turntables, I came away with a deep respect for the musicianship and dedication of the best DJs. I also came to appreciate turntablism as a phonograph effect. To make an obvious point, it literally could not exist without recording technology. Just as clearly, turntablism, like the *Grammophonmusik* discussed in the last chapter and the digital sampling in the next, reveals the boundless manipulability of recorded sound. It is the intersection of technology and culture, however, that makes this subject especially fascinating and instructive. Although it seemingly embraces violence, the DJ battle is in fact a safe space—one that allows young men (for the battle scene is male-dominated) to develop skills and confidence, engage in role play, and express themselves constructively and creatively. Further, perhaps more than any other phenomenon discussed in this book, turntablism demonstrates that users may shape recording as much as the technology influences them. In their utter subversion of the phonograph's intended function, turntablists have developed a rich musical and social discourse on their own terms.

WHAT IS TURNTABLISM?

Broadly defined, turntablism is a musical practice in which prerecorded phonograph discs are manipulated in live performance. While in this sense it is not limited to any one style or genre, turntablism is most closely associated with hip-hop. The term *turntablism* itself deserves some comment. Although it sounds like an academic neologism, it was in fact DJ Babu, a member of the DJ crew known as the Beat Junkies, who introduced it in 1995.[1] The new name distinguishes the turntablist from the traditional DJ, someone who plays records but is not typically thought of as a musician.[2] Although turntablists consider themselves—and are—musicians, their originality is sometimes questioned because they perform on machines designed for automatic playback. The use of an "ism," therefore, lends weight to the practice, suggesting an art form with a cohesive doctrine and conferring a seriousness that demands respect.

Despite its recent coinage, the origins of turntablism predate the term by two decades. (Before 1995, the practice was usually called DJing or scratching.) The oft-told story, which circulates in several slightly different versions, goes something like this:

The Bronx, New York. One day in the late 1970s a teenager named Theodore Livingston was listening to a record player in his home when his mother angrily pounded on his bedroom door, complaining of the noise. Not wanting to lose his place in the song, Theodore did not turn the table off when his mother entered the room. But instead of holding the disc in place, which would have risked damaging the motor, he chose a third route: he let the record rotate under the needle a fraction of a turn, and then pulled the disc back to its starting point, repeating the action over and again as his mother lectured him. His simple action transformed the music, and what he now heard was an unpitched rasping sound. And he liked what he heard. He worked to harness this newfound sound, and later, as a professional DJ calling himself GrandWizzard Theodore, he publicly introduced what came to be known as "scratching."[3]

This story has mythic status in DJ circles, and is reverently recounted by turntablists. While no one seriously disputes Theodore's claim, it is important to realize that his scratching rose out of an already thriving DJ scene in the Bronx. The DJs Theodore tried to emulate—neighborhood stars like Afrika Bambaataa, Kool Herc, and especially Theodore's mentor, Grandmaster Flash—did more than just select and play records. Often they would use two turntables to isolate and repeat their favorite parts. Using two copies of the same disc, they would switch from turntable to turntable, letting the passage play on one record and then the other, "backspinning" the silent record to the right point just in time to create a seamless repetition of the passage. This process, called "looping," could be sustained indefinitely, given the skill of the DJ. (Incidentally, the passages were often instrumental solos called breaks, and it was during these solos that individual dancers would showcase their talents, hence the term *breakdancing*.)[4] Theodore would have seen DJs moving records back and forth in search of a particular passage (though they would have had their headphones on so the crowd couldn't hear); he also knew that Grandmaster Flash had a move called the rub, where he pushed the record under the needle once and then let it spin. (Flash later described his protégé's innovation as "adding rhythm to the rub.")[5] Nevertheless, Theodore Livingston, we may presume, was the first to harness this sound for its musical potential.[6]

DJing itself is part of a larger hip-hop scene. Although the term *hip-hop* is often used to describe music, it refers more broadly to a set of cultural practices that arose in New York City's black and Latino community in the 1970s, one that later became a global and multicultural phenomenon. There are four elements of hip-hop art: DJing, MCing (rapping), b-boying (breakdancing), and graffiti writing. Turntablism is actually only a subset of DJing. In addition to turntablists, there are club DJs (who spin and mix records in nightclubs for dancing), production DJs (who, among other things, create the instrumental tracks, or beats, for hip-hop recordings), and so-called bedroom DJs (not strictly a separate category, but those who practice one or more of the other types as amateurs and mostly in private).[7] Turntablists themselves are a varied group. Many never leave the bedroom, but those who do may perform solo or in a "crew" of other DJs, or with other types of musicians, whether as part of a rap group, rock band, jazz combo, or even a classical ensemble.[8] Battling, in turn, is a subset of turntablism. Only a small percentage of turntablists compete, and those who do typically retire from battling after several years to turn their attention to professional performance, producing, or judging competitions. (We might compare them to certain types of Olympic athletes who turn professional to perform or coach.) The battle DJ, then, is a rare breed of hip-hop musician.

BATTLE GEAR

To do battle, the hip-hop turntablist needs two turntables, a mixer, and records.[9] In the early days, DJs used whatever equipment was available. Through trial and error, they identified certain machines and characteristics that suited their needs, or modified those that did not. The industry responded by designing turntables for DJ use. Specialty machines now offered by Technics, Vestax, and Numark, among others, differ from the average, inexpensive record player in a number of ways. Generally they are heavy and sturdy, so as to absorb shock and avoid skips. Moreover, the turntable's motor connects directly to the spindle that turns the platter (as opposed to being connected to a belt). Direct drive motors, as they are called, are more consistent, durable, and reliable, and allow records to start and stop more quickly. Just as crucial is a strong and durable stylus that can take the quick back-and-forth motion of scratching. Other features include pitch adjust sliders and BPM (beats per minute) displays. The humble slip mat also deserves mention. Turntablists replace the standard rubber mat that covers the record platter with a round piece of felt—the slip mat—which allows them to hold a record still or move it back and forth while the platter continues to spin, minimizing wear on the motor. To reduce friction even further, many DJs use an additional mat cut from a plastic record sleeve, or a "Butter Rug" (developed by DJ QBert)—a slip mat with the plastic already attached.

The turntables are connected to a mixer, a piece of electronic equipment that regulates the signal being sent from the two machines to the speakers. DJs manipulate the mixer through a variety of sliders and knobs, most crucially the crossfader, which determines whether the sound is coming from one turntable, the other, or some degree of both. Other important features include the upfaders, used to adjust the volume of each machine, and the tone controls, which allow the performer to adjust the bass, midrange, and treble frequencies. The mixer is incredibly important to the DJ's sound—a turntablist playing without a mixer would be akin to a guitarist playing with only the right hand. A typical set-up is illustrated in Figure 4. This particular configuration is called "battle mode," and the turntables' tone arms are placed out of the way so as not to interfere with the DJ's quickly moving hands.

Then, of course, there are the records. DJs value large and eclectic collections, gathered by "digging in the crates" of used record shops, Salvation Army stores, or garage sales.[10] DJs search for strong, catchy beats to scratch over, novel sounds to combine, and vocal phrases they can use in their "messages," as I'll explain later. Most of the records are funk, soul, or rap, but

Pitch adjust · Tone arm · Tone controls

Forward and Reverse buttons

33 & 45 rpm controls

Upfaders

Crossfader

Start/Stop

FIGURE 4 Turntables and mixer in "battle mode." Illustration by Nicole Jakub.

anything goes, from spoken word to Broadway to classical. Although originality and novelty are prized in the selection of records, turntablists often employ compilation discs. In the late 1980s many DJs drew on the massive twenty-five-volume series *Ultimate Breaks and Beats,* which collected dozens of funk, soul, and rock songs from the 1970s for their catchy drum breaks.[11] More commonly DJs now use what are called breakbeat or battle records. These discs, typically compiled by the better-known DJs, contain not whole songs but a variety of repeated musical or spoken fragments; examples include Babu's *Super Duck Breaks,* A-Trak's *Gangsta Breaks,* and QBert's *100 mph Backsliding Turkey Kutz.* These LPs offer the DJ several advantages: they excerpt records that are often difficult to find in their original form; they extract only the parts of the record likely to be used in a routine so that the DJ need not search a whole disc for a single passage; and because they compile a variety of passages and sounds in a single place, they minimize the number of times the DJ must replace records during a routine. Although these discs are widely accepted and used, many DJs try not to depend on them exclusively, so that they can demonstrate their originality and creativity through their own choice of records and combination of sounds.

All this equipment can be very expensive. The highly touted Technics 1200 turntables, which have been the standard for years, can run up to $700 apiece, and tables of comparable quality extract a similar price. Cartridges, which house the stylus, are typically sold separately and can cost well over $100. A good mixer can be had for about $300, the best for over $1,000. Records—ranging from just a few cents for used LPs to $20 or more for new breakbeat records or vintage vinyl—represent a potentially unlimited expense. Of course, it is possible to find cheaper used and lesser-quality equipment, but for most the outlay is considerable. I have talked with many turntablists who spoke of taking out loans, working extra jobs, and even then spending months or years to put together their systems. (Bartering is common, too. I recently came across an Internet want ad looking to trade a pair of Technics 1200s and a mixer for a 1989 van.)

DJing arose when turntables were the standard playback equipment, and turntablists remain, for the most part, resolutely analog in a digital age. DJs value the immediacy of the physical contact between hand and disc that turntables allow; they enjoy searching for rare or unusual records that exist only on vinyl. Since the late 1990s, however, technological developments have challenged the primacy of the older equipment, creating something of a crisis in the battle world. Although digital machines have yet to replace turntables as the battle DJ's weapon of choice, it is worth a brief digression here to discuss the equipment, for the responses it has generated are revealing.

In recent years companies such as Pioneer, Gemini, and Numark have developed CD players that can reproduce nearly everything that can be done on a turntable, even scratching (simulated digitally). With these players it is a much simpler matter to find, repeat, and manipulate particular recorded passages. What's more, with inexpensive CD burners, DJs can easily compile their own individualized battle records from other CDs or from digital files pulled from the Internet. An interesting hybrid approach is Stanton's Final Scratch. The traditional two turntables, mixer, and vinyl records are still used, but a software program (operated on a laptop computer) is added. The specially designed discs that come with the system contain no music themselves, but they can play any sound digitally stored on the connected laptop. Thus DJs can play thousands of records' worth of music on turntables without carrying thousands of records.[12]

Turntablists have mixed opinions about the incursion of digital technology into their world. I encountered this ambivalence at a battle in 2002. Before the first round, a representative from Stanton (one of the battle sponsors) introduced Final Scratch to the crowd. Several members of the audience heckled the Stanton rep, chanting, "We want wax!" and "Vinyl! Vinyl!" When one of the battle promoters came on stage to defend Final Scratch, saying, "Like it or not, this is the future [of turntablism]," he was roundly booed. A more considered response to digital technology comes from former world-champion DJ A-Trak: "I definitely think that vinyl is fundamental to turntablism, but these new technologies can be good tools. For a while I wasn't even paying attention to any of them, but now . . . you can't help but want to try it out and see how you can integrate it into what you do. But what you do as a turntablist stays essentially rooted in vinyl."[13] While some embrace the new possibilities, many feel that the art is diminished when the craft is made easier. Others lament the loss of a strong sense of authenticity surrounding turntables and prerecorded discs. This sense of authenticity may be hard for outsiders to understand, since LPs and CDs are equally mediated forms of music when compared to live performance. Yet LPs and turntables were present at—and largely responsible for—the birth of hip-hop, and many contemporary DJs value and celebrate this link to the "old school." This technological resistance demonstrates a crucial point about phonograph effects, which is that cultural and aesthetic values—as much as the design or possibilities of a particular machine—can determine how users interact with technology.

THE BATTLE: ORIGINS AND DEMOGRAPHICS

In the 1970s informal DJ contests were taking place in the streets, schools, and apartment buildings of the Bronx, but it was several years before formal battles were established. One of the earliest was held in 1981 as part of the New Music Seminar, an annual music industry convention in New York. In 1986 the British organization DMC, then known as the Disco Mix Club (now the Dance Music Community), held its first annual battle; the DMC is now the best-known battle organizer. Since the 1980s the DJ battle has blossomed into an international phenomenon with governing bodies and corporate sponsorship. Battles now take place around the world and feature entrants from dozens of countries.

The structure and rules of a battle vary from event to event. The larger battles, like those sponsored by the DMC or ITF (the International Turntablist Federation), have multiple rounds that progress from regional to national to international finals over the course of several months, usually during the summer. Smaller battles last only an evening. In some, DJs compete head to head, while in others performers are judged individually. Most cater only to single DJs, while some also allow crews made up of three or more turntablists to enter. The length of routines may be set at anywhere from one to six minutes, with the longer routines usually reserved for the final rounds of the larger battles. Typically there are three judges, themselves DJs, who evaluate the skill, originality, and showmanship of the routines. Christie Z-Pabon, former DMC events coordinator, explains that battle judges also have a symbolic role: "Having Hip Hop DJ legends and pioneers present as judges and honored guests is very important to the sense of community within Hip Hop DJ culture. The newer DJs basically try to gain the approval from the 'tribal elders' (as judges) and the elders in turn, who have long since retired from battling, give their blessings (bestowing championship status) to those who they feel best represent the artform."[14] Occasionally cash is awarded, but often winners receive gear from a sponsor or local store. The more impressive awards may be gold-plated turntables and mixers, or oversized belts like those awarded to championship boxers. Mostly what DJs earn are bragging rights.

DJ battles—specifically those in the United States—offer a varied demographic mix. Competitors are usually in their late teens or twenties, and may be black, white, Asian, Latino, or some or all of the above. (The audiences are similarly composed, though young white men tend to be the largest constituency.) There is little obvious racial tension in the battle scene. Every DJ I have spoken with has said that race, though not invisible, truly is not an issue of contention. As Rob Swift, a member of the X-Ecutioners and an African American of Colombian descent, told me, "If you're white and you have skill and you're creative I'm going to respect you. But if you're black and you're not creative and you don't have skills and you suck, I'm not going to respect you."[15] He could well say the same thing about Latinos and Asians, who have come to have a strong presence in the battle scene. (For example, the Filipino community boasts a disproportionate number of the country's most renowned DJs.)[16] When I asked DJ A-Trak if he felt he had anything to prove as a white man, he responded, "No, not at all. DJs come from all backgrounds. It's not like the rap scene which is predominantly black, and where you constantly hear about white MCs having to prove themselves. It's really great, actually, how multicultural DJing is."[17] In contrast to the multiculturalism of the DJ battle, there is little gender diversity. Audiences are largely male and the DJs overwhelmingly so. (I speak here specifically of turntablists; women make up a larger minority of club DJs.) One notable exception is Kuttin' Kandi, who made it to the U.S. finals of the DMC competition in 1998. Still, the lack of women in battles is striking, an issue I will revisit later in the chapter.

THE BATTLE ROUTINE

Once on stage, the battle DJ has a scant few minutes to demonstrate his (and occasionally her) virtuosity, originality, and crowd appeal. Battle routines are therefore rarely leisurely affairs, and aspire to demonstrate every facet of the turntablist's art, from boasting and dissing to scratching and beat juggling.

Routines often begin with the verbal element—what some DJs call their "messages." These are recorded fragments of dialogue or song that, when recontextualized within the routine, typically boast of the DJ's skills or denigrate—"dis"—his rivals. The DJs never say a thing, but in a kind of reverse ventriloquism they often mouth the words or gesture while the records play. As turntablists like to say, "We speak with our hands."

Simple messages borrow a phrase from a single record, such as the boast "Let me tell you baby that I'm a talented boy" from Prince's 1991 song "Gett Off." Prince is bragging about his sexual prowess; DJ Dexta, who incorporated the song into a 1999 routine, is touting a different type of dexterity, though surely he wanted to keep some sense of the original as well.[18] Often messages are created by combining fragments from two different records. In a battle routine from 2001, DJ Dopey took the following line from an old-school rap called "Reckless": "The DJ named Glove has reigned supreme as the turntable wizard of the hip-hop scene." But when the name

Glove would have come in, Dopey quickly and seamlessly switched to the other turntable and played the word *dopey*, which he had found buried in another record. So the result was the personalized boast "The DJ named *Dopey* has reigned supreme . . ."[19] Disses, too, may refer to a specific DJ (and are often, as we will see, laced with obscenities and epithets). For example: "Precision" (the name of a rival DJ) is played on one record, then the dis, "That shit is wack" (from Kool Keith's song "In Your Face") is played on the other. Even more complex messages are strung together from three or more sources, and are typically called "scratch sentences."

Battle messages are often extracted from rap songs, but they can come from anywhere. I have heard messages borrowed from the Smothers Brothers, Tom T. Hall, Irving Berlin, Chris Rock, and the film *Shrek*. The turntablist Roli Rho has come up with an even more eccentric source: Morse code. As he explained in a recent interview, he hopes to create subliminal disses by arranging snare hits into obscene strings of dots and dashes.[20]

Battle DJs consider their messages crucial to their art, and spend much time and energy locating, cataloging, and jealously guarding recorded names and phrases for use in their routines. In the weeks before a battle there is typically a flurry of intelligence gathering among the entrants (usually over the Internet), who try to identify competitors in order to customize their messages. One DJ told me that at long last he had found his battle name on an obscure record, and refused to identify it to anyone, even his closest friends, lest the information fall into the wrong hands—literally.[21]

It is usually understood that disses are just part of the game and shouldn't be taken personally. Some think, however, that dissing goes too far. The Zulu Nation battle held in November 2001 actually forbade obscene and discriminatory dissing. Its rules stated:

NO FOUL LANGUAGE . . . NO USE OF WORDS THAT WOULD BE CONSIDERED DEROGATORY TO ANYONE'S RACE, RELIGION, GENDER. Employing such language in your disses will result in your opponent automatically winning, whether he's wack or not.[22]

Christie Z-Pabon, the organizer of the Zulu Nation battle, later elaborated on this policy. "Many feel that the dissing is essential to battles, and I agree. It's not the dissing that I try to prevent, I want to discourage DJs from using racial slurs, misogynistic language, cursing, and other offensive words. There's a lot of battle disses that can still serve to humiliate one's opponent but which don't involve the ugly language that many rappers are putting on wax these days."[23] Despite Z-Pabon's efforts, however, profane and defamatory dissing continues to be the norm at battles and, for the most part, seems to generate little animosity among the DJs. As Rob Swift observed, "Once you get off stage it's all cool. You shake hands, you hug, and that's it."[24]

While messages often open and close routines, the instrumental techniques of scratching and beat juggling take center stage at any battle. The most basic scratch, typically known as the baby (because of its simplicity), requires one hand to move the disc back and forth while the stylus is on the record, and can be done in any rhythm; the mixer isn't used. A broader vocabulary of scratches is available with two hands, one on the record and the other operating the mixer to shape the sound. (Turntablism does not require that each hand have a particular function, as with guitar playing, for example. Good turntablists will be able to manipulate the records and the mixer with either hand.) The crab is one of the most impressive scratches to see (though not the most difficult to perform): while the record hand does a baby scratch, the other hand—in a movement that suggests a skittering crustacean—bounces the crossfader between the thumb and each of the other fingers in quick succession to create a rapid burst of sound. Other scratches include the scribble, the twiddle, the ripple, the tear, the flare, the stab, the transformer, and the hydroplane, to name just a few.[25]

Beat juggling, another crucial element in most routines, requires two turntables and involves isolating and repeating discrete passages, alternating ("juggling") them between the turntables in counterpoint. When done well, it looks easy, but as with juggling chain saws, the smallest error in timing can have disastrous results. Dick Hebdige's description of Grandmaster Flash applies nicely to beat juggling generally: "Taking sound to the very edge of chaos and pulling it back from the brink at the very last millisecond. [It] is playing chicken with a stylus."[26] Any record can be scratched or juggled, but turntablists often use breakbeat or battle records for their convenience. Whether scratching or juggling, the DJ's actions inevitably alter the sound of the discs; such transformation is in fact what separates turntablism from simple mechanical reproduction.

In addition to the verbal and instrumental aspects of a routine, the physical element can be just as crucial. Part of the appeal of a successful routine is the sight of the swift and intricate motion of the DJ's hands; in fact, it is sometimes hard to appreciate the difficulty of a routine without seeing it. (This is true to a certain extent of all music making, and reveals once again the challenge created by the invisibility of recorded performers.) To make their virtuosity clear to audiences and judges—and in fact, to make their routines even more demanding—DJs often employ what are called "body tricks." These moves do not—or should not—affect the sound of the routine, but add to its visual appeal and level of difficulty. This may involve spinning in place between beats, or scratching or juggling the records with the hands under the legs or behind the back. Sometimes DJs will use any part of the body *other* than the hands (which can lead to rather lewd gestures). Body tricks often act as self-imposed hurdles for the performer to overcome, though sometimes they're purely for show. One celebrated trick involved a DJ mounting the turntable, balancing his body on one hand, and spinning like a breakdancer. By the 1990s, however, turntablists were eschewing the more outrageous moves, with some calling for a greater emphasis on the musicality of routines.

The best routines not only combine the various verbal, instrumental, and physical elements, but do so in fresh, new ways. Originality is the highest value. No one performs someone else's routine, as a rock band might cover another group's song or a pianist play Mozart. DJs will even avoid doing a particular scratch over a certain beat if that combination is associated with someone else—that would be "biting." There is no lower form of life in the battle world than the biter, and no quicker way to lose battles and respect than if you steal someone else's moves. But DJs recognize that most new routines arise out of old ones and that the best way to learn the craft is to imitate others. There is, therefore, a fine and often moving line between biting someone's moves and creating one's own.

It might seem ironic that originality is the highest virtue in what might be called an art of recycling. Originality, however, is not judged on the source of the raw materials, but in their selection, juxtaposition, and transformation. To illustrate the turntablist view of originality, consider two battle routines, both using M.O.P.'s "Ante Up" (2000). For a time, this rap song popped up frequently at battles, and usually drew a positive reaction from crowds within the first seconds of its appearance in a routine. Typically, the DJ would play the opening, which begins with a long, stuttering note that leads into a repeated four-note pattern, and then juggle it or scratch over it. In one routine, the DJ played the figure several times, but always withheld the final note, replacing it with various scratches. In doing so, he created an air of intense expectancy among the listeners (who all knew the song), and when he finally let the last note drop, the crowd roared in appreciation. In the other routine (at a battle about nine months later), in contrast, the DJ was heckled after using "Ante Up." Afterward I asked a DJ/producer (and frequent battle judge) also in attendance about the crowd's reaction. Was "Ante Up" out of fashion now? No, it was that the DJ "didn't do anything with it," he simply let the song play without adding his own touch. The whole routine, in fact, was poorly received, and I wondered if it was perhaps because the DJ, a white man, offended the crowd when he used the word *nigga* several times in his messages. No, I was told, DJs of all races use the "n-word" without typically incurring the displeasure of the crowd. The whole routine "sucked," he explained, simply because "it wasn't original."[27]

Finally, a good routine will not only be original and inventive, but will also be customized for the given battle. Here's how Rob Swift explained it: "If I'm going to be in a battle and I know that your specialty is scratching, I'm going to practice a scratch routine to take you out. It's almost like you're preparing yourself for combat. You come up with strategies, it's like a war. If I go up against this DJ, I want to intercept whatever style he may come at me with. And when I go up against this other DJ, he DJs like this, so I need to be prepared for this and that and the third." As Swift implies, routines are painstakingly planned and therefore leave little room for improvisation. He points out that although good battle DJs communicate a sense of spontaneity "improv is really at a minimum. I know exactly what records I'm bringing, what I'm going to do with each record."[28]

With all of this in mind, let's consider a specific routine, included on the accompanying CD as Track 9. "Hardcore Scratching," a two-minute routine by I.Emerge, was recorded for the 2003 World Series Turntable Championships, which he went on to win; a slightly longer version won him the title of ITF World Scratch Champion in 2002.[29] As I.Emerge himself has pointed out, this is a highly technical routine aimed primarily to impress judges rather than please crowds.[30] To the uninitiated, routines such as this may be difficult to follow, which is why a rather detailed analysis (and repeated listening) will help one understand and appreciate this complex work.

I.Emerge begins with a message to his competitors, a brief sample of Eddie Murphy shouting, "Just shut up and pay attention!"[31] I.Emerge then switches records and devotes the remainder of the first half of the routine to beat juggling. First he simply plays the record (0:01–0:05), introducing the material that will be juggled. Next come the "set-up patterns" (0:08–0:13), where he changes the speed from 33 to 45 and alternates the beat between the two turntables (which have the same record playing on both of them). From 0:17 to 0:24 he demonstrates what's called a three-four pattern, creating a short-short-short-long figure on the word *yeah*. At 0:27 he moves into his "kill pattern," a term that describes the showiest or most technical juggle or scratch in a routine. His kill pattern has four smaller sections. The set-up and outro (0:27–0:30 and 0:50–0:54) both consist of a simple pattern of snare drum hits, and frame the inner sections (0:30–0:41 and 0:41–0:50). These use the same snare hits but are much more complex: the first interpolates jittery rhythms created by a rapidly moving crossfader, while the second is more halting. He finishes the juggling portion of his routine by hitting the turntable's start/stop button, giving a distinctive "winding-down" sound. This is an important technique for shaping the structure of a routine, for this sound acts as a cadence, signaling the end of a phrase. (It can also be heard at 0:13 and 0:24, among other places.)

The second half of the routine (0:55–2:04) showcases I.Emerge's scratching, though, like the first half, it opens with some messages. Using a battle record, which plays a sample from a Beatnuts song, he testifies to his skills and confidence (e.g., "Come test me, and I'ma have to bust yo . . ."). We then hear a "scratch sentence"—a statement pieced together from different sources: "How about some hardcore/motherfuckin'/scratchin'?" The first time he plays it straight; next he uses just the last three words, scratching *hardcore* and, appropriately enough, *scratchin'*; at 1:15 he creates an echo on *scratchin'* (by decreasing the volume using the upfader as he repeats the word). All of this serves as an introduction to the virtuosic scratching that begins at 1:18. The first pattern (1:18–1:30) employs rapid combinations of the drag (a slow push or pull on the record), the transformer (a drag fragmented by rapidly cutting the sound on and off with the crossfader), the scribble (a tremolo baby scratch), and the tear (a halting sound created by pausing the record briefly while moving it forward or backward).

It's important to note that I.Emerge is scratching on the word *ah,* taken from Fab Five Freddy's classic hip-hop record "Change the Beat" (1982). *Ah* is considered a "standard," a sound whose timbre is immediately recognizable even if the word is unclear. (The other main standard is *fresh,* also from "Change the Beat.") The reason for using one of the standards is that knowledgeable listeners will know exactly how the DJ is transforming the sound, and thus be better able to judge the scratching.

The next set of scratches (1:30–1:40) consists of a combination three-click forward and four-tear reverse. It begins with the reverse, with I.Emerge pulling the record back in a stuttering motion that creates four distinct sounds. He then pushes the record forward smoothly while the other hand cuts the sound off three times in rapid succession with the crossfader. (The "click" is the sound the crossfader makes when it is pushed to the extreme left or right.) He repeats this tricky combo several times, so fast that it is hard to know where one ends and the next begins. Although the battle judges obviously appreciated this section, inexperienced listeners, unaware of its difficulty, may hear only a series of staccato notes.

The subsequent passage (1:41–1:52) uses a new scratching technique that I.Emerge helped develop called "hydraulics." (The name comes from the rapid combination of horizontal and vertical motion in the crossfader and upfader that suggests the movement of rods and pistons in a car engine.) The listener will have noticed that interspersed among the scratches is the verbal fragment "What you know about." Now we hear the last word—*that*—but instead of playing it straight, I.Emerge uses the upfader to stutter it, creating an irregular pattern of *that*s: first four, then two, three, two, and then six. The rhythm is far from arbitrary; it was devised to mesh perfectly with the music on the other turntable. That record is playing a complex drum pattern, in which the snare hits come (rather unexpectedly) on the fifth, eighth, twelfth, fifteenth, and twenty-second notes of the pattern. Every time there is a snare, I.Emerge uses the crossfader to switch from the turntable with the word *that* to the one with the drums. In doing

TABLE 1. Rhythm in I.Emerge, "Hardcore Scratching"
(1:41–1:44 and 1:46–1:50)

16th note	1	2	3	4	5	6	7	8	9	10	11
Turntable 1	that	that	that	that		that	that		that	that	that
Turntable 2					snare		snare				

16th note	12	13	14	15	16	17	18	19	20	21	22
Turntable 1		that	that		that	that	that	that	that	that	
Turntable 2	snare			snare							snare

so, he creates a seamless flow of sixteenth notes (represented in Table 1). He actually does this twice (1:41–1:44 and 1:46–1:50); in between, he creates a complementary pattern that uses a series of kicks (notes played on the bass drum) from the second record. For all its Stravinskian complexity, this is one of the catchiest parts of the routine, and would be sure to please any crowd. It probably did not please his competitors, however, who may have lost all hope upon hearing it.

The final scratch section uses the hydroplane (or rub) on the words *ah yeah*. The effect is created by lightly pressing a moistened finger to the record as it spins; just the right amount of resistance vibrates the disc, resulting in a distinctive wobbly sound. I.Emerge is able to repeat *ah yeah* several times by "stickering" the disc. As the term suggests, a small sticker is placed on the record; its edge just barely juts out onto the groove with *ah yeah*, so that when the needle hits the sticker it jumps back into the same groove, creating a loop.

The routine closes with a final message. With one brief exception, every previous statement of "What you know about that?" omitted the last word, its obvious incompleteness generating tension each time it was repeated. Now I.Emerge provides the full statement, resolving this tension while taunting his rivals one last time.

I.Emerge's routine is both a typical and remarkable—or perhaps typically remarkable—example of the battle DJ's art. It takes extraordinary coordination and an exquisite sense of timing to fashion such intricate rhythmic and contrapuntal structures from rotating pieces of vinyl. Even short routines such as this may require weeks or months of daily practice to craft and perfect. In the end, using two turntables, a mixer, and five records, I.Emerge has created a tightly constructed, virtuosic, and engaging routine that should dispel any doubts about the musical and creative possibilities of turntablism.

GENDER AND THE DJ BATTLE

I noted earlier that the battle scene, in both its participants and audience, is overwhelmingly male. This is hardly an incidental point, and provides a key to appreciating the function and significance of the DJ battle. In fact, I propose that one way to understand the battle is as what I would call a "safe space" for young men. This may seem counterintuitive—after all, battles (in the general sense of the word) are sites of violence and danger. Yet DJ battles offer an array of opportunities for young men to express themselves constructively and creatively. What Robert Walser has written of white heavy metal fans can also be said of the multicultural turntablist community: "It is a group," Walser explains, "generally lacking in social, physical, and economic power but besieged by cultural messages promoting such forms of power, insisting on them as vital attributes of an obligatory masculinity."[32] This is not to say that turntablists are typically poor and oppressed. But nearly all would-be battlers, regardless of wealth, lack the economic power to purchase good DJ equipment easily. Walser's observation is applicable here, not because it singles out a certain class of young men, but because it describes male adolescence as it is experienced in many cultures, where young men are expected (or strive) to be powerful but have little access to power of any sort.

But if power is not available in the larger world, it is available in the battle world. DJs engage in symbolic and bloodless violence, and can make outrageous claims about themselves or others without, for the most part, seeming arrogant or hateful. DJs construct fantasy selves—they take on new names and identities in battle—and can vanquish foes and even claim world domination. Battles further provide an outlet for self-expression through music. In the United States, where little funding is available for school and community music, this is especially significant. DJ Babu spoke for many when he explained, "DJing is the main source of my expression, it's my only outlet."[33] Battles allow—in fact, demand—a devotion to an art that requires hours of daily practice, yet they shield the musicians from the ridicule that a similar dedication to, say, the piano or clarinet might bring from their peers. Battles celebrate cleverness, intelligence, even geekiness, all qualities held in low esteem in some youth cultures. Of course, battles *are* fraught with tension. But it is a constructive tension that provides DJs with an outlet through which to express themselves, to socialize, and to navigate the straits of male adolescence.

Moreover, battling allows a safe subversiveness. On the most basic level, turntablism subverts the intended functions of the phonograph and the disc. It transforms a sound reproduction mechanism into a musical instrument and treats records—typically finished musical products—as raw material. It denies technological determinism by proving that a machine designed for passive reception may foster musical activity and promote a flourishing new class of musical amateurs. Turntablism is creation through destruction. It breaks down, isolates, reorders, and decontextualizes. Yet at the same time, turntablism recontextualizes sound, playing matchmaker to seemingly incompatible genres. The term *scratching* suggests an art of vandalism; like its hip-hop cousin, graffiti writing, it can only be realized by violating its own medium. (In fact, now that New York City subway cars are more or less spray paint proof, graffiti is typically scratched into the Plexiglas windows, giving rise to the art of "scratchiti" and bringing the elements of hip-hop even closer together.)[34] Yet as scratching renders its source material into noise, it simultaneously transmogrifies it into a wholly new form of music.

It would be a mistake, however, to assume that such recontextualization is solely a function of technology. Even in today's racially and ethnically diverse scene, the battle's continuity with certain cultural practices is clear. This is especially true of two related practices in African American culture: playing the dozens and cutting contests.

Playing the dozens arose in the black community at least a century ago. Like the DJ battle, it is ritualistic and usually amicable combat engaged in mostly by young men. But there is no music; it is wholly verbal. Competitors trade insults intended to demonstrate one's rhetorical skills while denigrating a rival's masculinity, intelligence, hygiene, or heritage (it is perhaps the origin of the "yo mama" put-down). As in DJ battles, obscenities abound in these disses and boasts (though there are "clean" versions of both practices), but the purpose is less to crush opponents as it is to elevate oneself and draw laughs and cheers from spectators.

One way to understand why battle messages are seldom taken to heart is to see them as a form of signifying, an important practice in the dozens. A traditionally African American rhetorical device, signifying is marked by a linguistic legerdemain that plays on the possible meanings of a given statement.[35] All the messages in a battle routine may be considered examples of signifying, for in removing texts from their original sources (and by cutting and combining them) DJs generate new meanings. Traditional signifying is often a form of play, and its indirection and ambiguity help avoid real confrontation. Battle messages provide further distance between sender and receiver, for all messages are spoken through a proxy—the records. This helps explain why apparently vicious disses are usually accepted with equanimity, and likewise, why outrageous boasts need not suggest arrogance.

If the dozens may be understood as a DJ battle without the music, cutting contests can be seen as DJ battles without the verbal component. Perhaps as old as jazz itself (and more common in the early 1900s than today), cutting contests typically pitted two performers or bands (again, usually young men) in head-to-head displays of instrumental virtuosity, the victor decided by the crowd's acclamation or a contestant's capitulation.[36]

The cutting contest and the dozens are rich in interpretive possibilities, and we can look to studies of these phenomena to help us understand the DJ battle. Thurmon Garner sees the dozens as a way to learn conflict resolution in a nonviolent setting; Robin D. G. Kelley emphasizes its play and verbal outrageousness.[37] And although earlier studies by John Dollard and Roger Abrahams focused on the dozens as responses to white oppression and the matriarchal structure of black family life—neither of which seems applicable here—their insistence that the dozens was a means for young men to assert and explore their masculinity is apt.[38] In his study of early jazz in New Orleans, Burton Peretti describes cutting contests as "vicarious violence" and notes that they "provided a workshop environment for exchanging ideas and honing skills"; we can say the same of the

DJ battle.[39] Even though the music of the cutting contests was typically instrumental, the musicians sometimes added a verbal component. New Orleans bandleader Kid Ory was known to instruct his band to sing to the rival group, "If you don't like the way I play, then kiss my funky ass," a dis that would be right at home in a DJ's battle routine.[40] Despite their differences, the similarities between the dozens, the cutting contest, and the DJ battle are too many and close to be ignored, suggesting that the battle both draws upon these earlier traditions and serves similar functions in the lives of DJs.

It is important to remember, however, that the DJ battle is now a multicultural phenomenon, not a solely African American one. Nevertheless, the core functions of the dozens and the cutting contest that the battle retains—pushing and testing one's abilities, asserting one's masculinity, and engaging in playful and safe confrontation—can have a strong crosscultural appeal to young *men,* regardless of their heritage. This may be one reason there is such little (at least overt) racial or ethnic tension among turntablists. Battles, ironically, address the competitors' similarities, not their differences.

One question remains: Why are so few women involved in the battle scene? By all accounts, girls and women are not actively discouraged from battling, and are warmly received when they do participate. (When QBert was once asked what he hoped the future of turntablism would bring, he immediately responded, "More girl DJs.")[41] There are many reasons for the dearth of women, but direct discrimination seems not to be one of them. One possibility, as Christie Z-Pabon suggests, is that rap has tainted the battle scene for women: "Considering that so much misogyny exists in today's rap music, perhaps many conscientious women and girls just shut it out all together, not realizing that they could get involved in the non-rap elements."[42] Certainly, battles are not free of misogyny: rival male DJs often dismiss each other in their routines as "bitches" or use similar epithets at the expense of women. More generally, the situation may reflect differences in the way girls and boys are socialized in American society. Traditionally, competition and conquest are not culturally valued for girls and women; although the growing popularity of women's sports suggests a change in attitudes, battling, in its various senses, is apparently still seen as unladylike. Broad differences in conversational styles are likely at work as well, for verbal confrontation among women tends to be frowned upon, while among men it is supported, even expected. As linguist Deborah Tannen explains, "Females may well fight, but males are more likely to fight often, openly, and for the fun of it."[43] In this sense, the very structure of the DJ battle may discourage women from participating, even if the male DJs are welcoming.

The scarcity of female turntablists also implicates an old but still pervasive view of recording as a gendered technology. As I explained in chapter 2, the phonograph helped remove the taint of effeminacy from music in early-twentieth-century America because it allowed the art to be enjoyed in combination with the traditionally male pursuits of tinkering and "shop talk." The phonograph, specifically in connection with equipment repair and record collecting, came to be seen as the domain of men, a view still common today. Given that turntablism demands an intimate knowledge of the equipment and requires "digging in the crates" for records (a term with resonances of the hunt), it is understandable that DJing has been and continues to be largely associated with men. Moreover, although women are not barred from DJ battles, they have long been discouraged from pursuing technical interests or careers. Tricia Rose makes this point in connection with rap, but the same could be said for turntablism:

> Women in general are not encouraged in and often actively discouraged from learning about and using mechanical equipment. This takes place informally in socialization and formally in gender-segregated vocational tracking in public school curriculum. Given rap music's early reliance on stereo equipment, participating in rap music production requires mechanical and technical skills that women are much less likely to have developed.[44]

Young men, in contrast, have access to informal networks of male relatives, friends, or neighbors that allow them to develop DJ skills in a supportive environment. These networks, though not necessarily discriminatory, tend to perpetuate the underrepresentation of women in the field, for young women might not feel comfortable spending time alone with groups of male DJs in the bedrooms and basements where they usually gather. None of this is to say that gender parity in the battle scene will never be achieved. Rather, I would suggest that if the demographics are to change it will be because women establish parallel DJ networks that offer them a safe space of their own.

ooo

Turntablism is a manifestation of a radical phonograph effect—one in which record players are no longer record *players,* but musical instruments capable of creating and manipulating sound in the most sophisticated ways. Although turntablism encompasses much more than the battle scene, the DJ battle showcases, advances, and keeps the record, so to speak, of turntablist technique.[45] Using turntables, mixers, and lightning-fast hands, DJs reorganize and recontextualize fragments of recorded sound and, in a kind of musical husbandry, breed rich new meaning from their juxtaposition. In doing so, they explore and construct their identities and enter into a dialogue in which no one speaks, but so much is said.

CHAPTER SEVEN

MUSIC IN 1s AND 0s

THE ART AND POLITICS OF DIGITAL SAMPLING

A fragment of a drum solo: the thump of the bass, the crack of the snare, the sting of the hi-hat, all combined in a distinctively syncopated pattern. Common sense suggests that this solo was fixed long ago, on the day drummer Clyde Stubblefield recorded it as part of James Brown's 1970 R&B song "Funky Drummer, Part 1 and 2."[1] Yet this two-second sequence enjoys a promiscuous, chameleonic existence. Accelerated, equalized to sound muffled and distant, and repeated continuously in Eric B. and Rakim's "Lyrics of Fury" (1988), it takes on a menacing tone, matching the intensity of the rap. Similarly looped, but slowed slightly and placed underneath a haunting folklike melody, it occupies a completely different sound world on Sinéad O'Connor's "I Am Stretched on Your Grave" (1990)— that of the Irish lament. It masquerades as a reggae beat in Sublime's "Scarlet Begonias" (1992) and turns wistful in George Michael's pop ballad "Waiting for That Day" (1994). In each example, and in scores of others that appropriate Stubblefield, something of the original sound is maintained, yet its meaning changes in every new setting.[2]

The multiple incarnations of Clyde Stubblefield's "Funky Drummer" arise from the practice of digital sampling, a form of musical borrowing in which a portion of one recording is incorporated into another. Since the 1980s, musicians of every stripe have embraced the technology. Their work raises a host of questions, from the aesthetic and the technical to the ethical and the legal. How have composers changed their work in response to the possibilities of this technology? Has digital sampling introduced a fundamentally new compositional aesthetic, or is it best understood as an extension of older practices? What is it about the technology and its applications that have exposed the practice to charges of being inartistic, immoral, and illegal? Three case studies will address these questions. The first examines *Notjustmoreidlechatter,* a work by composer Paul Lansky that transforms speech into music. The second explores the complex relationship between two pop songs, one of which, Camille Yarbrough's "Take Yo' Praise," is sampled by the other, Fatboy Slim's "Praise You." The final case study focuses on Public Enemy's "Fight the Power," whose extravagant sampling serves to enact the group's political and cultural agendas. But before addressing the complex questions just raised, we must first answer a more straightforward one.

WHAT IS DIGITAL SAMPLING?

Digital sampling is a type of computer synthesis in which sound is rendered into data, data that in turn comprise instructions for reconstructing that sound. Sampling is typically regarded as a type of musical quotation, usually of one pop song by another, but it encompasses the digital incorporation of any prerecorded sound into a new recorded work. The equipment used to create samples varies widely, from traditional-looking keyboards to purpose-built machines dominated by buttons, knobs, and sliders that look nothing like musical instruments, to software used on personal computers. Regardless of the gear, on the simplest level sampling works like a jigsaw puzzle: a sound is cut up into pieces and then put back together to form a digitized "picture" of that sound. When a sound wave is digitized, using what is called an analog-to-digital converter (ADC), it is not reproduced in its entirety; rather, select "samples" of the wave are assigned binary numbers. Each of these numbers represents the amplitude, or height, of a wave at a given point. When a sound is reconstructed, a digital-to-analog converter (DAC) emits voltages corresponding to each of these binary numbers. When all of these various voltages are emitted in a particular order, the result very closely approximates the original. This may seem to be an odd way of reproducing sound—breaking it down and then putting it back together—but in fact it works very well. At present, the standard sampling rate is 44,100 Hz, meaning that every second of sound that is sampled is cut into 44,100 slices; typically, each of these slices is given a sixteen-digit binary number, which allows for extremely fine gradations (2^{16}, or 65,536) in measuring the amplitude of a wave. Sampling can therefore be fast and fine enough so that the human ear perceives a continuous and faithfully rendered reproduction.

The advantage of digitization is that sound, once rendered into data, can be manipulated in a variety of ways down to the smallest details. Tempo and pitch can be increased or decreased in any increment, and the two can be manipulated independently. (In the predigital age, when the speed of a recording was increased, the pitch rose, and when the record slowed, the pitch fell. Think of the sound of a phonograph switching from 33⅓ to 45 rpm or vice versa.) Sounds can be reversed, cut, looped, and layered; reverberation can be added; certain frequencies within a sound can be boosted or deemphasized. Noise can be removed to make an old recording sound pristine, or even added to make a pristine recording sound old, as can often be heard in recent popular music.[3] All of these manipulations can be visited upon any sound, musical or otherwise, and on any length of sound that can be recorded. A sample can be a fraction of a waveform, a single note from an instrument or voice, a rhythm, a melody, a harmony, or an entire work or album. Although sampling, particularly when done well, is far from a simple matter, the possibilities it offers are nearly limitless.

As a form of musical borrowing, the roots of digital sampling reach back more than a millennium. Consider just the Western musical tradition: medieval chants freely incorporated and adapted melodic patterns from earlier chants; dozens of Renaissance masses were based on the melody of the secular song "L'homme armé"; a similar craze raged centuries later when composers such as Berlioz, Liszt, Rachmaninoff, Saint-Saëns, and Ysaÿe "sampled" the chant *Dies irae* ("The Day of Wrath") in their instrumental works; Bach reworked Vivaldi's music; more than a century later Gounod returned the favor, adding a new melody to Bach's Prelude in C Major and calling it *Ave Maria;* Mahler cannibalized his own earlier vocal works in several of his symphonies; Ives quoted George M. Cohan's "Over There" in his song "Tom Sails Away"; Bartók parodied Shostakovich's *Leningrad* Symphony in his Concerto for Orchestra; and so on and on.

Yet isn't there something fundamentally different between such traditional acts of borrowing and digital sampling? It is sometimes said that while a quotation is simply a representation of another piece, a sampled passage of music *is* that music. But that depends on what the meaning of "is" is. Consider a conventional example of musical quotation: in the third movement of Luciano Berio's *Sinfonia,* an enormous five-movement work for orchestra and vocalists from 1968, the composer quotes music by Brahms, Debussy, Hindemith, Mahler, Ravel, Schoenberg, and Strauss, among many others. These quotations are notational—that is, Berio reproduces not the sounds themselves, but the instructions for recreating them. The quotations are only complete when performed. Digital sampling also involves symbols—1s and 0s instead of the various lines, dots, and squiggles of traditional notation. As a standard textbook on computer music explains, "What computers manipulate is not sound itself but representations of sounds."[4] Therefore, if sampling *represents* sound, we cannot say that a sampled passage of music *is* that music.

But if sampling does not differ from traditional musical borrowing in kind, it certainly differs in degree. Consider a hypothetical quotation, in which the score of an otherwise original work notates the two-second "Funky Drummer" solo. At most, only a dozen or so instructions (in the form of various symbols) would be used: several to indicate the parts of the drum kit (bass, snare, tom-tom, hi-hat, etc.), a handful for the duration of each note, and a few for dynamics, accentuation, and meter. But the equivalent digital sample would require nearly a hundred thousand distinct instructions, a level of specificity impossible to notate. With all of these instructions, so much more can be indicated: the sound of a particular drum being hit with a certain amount of force using a specific stick, or the exact number of milliseconds a note enters before or after the beat. Moreover, the sonic aura surrounding the sound can also be captured. By "aura" I mean two things: the reverberation that imparts a sense of space, and the slight but constant ambient noise—a patina, perhaps—that is a by-product of imperfect recording fidelity. Digital sampling offers the possibility of what I would call performative quotation: quotation that recreates all the details of timbre and timing that evoke and identify a unique sound event, whether two seconds of Clyde Stubblefield's drumming or the slow, unsteady tapping rhythms produced as I type this sentence. In other words, traditional musical quotations typically cite works; samples cite performances. As we will see, it is the possibility of performative quotation, including the ability to manipulate those sounds, that sets sampling apart from traditional quotation and has led to some astonishingly creative works of modern music.

THE UNCOMMON PARLANCE OF PAUL LANSKY

I was sitting on a plane just before takeoff when an announcement came over the loudspeaker. It was no doubt the usual welcome, but for some reason I could not quite understand what the attendant was saying. At first I thought the loudspeaker was faulty, and then I put the difficulty to the noise of the engines. I leaned forward, closed my eyes, and concentrated, yet I still could not make sense of the words. My frustration mounted, but then suddenly I could understand her perfectly. I quickly realized why, much to my chagrin: I was on a KLM flight to Amsterdam, and it dawned on me that the attendant had given the announcement twice—first in Dutch, and then in English. Dutch, at least to my ears, sounded quite a bit like English. But it did not occur to me that she was speaking a different language. Rather, it seemed as if she were using all the basic and familiar sounds of English, but in a completely unfamiliar (and rather maddening) way.

I am reminded of this incident when I listen to *Notjustmoreidlechatter,* a 1988 work by composer Paul Lansky. Lansky, a professor of music at Princeton University, creates his music almost exclusively with computers, and the eight-minute *Notjustmoreidlechatter* is one in a series of works in which he digitally manipulates speech—English speech—to create fantastic musical textures in which semantic meaning is tantalizingly out of reach.[5] Lansky has long been interested in using the computer to transform the everyday into music, or perhaps to extract the music from the everyday. He finds inspiration in unexpected places—conversations, highway traffic, a bustling shopping mall, his own kitchen. Rather than sampling preexisting works (as the other composers discussed in this chapter do), he mines raw sonic material; moreover, these works bear little connection to the world of traditional performance. Lansky is thus presented with a distinct compositional challenge: How does a composer write music that lives only on recordings? That is, how does one write a work that not only must stand up to exact and frequent repetition, but must also create its own self-sufficient world outside the familiar traditional concert venues? Lansky answers these challenges in the form of *Notjustmoreidlechatter.*

Notjustmoreidlechatter (Track 10 on the accompanying CD) opens with what one might take for the Babel of legend. Countless unintelligible voices—high, low, fast, slow—bombard the listener from every direction. Heard on headphones (perhaps the "natural" venue for such a piece), the voices seem to be inside one's head, bouncing and darting chaotically. In fact, we are hearing only one voice, that of Lansky's wife, Hannah MacKay. MacKay is reading from chapter 25 of Charlotte Brontë's *Jane Eyre,* in which Jane tells Rochester of her unusual dreams. The subject seems appropriate to the piece, for the disembodied voices have an unreal, otherworldly sound. While MacKay's voice is digitally multiplied, fractured, and transformed so that no single word is long or distinct enough to be understood, it is still possible to pick out recognizable syllables or phonemes. Here Lansky strikes a balance between familiarity and strangeness, in which listeners instinctively "squint" their ears, as Lansky puts it, in an attempt to understand what is being said. (Much as I did when I tried to make sense of Dutch on the KLM flight.) This is a canny compositional strategy, for it not only encourages attentive listening but also addresses the problem of repeatability. Even the most careful scrutiny will not reveal the text, but with every successive hearing the listener cannot help trying to extrapolate meaning from these verbal scraps. Here Lansky exploits the human tendency to fill in missing or unclear information to form whole structures. This is the same tendency that leads listeners to misinterpret indistinct song lyrics, even if the result makes little sense, for nonsense seems always to be more tolerable than uncertainty. (Examples of misheard lyrics are legion: "Excuse me while I kiss this guy," instead of "Excuse me while I kiss the sky"; "The ants are my friends, they're blowin' in the wind," instead of "The answer, my friends . . ."; and so on.) Play *Notjustmoreidlechatter* to a group of listeners and you will find that they all think (and even insist) that they hear particular words, though few if any will agree on what is being said.

Lansky responded to the repeatability issue in another way as well. Using what he describes as stochastic mixing techniques, he essentially instructed a computer to determine certain aspects of the chattering at random. As Lansky has explained, the purpose of this unpredictability is to compensate for the fixity of the recorded medium, and in doing so simulate the spontaneity, the "danger," of live performance:

> My view is that in order to recreate that sense of danger you have to make
> the listener into the performer. The listener has to take an active part in the
> experience in fundamentally different ways than in live performance, and
> in order to do this I think that it's necessary to compose elements into the
> music that are non-linear, sometimes random, sometimes noisy and not
> discursive in the ways that a lot of traditional music is. I want the music
> to challenge the listener anew on each hearing, so that identical sounds will
> end up sounding different depending on the performance the listener creates
> in his own mind and ear.[6]

In *Notjustmoreidlechatter* there is no performer in the traditional sense. So the performer's task—to create a fresh interpretation of a work with each performance—is split between composer and listener. The composer imbues the work with the unpredictability of a live performance, while the listener assumes the executant's interpretive duties. In fact, for Lansky it is the listener who truly defines the music: "The essence of the music," he argues, "doesn't lie as much in its details as in the act of trying to understand them."[7] If we compare Lansky's response to repeatability with that of the recording performer, we see a fascinating inversion. I suggested in chapter 1 (see p. 25) that recording artists transform performances into works by creating unchanging texts that transcend the temporal vicissitudes of the concert. Lansky has done exactly the opposite: he has composed a work with the qualities of a performance.

As its title suggests, there is more to the work than chaotic chatter, which alone might well drive listeners to distraction. Just as Lansky seeks a balance between familiarity and strangeness, he also leavens complexity with simplicity. Anchoring the swiftly moving surface voices are what Lansky refers to as background singers. Where the former move randomly in complicated rhythms guided by no perceivable system of tonality, the latter do the opposite. These voices sing slowly in simple harmonies on vowel sounds, meandering in stepwise motion within a diatonic scale. Although they do not follow the traditional rules of tonal voice-leading, their deliberate and predictable movement provides structure to the piece. A broader organizing principle also helps unify the work. The chatter voices chart a gradual path from lesser to greater intelligibility and back again, providing a kind of arch form to the work. At the midpoint of the piece, the background voices fade while the chattering becomes more prominent and distinct. Lansky seems to be rewarding careful listeners; for example, I hear "dream" and "a long way" (4:23–4:24), both of which are in the source text. (Then again, I would swear that I hear certain words and phrases that are not in the source text, so at any point in the piece it is impossible to know whether I hear what I think I hear.) After this section of relative clarity, the distinctness of the text diminishes as the chattering recedes into the background. After nearly eight minutes, the piece slowly fades from one's consciousness, the voices dying away inarticulate, to paraphrase Jane Eyre's description of her own voice disappearing in a dream.

Notjustmoreidlechatter wonderfully demonstrates the musical and aesthetic potential of digital technologies. Like an alchemist, Lansky transforms the ordinary into the precious, where a spoken word becomes a superhuman chorus. But this is no black magic—it is virtuosic handicraft developed from an understanding of both computer software and human perception. If Lansky exploits the possibilities of the technology to the fullest, he also confronts its limitations. The 1s and 0s of *Notjustmoreidlechatter* will not change no matter how many times we hear the piece. But he uses those same fixed digits to create the illusion of spontaneity, and makes us squint our ears in an attempt to hear more. The piece also raises questions about the definition of music. How does mere sound become music? Can we pinpoint the transformation? Or is the transformation in the listener, achieved when something is heard *as* music? Lansky does not answer these questions, but he does suggest (as John Cage had done before, but with very different sonic results) that the line between noise and music is far from clear, if such a line exists at all.

Paul Lansky hopes that listeners will not dwell on the technology with which he creates his music. "Music succeeds when its machinery is less interesting than its tunes."[8] His stance is understandable, for he certainly would not want the medium to overshadow the message. While I do not agree with Marshall McLuhan that the medium *is* the message, a rich understanding can come of investigating both. Although the world of *Notjustmoreidlechatter* springs from the imagination of the composer, it is the technology that renders it audible.

FROM "TAKE YO' PRAISE" TO "PRAISE YOU"

The recording opens with a piano playing an eight-bar introduction in a gospel style. We can imagine the pianist sitting at a battered upright, vamping an introduction for a nervous amateur singer. Oblivious to the proceedings, some members of the audience continue their neighborly chitchat. The singer then enters tentatively:

We've come a long, long way together,
Through the hard times and the good.
I have to celebrate you baby,
I have to praise you like I should.

At the end of the phrase something very strange happens, disrupting our mental image of the proceedings. The singer starts to stutter unnaturally on the word *should,* as a complement of percussion instruments and then an electric bass thicken the texture. The woman holds the note for ten, twenty, thirty seconds. A synthesized drum joins in, pounding out quarter, then eighth, then sixteenth, then thirty-second notes before the texture erupts into an up-tempo dance.

The minute and twenty seconds of music I just described opens "Praise You" (Track 11 on the accompanying CD), the 1998 electronic dance music hit by Norman Cook, better known in his native Britain and throughout the world as Fatboy Slim. At the core of "Praise You," however, is another song, representing a different era and genre. The voice we hear belongs to Camille Yarbrough and was recorded in 1975 as the opening of her soul/funk song "Take Yo' Praise" (Track 12).[9] Through the technology of digital sampling, Cook has at once decontextualized and recontextualized Yarbrough's voice, giving it new sounds, functions, and meanings. What makes this case study fascinating, however, is that the relationship between these two songs simultaneously confirms and confounds our expectations of digital sampling, and in the process raises some of the complex aesthetic and ethical issues arising from this new form of musical borrowing.

Cook samples only the first twenty seconds of "Take Yo' Praise," which consist of Yarbrough's unaccompanied singing—nothing more. This comes as a surprise to most listeners, who assume that the opening of "Praise You" is an unretouched aural snapshot of an actual performance. It was Cook, then, who added the piano and the background voices; he even manipulated the crackling sound of the LP from which he sampled the piano, making it more prominent. (He also altered Yarbrough's singing, increasing the tempo and flattening the melodic contour.) Cook demonstrates his mastery of the sampler here, providing a sense of wholeness to this olio. He does this not only through the harmonization of the vocal line, but with noise. The background chatter offers a sense of occasion, of liveness, and of place; the foreground crackling offers a sense of time, evoking the unspecified past of the vinyl age. The latter can now be produced digitally and is aptly known as the phonograph effect. A phonograph effect indeed, for it is a palpable manifestation of recording's influence. This noise, real or digitally simulated, is now firmly part of our modern sonic vocabulary, and can be powerfully evocative to listeners. It was long deemed an unwanted addition to the phonographic experience by both the industry and listeners, but ironically became a valued and meaningful sound when digital technology finally eliminated it. In the age of noiseless digital recordings, this sonic patina prompts nostalgia, transporting listeners to days gone by (whether of their own or some generalized past), an effect Cook exploits in "Praise You."

In the original, Yarbrough's line "I have to praise you like I should" leads to the entrance of a sublimely funky electric bass line, with guitar and percussion filling in the accompaniment. As the song continues through several more verses, text and tone become increasingly passionate and erotic before subsiding into a postcoital coda. Cook, however, takes another path. The music following the opening sixteen measures, when Yarbrough's voice starts to skip, seems rather unimaginative, even inept. The vocal stutter suggests a failed attempt to create a superhuman fermata; the synthesized sound of the throbbing drum is clearly foreign to the rest of the musical texture; and the successive doubling of the pulse is a dance music cliché. Yet whatever else he is, Cook is not inept. He is actually playing a sly joke on us, for his intentionally ham-fisted sampling convinces us all the more of the "authenticity" and "naturalness" of the opening, which, as we now know, is neither. Cook himself admits that the vocal stutter was "a gag, a way of saying, 'Look, I sampled this.'"[10] With this heavy-handedness he thus makes his presence known; the man behind the curtain has revealed himself. Of course, he was there from the start. Attentive listening reveals that the first four seconds of "Praise You" are looped, so that the two measures in the piano, the fragment of conversation, even the pattern of pops and clicks are repeated in exactly the same form. His portrait of an artist as a young woman is clearly a construct.

The introduction now over, Cook proceeds to use the twenty seconds of Yarbrough's singing, and various parts of it, through the rest of the five-minute song. The entire sample is heard only three times. All other appearances of Yarbrough's voice come from the last line, "I have to praise you like I should." Cook does not further alter the sample; rather, variation in the music comes from the accompaniment, which changes throughout the piece. Although this is dance music, which requires repetition and a steady beat, it has a subtlety that rewards close listening. Cook himself might argue to the contrary, however. According to him, with dance music, and his music by extension, "There's nothing to sit and listen to. It's the sound-track of your nights out rather than anything that's supposed to be heard or discussed at home at great length."[11] Yet notice the male voice singing along to the bass in nonsense syllables at 0:57, the faint vocal echoes accompanying "I have to praise you" starting at 1:57, the human beat-box rhythm at 2:11, and the variety of glissandos, cymbal hits, and robotic chirps that pepper the texture. Most of these can only be heard with careful attention and headphones—that is, at home, rather than at the club.

If Cook adds a good deal musically, he also strips much away from the original. Camille Yarbrough's "Take Yo' Praise" offers a complex message, one absent in "Praise You." Yarbrough's is a multifaceted love song, one woman's moving and sensual tribute to the man in her life. As the composer reveals, the lyrics are autobiographical: "I wanted the brother with whom I was attached to know that . . . he had contributed a lot to my growth."[12] The song has broader implications as well. Yarbrough wrote

"Take Yo' Praise" during the civil rights movement, in which she, an African American woman, was deeply involved. "I had decided to give it a double meaning," she explains. "It was also directed at all people of African ancestry . . . who had at that time been in the front lines of the battle to turn racism around." The opening line—"We've come a long, long way together"—refers, then, to her people, not just her man. In Cook's hands, however, both the personal and political meanings of the original evaporate. In fact, after so much sheer repetition, it's unclear whether these words mean much beyond what the timbre and rhythms of Yarbrough's voice communicate musically. In a survey of informal reviews of "Praise You" posted on the Internet I found very few that even mentioned the lyrics. Of those that did, most were dismissive. "I can't really say the lyrics are deep, because they're not," one reviewer noted. He summed up the song in this way: "I think one of my friends described 'Praise You' best when she said it felt like one of those songs you cruise around town with all your friends listening to and doing fun, crazy stuff. And if you know that feeling, you know what 'Praise You' feels like. It's just a fun song."[13] While it might be tempting to dismiss this assessment as superficial, it is important to remember that Cook omits the vast majority of the text, repeating just a few words over and again. No wonder fans of the song have had little to say about its lyrics.

One could also argue that through his sampling Cook digitally neuters Yarbrough. On first hearing, many people think that the singer is a man or are unsure of the gender.[14] Cook changes Yarbrough's voice in such a way that it is less nuanced than the original, and the lack of timbral clues makes it possible to hear it as a tenor or alto. (Interestingly, Cook points out that the quality of Yarbrough's sampled voice was an unintended consequence of time-stretching, at the time a relatively new and rather unrefined technique used to change the tempo of a recording without affecting its pitch. He nevertheless appreciated the resulting gender ambiguity.)[15] Nor does the sample offer any textual clues as to gender, whereas in the original the second verse leaves no doubt as Yarbrough sings, "You make me glad I'm a woman, because you're a feeling, thinking man." The lack of any eroticism in "Praise You," so clear in "Take Yo' Praise," also renders the voice asexual. The effect of this digital denaturing is ambiguous. It is possible to hear Yarbrough's bodiless voice as a free-floating signifier, one that transforms the personal into the universal and allows the song to be heard from a male or female, heterosexual or homosexual, frame of reference. Another possibility, perhaps not mutually exclusive, is that Cook is disempowering Yarbrough, erasing her history, identity, and vitality. As Kay Dickinson has pointed out, "In the case of sampling, it would not seem untoward to derive extremely disempowering readings from male producers chopping chunks out of women's performance."[16] It would certainly be fair to say that Cook has "chopped chunks" out of Yarbrough's performance.

What should we make of "Praise You"? Is this just another example of a white musician—Cook—appropriating and denuding black culture for profit and fame? Certainly there was an unequal power relationship. Cook was a popular and wealthy musician (becoming much more so after the release of "Praise You"), while Yarbrough's musical career brought her rather less money and notoriety, and was all but forgotten by 1998. (Even by Yarbrough herself; she had long since moved on in her varied career as a dancer, actress, radio host, writer, and teacher.) Notice, too, the "whitening" of the title as the black vernacular "Take Yo' Praise" becomes "Praise You."

Yet the story is *not* so black and white. It turns out that Yarbrough was actually "pleasantly surprised" when she first heard the song. She was pleased that Cook had sampled the hook from "Take Yo' Praise," which she considers the emotional core of her song, with an important message to offer. "We need to praise one another," she explains, "we need to stop all the negativity. Once you begin to fill your mouth and your mind and your heart with praising something or someone the put-down lessens." Yarbrough also feels that the gospel quality Cook lent the sample was appropriate, and brought out the spirituality of her song, at least in the opening of "Praise You." (While Cook acknowledges the influence of gospel, he denies that there is anything spiritual about his song. Ironically, it is the gospel sound of the Rolling Stones' "Sympathy for the Devil" that he cites as inspiration. As Cook points out, "I'm a big fan of gospel music, more than I am of God.")[17] And although Yarbrough seems ambivalent about what she calls the "dance hall" sound of the remainder of the song, she does not feel that it in any way devalues her work. After all, she points out, "I can still do that song as I do it. And so what he did, that's on him; what I do, that's me."

For his part, Cook understands that what he did is on him. "I'm always aware that white artists who are fans of black music tend to have big hits when they cover black records. All I can say is, I don't do it for profit, I do it because that's the music I love, that's the music I want to make in my way. I always try to make sure that the original artist gets the credit and the money."[18] To be sure, Yarbrough received both. Cook gave her co-composer credit and a *60 percent* share of the royalties, a generous arrangement indeed. Cook, however, may have learned from experience. On his previous album, *Better Living through Chemistry*, he sampled guitar chords from The Who's "I Can't Explain" without permission. Not until a year after its release did Cook approach Pete Townshend, the composer and copyright holder of the song. The ensuing negotiations between their respective lawyers ended badly for Cook: Townshend was given sole composer credit for the song and 100 percent of the royalties.[19] Cook obviously wanted to avoid such a debacle with "Praise You." Nevertheless, Yarbrough received (and still receives) a considerable amount of money from the song not only from album sales, but from licensing fees paid by the many film and television producers who have used the song. She does not downplay the significance of this windfall, which she has described as "a gift." She later joked, "I have a platinum card, so now I praise Fatboy Slim!"[20] Moreover, "Praise You" has brought a good deal of positive attention to Yarbrough and her music, leading to the re-release of her 1975 album *The Iron Pot Cooker*, two remixes of the song, and a reevaluation of her place in popular music by the press. Cook may have "chopped chunks" out of Yarbrough's song, but the result hardly seems to have been disempowering.

In 2002 I presented this case study to an undergraduate class on popular music and invited Yarbrough to speak to the students. The students were enchanted by Yarbrough and fell in love with her music. Yet as impressed as they were with Yarbrough's talent and integrity—or perhaps because of it—a number of students were disappointed that she so readily accepted Cook's "Praise You." In a later discussion, these students said that Cook's treatment of "Take Yo' Praise" was demeaning, and found it disturbing that Yarbrough, who spoke so forcefully to us about racism and injustice, did not see that she herself had been exploited. Regardless of how Yarbrough felt about the matter or how well she was paid, these students still felt there was something wrong about the whole affair.

Although I sympathize with their viewpoint, I disagree with it, and will persist in resisting an unambiguous view of these two songs and their relationship, and of digital sampling in general. Sampling has often been criticized as fundamentally uncreative, even unethical.[21] True, one can hear unimaginative borrowings that capitalize on a sample's familiarity, neither revealing new ways of hearing the sample nor enriching its musical surroundings. And many musicians have had their work sampled without credit or payment, with others profiting from their creativity. Fatboy Slim's "Praise You," however, does not allow us the luxury of a blanket condemnation (or celebration, for that matter); it can be understood as derivative *and* novel, exploitative *and* respectful, awkward *and* subtle. The song, moreover, raises questions of creativity and originality, and forces us to confront issues of gender, class, and race. In that sense, the relationship between "Praise You" and "Take Yo' Praise" brings into focus some of the crucial questions, issues, and ambiguities that face the study of digital sampling, as it presents to us the practice in microcosm.

DIGITAL AESTHETICS AND POLITICS IN "FIGHT THE POWER"

Consider the opening of Public Enemy's 1990 rap song "Fight the Power" (Track 13 on the accompanying CD). In less than a minute, more than a dozen samples fly by, chopped, looped, layered, and transformed in any number of other ways. The tone is set in the opening seconds by a resonant, agitated voice: "Yet our best trained, best educated, best equipped, best prepared troops refuse to fight. Matter of fact, it's safe to say that they would rather switch than fight." The second section (0:17–0:24), a mere three measures long, is anchored by the dotted rhythm of a vocal sample repeated six times. The words are indistinct, and with good reason—they're backwards. The words are "pump me up," from Trouble Funk's 1982 song of the same name. Against this pattern a melodic line, sunk deep into the mix, snakes upward in triplets over the three measures. The sound, obviously electronically processed, may be the saxophone playing of Branford Marsalis, the only instrumentalist (in addition to Terminator X, who provided the turntable scratches) who performed specifically for this song. Eight hits of a snare drum in the second measure and some vocal exclamations in the third fill out the texture. (One of these exclamations, a non-semantic "chuck chuck" from the 1972 soul song "Whatcha See Is Whatcha Get" by the Dramatics, may well be a sly nod to Public Enemy's rapper, Chuck D.) The next section (0:24–0:44), which leads up to the entrance of the rappers, is even more complex. Clyde Stubblefield's "Funky Drummer" solo makes an appearance, though it is submerged within a dense web of other samples. Only the first two eighth-notes in the bass drum (or kick) and the snare hit are clearly heard. Competing for the listener's attention is a host of other sounds: four fragmented vocal samples (three have text and the other is one of James Brown's famous grunts) as well as guitar, synthesizer, bass (from James Brown's 1971 "Hot Pants"), and various percussion samples.[22] The effect created by Public Enemy's production team is dizzying, exhilarating, and tantalizing—one clearly cannot take it all in at once.[23]

When Public Enemy rapper and spokesman Chuck D. explains, "Our music is all about samples," he reveals the centrality of recording technology to the group's work.[24] Simply put, "Fight the Power," and likely Public Enemy itself, could not exist without it. "Fight the Power" is a complex and subtle testament to the influence and possibilities of sound recording; but at the same time, it reveals how the aesthetic, cultural, and political priorities of musicians shape how the technology is understood and used. A look at Public Enemy's use of looping and performative quotation in "Fight the Power" will illuminate the mutual influences between musician and machine.

The looping in "Fight the Power," and in rap generally, directly arose from the hip-hop DJs of the 1970s. As we know from chapter 6, a recorded passage—typically an instrumental solo, or "break"—would be repeated by switching back and forth between two turntables playing the same record. Although looping in most rap ("Fight the Power" included) is no longer created on turntables, its connection to DJing remains crucial. Many hip-hop producers were once (or are simultaneously) DJs, and the skills in selecting and assembling beats are required of both. Moreover, the DJ is a central, founding figure in hip-hop music and a constant point of reference in its discourse; producers who stray too far from the practices and aesthetics of DJing risk compromising their hip-hop credentials.[25]

Although "Fight the Power" samples dozens of different works, the total length of those fragments is fairly short, as most are less than a second long. From such an economy of material, the four-and-a-half-minute track can only exist through an extravagance of looping. Indeed, as Chuck D. once told an interviewer, "We put loops on top of loops on top of loops."[26] For example, in just one four-second segment (0:24–0:28), at least ten distinct samples are being looped; the whole texture is then repeated four more times as a meta-loop until the rappers enter. The section is wildly polyrhythmic; with no two samples overlapping completely, each one competes for the listener's attention. This raises an interesting musical question: What is the effect of weaving together so many distinct and opposing rhythms into an ostinato? An uneasy balance is struck. The repetition provides a consistent pulse, yet the angular syncopation of the various fragments hardly provides a model of stability. The result is something of a paradox—a groove that somehow resists inevitability however many times it is repeated. This practice is also characteristic of various African American musics that do not make use of digital sampling. One need only listen to, say, James Brown's "Papa's Got a Brand New Bag" or "Funky President," both densely packed with competing ostinatos, to understand that looping represents an extension of earlier practices, not a break from them. The loops in "Fight the Power" are not only polymetric, they are polytimbral, representing what composer Olly Wilson calls the "heterogeneous sound ideal."[27] Such an ideal values a diversity of tone colors sounding simultaneously and is demonstrated in a wide variety of African and African American repertoires. Listen again to the section following the opening spoken sample: the combination of percussive grunts, singsong speech, throbbing bass, cracking drums, and high-pitched ringing defines "heterogeneous." This meta-loop is therefore not simply a technological manifestation, but a cultural one.

Public Enemy's sampling in "Fight the Power" serves political as well as musical ends. There is no mistaking the song's rhetoric. The lyrics express black pride, voice opposition to the white establishment, and address racism, freedom of speech, and the representation of blacks in American life and culture. Toward the end of the song (3:18–3:24) Chuck D. raps, "Most of my heroes don't appear on no stamps/Sample a look back you look and find/Nothing but rednecks for 400 years if you check."[28] The use of the word *sample* is significant. Public Enemy's remedy is to provide its own samples, literally in the form of digitized snippets—performative quotations—of the work of its underrepresented heroes. Among others, these samples pay homage to Afrika Bambaataa, Bobby Byrd, James Brown, George Clinton and Funkadelic, the Jacksons, Sly and the Family Stone, and Trouble Funk, all seminal figures in the development of late-twentieth-century African American popular music (and popular music, period). Although many of the samples in "Fight the Power" are disguised beyond recognizability, there is no mistaking Brown's grunts and Bambaataa's electronically processed exclamations. Even when not readily identifiable, the samples clearly draw from African American culture. Various exhortations common in black music and church services—"Let me hear you say," "Come on and get down," "Brothers and sisters"—dot the soundscape. Reinforcing the musical samples are textual references to the music of black Americans (many of them also quoted digitally), including "sound of the funky drummer" (James Brown and Clyde Stubblefield), "I know you got soul" (the title of a Bobby Byrd and, later, an Eric B. and Rakim song), "freedom or death" (a Stetsasonic song), "people, people" (from James Brown's "Funky President"), and "I'm black and I'm proud" (James Brown's famous anthem). The track's title itself invokes the Isley Brothers song of the same name.[29] Finally, a more general reference to African American music is implicit throughout the entire song—in its virtuosic sampling and looping, "Fight the Power" draws upon and honors the work of the hip-hop DJ.

In *Black Noise,* Tricia Rose argues that "although rap music is shaped by and articulated through advanced reproduction equipment, its stylistic priorities are not merely by-products of such equipment."[30] "Fight the Power" perfectly illustrates that claim. On the one hand, it would be extraordinarily difficult, perhaps impossible, to reproduce the dense polyphony and distinctive timbres of the rhythm track without digital sampling. Even if the sampled musicians were to perform their chopped and looped parts in concert (an unlikely prospect!), they themselves could not exactly reproduce the original. It is not simply their voices or their playing that is important, but specific and well-known performances as mediated through recording technologies and heard on discs of a certain vintage. And even if it were somehow possible to recreate the samples, to do so would be to miss the point of hip-hop sampling completely. As Joseph Schloss has demonstrated in his study of the practice, it is the sample—not the live performance—that is the real thing. As one producer explained to him, a live recreation "just doesn't sound *authentic*. There's something about the way old records sound when they're put together right. You can't really recapture 'em when you play [live]."[31] In other words, it is performative quotation—made available by digital sampling—that allows Public Enemy to call forth a pantheon of black figures with such vividness. And it is the manipulability offered by recording technology that makes it possible to interweave these sounds into a rich collage.

Yet the structure and texture of the music were not directly determined by the tools used to create them. Rather, Public Enemy employed these tools in ways that served their own musical and rhetorical ends. They would no doubt agree with Stetsasonic's Daddy O. (cited as a "lyrical inspiration" in the liner notes of *Fear of a Black Planet*) that "A sample's just a tactic/A portion of my method, a tool/In fact it's only of importance when I make it a priority."[32] Sampling serves to continue the predigital, prephonographic practice of signifying that arose in the African American community. Signifying, which can be used to boast, insult, praise, or moralize, generally plays on the many possible meanings and interpretations of a given statement; it is, in the words of Henry Louis Gates Jr., a "black double-voicedness."[33]

We can see how in "Fight the Power" sampling is a digital form of signifying. (Recall how in chapter 6 turntablism was invoked as an analog form of signifying.) The double-voicedness of the samples is clear, as two examples will illustrate. In its original context, the opening sample ("Yet our best trained . . . troops refuse to fight") most likely referred to the Vietnam War. In quoting this passage, Public Enemy preserves its bitterness and fury, but broadens the message, suggesting that real injustice comes not from without (in the form of the country's wartime rivals) but from within, in the form of racism, poverty, and crime, attributed here to the white establishment—"the power." The statement of "people, people" (1:45) is literally double-voiced: Flavor-Flav and a sampled James Brown (from "Funky President") speak simultaneously. But the double-voicedness is also rhetorical. Flavor-Flav proclaims "People, people we are the same," while Chuck D. retorts, "No we're not the same." On its own, the lyric expresses the conflict between assimilation and separatism within the black community. The addition of James Brown's voice taps into his cultural authority, while linking Public Enemy to the less complacent past of the civil rights era.

Yet the power of these sampled statements comes not just from their words, but from their voices, their digitally sampled voices. It is the "grain" of these voices—captured in sequences of 1s and 0s—that truly gives their words such power. And round and round we go: the message cannot be understood without examining the medium, while the nature of the medium is not fully apparent independent of the message. One way of understanding "Fight the Power," then, is as a four-and-a-half-minute treatise on the phonograph effect, one that reveals, as much as anything discussed in this book, the complex relationship between artist and technology.

○○○

Too often discussions of sampling treat the practice simply as technological quotation. However, as I have suggested throughout this chapter, sampling is most fundamentally an art of *transformation*. A sample changes the moment it is relocated. Any sound, placed into a new musical context, will take on some of the character of its new sonic environment. Every "Funky Drummer" sample, however recognizable, leads a distinct life in its new home. Thus, the sound and sense of a two-second drum break may change radically from song to song, even if the patterns of 1s and 0s do not.

Yet samples rarely leave home unchanged, and it is in the chopping, looping, tweaking, and shuffling that the art is truly found. The sampled sounds are really only raw materials, waiting to be mined and refined. This is made most clear in the work of Paul Lansky, whose sources are not songs but everyday sound, and it is up to him to give them musical meaning and syntax. But even finished compositions are ore in the sampler's hands. "Take Yo' Praise" is still recognizable in "Praise You," but in changing its sound, Norman Cook has transformed its function and meaning as well. By contrast, very little of the ore Public Enemy mines in "Fight the Power" is even recognizable, having been transformed so dramatically.

Sampling is also transformative in a less tangible way, in that it blurs the traditional distinction between ideas and expressions.[34] As they are typically understood in the discourse of intellectual property, an idea is a concept, principle, process, or system that is independent of any form, while an expression is a particular embodiment of that idea. For example, the concept that sound recording influences modern musical life is an idea, one that I and many other people share. On the other hand, *Capturing Sound* is a particular expression of that idea. In practice, the dichotomy is not always so clear-cut, but digital sampling muddies the distinction almost beyond recognition. Trouble Funk's 1982 song "Pump Me Up" is obviously not an abstract idea, but a concrete expression. But does the passage sampled in Public Enemy's "Fight the Power" remain Trouble Funk's expression when it no longer bears any resemblance to its unaltered state? Isn't Public Enemy's use of that sound an expression distinct from Trouble Funk's? And if so, does that make the Trouble Funk song the raw material of an idea (or even a wholly different idea) for Public Enemy?

The collapse of the idea-expression dichotomy could have considerable ramifications for copyright law, for while expressions are legally protected, ideas are not. If sampling can be more like taking inspiration from another's ideas than appropriating another's expressions, then sampling—in many cases—should be treated as a form of protected speech immune to prosecution for copyright infringement. My point, however, is not to argue the legal issues of sampling—an area I have intentionally avoided, as I believe it overshadows so many more interesting aspects of the practice. Rather, I raise the idea-expression dichotomy to demonstrate the radically transformative potential of digital sampling.

Finally, sampling has transformed the very art of composition. When composers sample existing works, they begin with expressions, transform them into ideas, and then again into new expressions. Sampling obviates the need for notation or performers, since the final product is not a score requiring interpretive realization, but a document of binary numbers requiring electronic conversion. Composers who work with samples work directly with sound, thus becoming more like their counterparts in the visual and plastic arts. As Public Enemy's Chuck D. explained, "We approach every record like it was a painting."[35] Sampling is a rich and complex practice, one that challenges our notions of originality, of borrowing, of craft, and even of composition itself.

CHAPTER EIGHT

LISTENING IN CYBERSPACE

I am exercising at the University Recreation Center and hear some unfamiliar rap coming from the weight room stereo. The attendant, a student, tells me that we're listening to a homemade compilation CD of songs he downloaded from the Internet. The music reminds me of another rapper, and I take out my portable MP3 player and bring up a song. I hand the headphones to the attendant, who listens, bobbing his head in appreciation.

I receive an e-mail from a professor of musicology in Rio De Janeiro who had recently downloaded my dissertation from the Internet. He wants to assign a chapter to his students but doesn't have access to certain recordings I cite. Could I possibly e-mail them to him as MP3s? I do, and within seconds he is able to listen to these recordings, now better able to make use of my work, whether to share, discuss, confirm, or contest it.

I am in a store and hear an unfamiliar R&B song that piques my interest, as it unexpectedly quotes a classical piano piece, Erik Satie's *Gymnopedies*, no. 1. When I get home to my computer I go to a search engine and enter a fragment of the lyrics I remember; I quickly find that the song is Janet Jackson's "Someone to Call My Lover." I then call up one of a series of file-sharing programs I've used since the demise of Napster and search for the song. Twenty-six copies are available, one of which I start to download. As I wait, I go to the All Music Guide, a useful online reference, and find that "Someone to Call My Lover" was released on Jackson's album *All for You* in 2001. The review notes that the song also appropriates America's "Ventura Highway" (1973).[1] (Later on, I download that song and find that what Jackson sampled was its acoustic guitar introduction.) After a few minutes, the Jackson song has finished downloading. I listen to it, and yes, it's the song I remember from the store. At some later date I may copy (or "burn") the three interconnected works (by Jackson, Satie, and America) onto a CD and use them as examples of musical borrowing in the seminar I teach on popular music.

Each scene I have just described is both remarkable and mundane. Remarkable, because not long ago each might have seemed as distant a possibility as the flying cars or interplanetary tourism of midcentury predictions. Imagine carrying the equivalent of an entire record collection in a device the size of a deck of cards, sending music to unseen colleagues thousands of miles away in the blink of an eye, or conjuring any desired piece of music out of the ether. Utter science fiction! But what I have described is in fact becoming utterly mundane. Similar scenarios repeat themselves daily across the planet, and soon—at least in certain parts of the world—an entire generation of listeners will come of age not knowing of a world *without* such possibilities.

The interactions I have described (and countless others like them) could only take place because of a transformative web of technologies that, at their root, enable all information—including music—to be represented, stored, and distributed as long strings of 1s and 0s. This is digital technology, and it is bringing about what musicologist Timothy D. Taylor describes as "the most fundamental change in the history of Western music since the invention of music notation in the ninth century."[2] In the previous chapter I considered the impact of the digital revolution on musicians; my purpose here is to explore its effect on listeners. In doing so, I will also delve into the conflicts between digital musical culture, the record industry, and U.S. copyright law. While I want to avoid the overheated rhetoric often heard from opposing sides, I have no intention of navigating a middle course. Rather, I will argue that the broad exchange of digital music files over the Internet can serve the public good; and although I recognize the problems of musical piracy, I also believe that the record industry can thrive in a world of widespread file-sharing—not despite it, but because of it.

MP3 AND P2P: PARTNERS IN CRIME

At the center of the three scenes that opened this chapter is a digital technology known as MP3, for the songs that I downloaded from the Internet, stored on my computer, carried around on my portable player, and zapped across continents over e-mail were all in the form of MP3 files.[3] MP3 stands for Motion Picture Experts Group 1, Layer 3, a name that reveals little about its current use. Like the phonograph, which Edison originally saw as a dictation device for businessmen, MP3 was not conceived with music in mind. Rather, it arose out of the work of engineers and executives connected with the film industry—dubbed the Motion Picture Experts Group—who sought to establish standards for the digitization of video and audio. As Leonardo Chiariglione, the Italian engineer who convened the first meeting of the group in 1988, later said, "Nobody, I promise you, had any idea of what this would mean to music."[4] An important goal of the group was to develop a way to compress the huge amount of data constituting video and audio files into sizes manageable for sending and storing on computers. The group engaged a team from the Fraunhofer Institute for Integrated Circuits in Germany to assist in the task, and in 1992 the German researchers created an audiovisual standard they called MPEG-1.

The system used a technique known as perceptual coding to remove "irrelevant" data from the recording (typically a CD) being compressed. The technique is based on the idea that when we listen to music (or any sound, for that matter), some frequencies are "masked"—rendered more or less imperceptible—by competing sounds. For example, a loud cymbal crash in an orchestral piece will momentarily cover the sound of the other instruments playing at the same time. In perceptual coding, those masked sounds are assigned fewer bits of data than the foreground sounds. This reduction allows digital sound to be stored quite compactly—depending on certain variables, about one-twelfth the size it would occupy on a compact disc—without compromising the sonic experience.[5]

MPEG-1 consisted of three different "layers," or levels of data compression. The first two layers were for high-performance use with state-of-the-art technology, the third a lower standard suitable for more modest systems, such as personal computers. To demonstrate MPEG-1, the Fraunhofer team created a free program using this third layer to compress digital music files. The program was a typical "demo"—it was just good enough to give prospective industry users an idea of its potential. Hardly a high-security item, the program was stored unprotected on a computer at the University of Erlangen in Germany. Not long thereafter, a Dutch programmer known as SoloH discovered the demo and downloaded it, tinkered with it, and then made it available to others to further refine. The modest demo soon spawned superior MP3 encoders that offered high-quality sound from highly compressed files. SoloH opened a box—Pandora's to some, a bottomless treasure chest to others—from which millions of files representing every conceivable type of music continue to pour forth.

MP3 did not have an immediate impact on modern musical life, however. In the early 1990s, few were aware of the format and fewer still had access to MP3 files. It was the rise of what is called peer-to-peer (P2P) networking later in the decade—most notably in the form of the Napster network—that endowed MP3 with its global influence. A P2P network is radically different from the more traditional client-server model, in which information flows from a centralized source (the server, a computer or group of computers that stores and distributes data) to its users (the clients, who request data from the server). Instead, P2P describes a decentralized network in which each computer has direct access to certain designated files stored on every other computer; the circulation of data among members of a network is known as file-sharing. If a public library is analogous to a client-server model, P2P is more like the arrangement my wife, her mother, and her aunt have to circulate their collections of mystery novels among one another. But on the Internet, P2P networks can exist on a much grander scale, linking millions of users who can share data almost instantaneously.[6]

Napster is the most famous example of a P2P network. Developed by two college students in 1999, it allowed users to share the MP3 files stored on their computers. At the height of its brief life Napster is said to have had tens of millions of users downloading hundreds of millions of sound files.[7] Its appeal was clear: it was free, easy to use, and provided access to an immense collection of music. After downloading a simple program from napster.com, one had only to connect to the Internet, open the straight-forward user interface, and type in the name of the composer, performer, composition, or album being sought. If anyone linked to the network at the time had that file, it was there for the taking (or more accurately, copy-ing, as I'll explain later). Napster, however, was not a pure P2P network. It relied on a centralized server, and while it held no actual files, it indexed them, linking those with particular songs to people searching for them. While this made searching and downloading relatively easy and efficient, it turned out to be Napster's downfall. Most of the music files circulating over the network were copyrighted and were being downloaded without the permission of the copyright holder. It was difficult for aggrieved par-ties to target any of the millions of individual network users, but it was possible to go after Napster itself, which was facilitating this illegal activ-ity. In July 2001, after nearly a year of intense litigation brought by the record industry, Napster was shut down. (In late 2003 Napster reemerged as a legal file-sharing service, though Napster 2.0, as it's called, shares lit-tle more than its name with the original enterprise.)

The end of the original Napster was not the end of file-sharing, how-ever. Although some similarly centralized networks that attracted large fol-lowings, like Audiogalaxy and Scour, also folded under legal pressure, other file-sharing services have been able to avoid disastrous litigation by being completely decentralized. Gnutella, for example, has no central server; in fact, it is not even a company, but a system for distributing digital files (and not only of music, but of photos, film, and software) that exists in numerous versions and is controlled by no one person or group. Perhaps the most popular network at this writing is Kazaa, which in 2002 was far more heavily used than Napster was at its peak.[8] Such decentralized net-works are immune to the kind of action that brought down Napster, though the record industry has developed alternative strategies for deal-ing with them. While it is unclear how long these networks will survive, their current influence is undeniable.

A great deal of ink has been spilled in the debate over the impact of file-sharing on musicians and the music industry. Rather less attention, how-ever, has been paid to its effect on listeners. Is listening to an MP3 different from listening to other recorded media, or to live music? What distinctive possibilities does musical file-sharing offer to listeners? Do users of MP3s think about music differently because of their use of the technology? What are the legal and ethical ramifications of listening in cyberspace? To address these questions, I propose that we apply the concept of the phonograph effect. This in turn requires that we first delineate the crucial qualities that distinguish the new technologies, and then explore how users respond to those characteristics.

MP3 VS. TRADITIONAL RECORDING MEDIA

I would suggest that the most distinctive and crucial attribute of MP3 files is their status as, in the language of economics, nonrivalrous resources. A resource is *rivalrous* if its consumption or use by one party limits its consumption or use by others. Most physical objects are rivalrous. If I eat a sandwich, no one else can eat it; if I build a house on a parcel of land, or even if I am simply standing on it, I am restricting its use by others. Traditional sound recordings are also rivalrous. In owning a copy of the Shaggs record *Philosophy of the World,* I am limiting everyone else's use of it. (Fortunately, there are plenty of copies to go around.) *Nonrivalrous* resources, in contrast, cannot be depleted by using them. Ideas are nonrivalrous. When I am done with the equation $2 + 2 = 4$, it is still there, intact and undiminished, quite unlike the tuna melt I just ate. Or as Thomas Jefferson more eloquently explained in 1813, "He who receives an idea from me, receives instruction himself without lessening mine; as he who lights his taper at mine, receives light himself without darkening me."[9] Digital sound files, like ideas, are also nonrivalrous. The analogy with ideas is not capricious. As law professor Lawrence Lessig maintains, "The digital world is closer to the world of ideas than the world of things"[10]—which is why copyright and other protections of physical property map uneasily onto the world of cyberspace, a point I will return to later in the chapter. Downloading a file is not like loading a shopping cart with groceries or a car trunk with suitcases, for no object is actually being moved. To download is not to use or take someone else's song file, but to copy it. This is the same with all digital files on the Internet. When I look at an image or read a newspaper online, it is not as if I am looking at a painting in a museum or reading the paper in the library (actions that would impinge on the access of other users). I am making and using my own copy of the images and texts. Of course, slow Internet connections, low bandwidth, and high network traffic can sometimes limit one's access to files. For the most part, however, when I use digital files, I receive light from another's taper, neither taking nor extinguishing the flame.

It is also important to realize that when I download a song (or an image or text, for that matter), I am making a *perfect* copy of that file. An MP3 is just a series of 1s and 0s that represent a given collection of sounds; when copied, the same arrangement of binary numbers is generated. It is not as if the 1s and 0s of the copy are slightly less crisp or true than the original MP3, as a second-generation cassette tape would be. In fact, copies and originals are indistinguishable. This is part of the great appeal of MP3s, for the sound does not degrade when copying.

The nonrivalrous nature of digital music files, moreover, has an important effect on the portability of recorded music. As I have pointed out, the tangibility of traditional recordings has made sound portable in unprecedented ways. But their very physicality places an upper limit on how easily and quickly music can be moved, even as recording media have become sturdier and smaller. Digital music files, however, are dramatically more portable than their more tangible kin. Depending on the speed of one's Internet connection, a three-minute pop song can be downloaded from or e-mailed to anywhere in the world in a matter of seconds. It cannot be long before even the largest music files will zip across the globe more or less instantaneously.

The nature of digital music files also affects cost. Throughout the history of recording, it has often been possible to hear certain kinds of music more cheaply on disc than live. The cost differential is even wider with MP3s and the like, with millions of tunes available for free. MP3s are not subject to the physical control exerted over traditional recorded media— they cannot be barcoded, pricetagged, shrinkwrapped, or sequestered on shelves or behind display cases—and most are downloaded on decentralized networks, subject to no one's control. Encryption, digital watermarks, self-implementing expiration dates, and the like have been sought as ways to control and affix prices to digital music files, but so far with little success.

Digital music files—nonrivalrous, endlessly reproducible, extremely portable, and frequently free—are clearly different from traditional recording media. How do these differences affect the listening habits of users? Before I venture some answers, I must pose a preliminary question: Who are the users? According to a December 2002 survey by the research firm Ipsos-Insight (formerly Ipsos-Reid), 19 percent of the American population aged twelve and over had recently downloaded one or more music files from an online file-sharing service. This translates to roughly 40 million users in the United States alone. Not surprisingly, teenagers and young adults were most likely to download music, but a sizable number of older adults did so as well; significantly more men (26 percent of the population) than women (12 percent) downloaded music.[11] Ipsos has also explored downloading habits throughout the world, and found significant activity. In Taiwan, Canada, Sweden, Hong Kong, and South Korea, eighteen- to twenty-four-year-olds were in fact more likely to have ever downloaded music from the Internet than their American counterparts.[12] In less economically developed regions, however, activity is quite low. In Africa in 2002, only 1 in 150 was even connected to the Internet, and certainly fewer still had downloaded MP3s.[13] (This figure is actually a huge increase over just a few years before.) The percentage of Internet users in Arab countries is even smaller: about 0.5 percent of the population has access.[14] Of those who do download, how representative are they of the general population? The average downloader is almost certainly wealthier than those not on the Internet, given the cost of computers and Internet service. (This disparity, again, is even more marked in poorer countries.) But the number of downloaders is growing and the cost of the technology is shrinking in every part of the world. So while we must be careful not to generalize from the experience of those who download digital music files to the rest of the population, we can speculate on downloading's impact on hundreds of millions of listeners.

Hundreds of millions of listeners, then, are likely to experience music in new ways given the differences between cyberspace and real space. In responding to these differences, users may enjoy greater access to music, discover new repertoire, and exercise an increased flexibility in the way they listen to music. Moreover, they may change their consumption of CDs, rethink their ideas about musical authenticity, and form virtual communities around shared musical interests. As will be clear, these are not theoretical possibilities, but represent the real-world experiences of a wide variety of users. In addition to Internet discussion forums and third-party surveys, I also draw on responses to a survey I conducted for this book as well as undergraduate student papers on file-sharing submitted in April 2002 in a course I taught at Johns Hopkins University.[15] I want to stress that I do not treat downloaders as if they are all of one mind. As we should expect, diverse and contradictory practices and attitudes abound. Still, the individual phonograph effects I describe represent the practices of many users and, taken collectively, help to paint a picture of musical life in cyberspace.

The clearest change that digital and networking technologies have introduced is the possibility of an unprecedented and unparalleled accessibility to music. This new accessibility may be understood in terms of speed, ease, and breadth. The first two traits can be seen in the last example from the opening of the chapter: I hear a bit of an unidentified song in a store, and a few minutes after I get home I am listening to it. The same accessibility also allows me to listen almost instantly to music I read or hear about. This is not a matter of instant versus delayed gratification, however, for before the advent of MP3s and the Internet I was simply never able to hear much of the music I heard about. Music delayed is often music denied.

File-sharing not only makes it possible to find particular pieces easily, it also allows users to explore unfamiliar territory. If one can imagine a particular type of music, it probably exists; if it exists, it can probably be found on the Internet. For example, here are two genres that may or may not exist: Swedish funk and Vietnamese hardcore rap. I will now try to find examples on MP3.

Success! After entering "Swedish Funk MP3" on a search engine, I am directed to a fan site for the group Electric Boys, a Stockholm quartet formed in 1988.[16] A number of their songs are posted on the site, and within moments I am listening to "Freaky Funksters" from their 1990 album *Funk-O-Metal Carpet Ride.* Now I am listening to "Around My Town," an as yet unreleased hardcore rap from a California-based Vietnamese group inexplicably known as Thai.[17] Thai posted the song themselves, it seems in the hope of generating enough interest to land a record contract. The song is not actually in Vietnamese, as I had expected, but the fact that it is playing only seconds after I wondered if such music even existed proves my point. I should admit that I did fail on a third search: I did not find any MP3s of Jewish gospel.[18]

Such broadened access to music is widely noted by downloaders. A June 2002 study found 29 percent of American respondents reporting that their favorite genre of music changed since they began downloading, while 21 percent indicated that they developed new radio listening habits.[19] But even if their musical tastes do not fundamentally change, downloaders seem to feel freer to explore unfamiliar genres without the risk of wasting their money or time; if the music is not to their liking, they can simply delete it. A number of downloaders noted that they ventured or stumbled into new musical territory in their file-sharing and were gratified by the results. One female Hopkins student explained: "File sharing has made music much more accessible for me. I never really enjoyed classical music as much as I do now . . . partly because I would rather purchase a Radiohead CD than some classical music CD with more than half of the songs I wasn't sure I'd like."[20] But without the risk of failure she delved much more deeply into the classical repertoire. A forty-year-old male survey respondent from Boise, Idaho, reported discovering the band the New Pornographers by accident. (One can imagine how this might have happened.) Others looked for out-of-print recordings, concert recordings by familiar artists, and remixes or covers of their favorite songs. A fifty-one-year-old consultant from Minneapolis, for example, reported that he has used P2P networks to collect more than seventy versions of the World War II–era song "Lili Marlene."

One fascinating manifestation of this new accessibility is what I would describe as a divergent approach to discovering music. Instead of seeking out particular pieces (a convergent approach), one initiates an intentionally general search in hope of broad and unfamiliar results. A search under the term "cello" yielded not only the expected (Bach's cello suites), it introduced me to Nick Drake's haunting "Cello Song," the works of Apocalyptica, the Finnish cello quartet known for its Metallica covers, as well as to the riches of Annette Funicello. What by all rights should be condemned as a poor search engine served as my trusted guide into the musical unknown.

In a similar vein, one college student wrote of her use of Napster, to search not for specific songs but for moods and emotions:

I typed "rain" into Napster, downloaded all my finds with the word in the title, and then listened to every song capturing the experience of a rainstorm. With this entire repertoire at my fingertips, I felt mighty— for the range of emotions responding to rain was mine—and paradoxically brighter. Voltaire once said, "Anything too stupid to be spoken is sung." What felt trite to say myself somehow sounded profound and weighty when artists added a backbeat and a melody. After a bad break-up I typed "cry," "love," "hurt," "heart," etc., and found the most soppy song (in this case a Neil Sedaka) that trumped my depression and therefore somehow uplifted me. Some of the music captured my pain, and helped me as though some artists completely understood me, and then others were so hyperbolic I felt relatively fortunate and therefore calmed.[21]

This divergent approach is an unexpected and valuable feature of musical life in cyberspace, one that simply cannot be duplicated in the physical world.

Another aspect of the accessibility downloaders enjoy is the flexibility to customize their musical experience. An oft-repeated complaint from fans of popular music is that any given album rarely has more than two or three tracks they want to hear. Many feel that they are forced to buy entire albums, and resent the record companies whom they see as foisting unwanted music on them. Over and over, survey respondents and contributors to P2P bulletin boards tout downloading as a way to avoid the all-or-nothing dilemma of CD buying; they, not the artist, producer, or record company, pick out the music, and only the music they want to hear. Although dissatisfaction with the album format preceded the advent of MP3s, file-sharing reinforces what might be called "singles listening." When listeners get to know an album intimately, the end of one song on the album strongly raises the expectation of the next. Beatles fans who wore out the grooves of *Sgt. Pepper's Lonely Hearts Club Band* will always anticipate "Lucy in the Sky with Diamonds" in the silence following "With a Little Help from My Friends" (even if they hear the latter on the radio), just as "Smells Like Teen Spirit" contains the seeds of "In Bloom" for initiates of Nirvana's *Nevermind*. For better or for worse, downloaders often miss out on the gestalt of the commercially produced album. Yet downloaders can decide how to group songs based on their own criteria. For example, I have numerous playlists on my computer's MP3 player: twelve-bar blues songs, works that I use in my classes, music my wife likes, and so on. These need not stay on the computer; I can "burn" these playlists onto CDs to create personalized compilations, which may in turn generate their own gestalt. As is clear from survey results, burning CD compilations is a common adjunct to downloading.

Downloaders can even go further and alter the very sound of their MP3s. Various software programs, many available free on the Internet, allow users to change pitch or tempo, add or subtract musical layers, reverse sounds, tweak frequencies, and much more. In other words, listeners can become amateur sound engineers, even composers. I use similar tools as a means of analysis: slowing Jascha Heifetz's performance of a Hungarian Dance allows me to hear variations in rhythm and tempo, changes in vibrato, and other performance nuances much more easily than at the normal speed; isolating certain frequencies in Public Enemy's "Fight the Power" helps me to unpack its incredibly dense web of samples. MP3s, so easily shuffled and manipulated, allow listening to be an active pursuit.

The most controversial aspect of MP3s that distinguishes them from rivalrous relatives is their affordability. Most MP3s are downloaded free over P2P networks, much to the delight of users, who can obtain CD-quality recordings without paying for CDs. The recording industry, of course, opposes such freeloading, arguing that file-sharing is responsible for the recent downturn in CD sales. One of the surprising findings of several file-sharing studies, however, is that collectively downloaders are not buying significantly fewer CDs than they would in a world without MP3s. In a February 2002 study, 57 percent of respondents reported that they bought the same number of CDs since starting to download; 24 percent said that their purchases *increased*.[22] In a separate study Jupiter Research found that 36 percent of "experienced file sharers" (those who have been active for more than six months) reported buying more CDs.[23] Of course, given that most songs are downloaded illegally, it is possible that survey respondents would misrepresent or simply lie about their buying habits. Yet by and large, downloaders see little wrong with their activities. In my survey, those who reported that they stopped buying CDs did so loudly and proudly. As I will explain later, many downloaders see their actions as a form of protest and are not averse to revealing what they do and why they do it.

Not only are many downloaders continuing to buy CDs, many claim that file-sharing has spurred them to spend more on concert tickets and other musical merchandise. Consider the example of this female college student:

> I started listening to a punk band called Midtown. They were giving out their songs on the Internet for free, and after listening to a few songs, I went to a concert. They put on an amazing show, and I was hooked right there. I quickly bought their CD and listened to it religiously for months. It had been years since I had spent any money on any musical product, but after listening to Midtown, I was spending money left and right on concerts, t-shirts, and CDs. I never would have discovered just how amazing these guys sounded if it weren't for file swapping.[24]

A self-identified forty-two-year-old male "Assistant VP" from my survey reported a similar experience: "I first heard The Strokes through a Kazaa download and now I am going to Milwaukee with my daughter (400 miles) to see them in concert—something that would not have happened without P2P file sharing."

That file-sharing would encourage CD buying might seem astonishing until we remember that CDs and MP3s are very different things. CDs are more or less permanent; they are immune to computer viruses and lightning strikes, are usually glitch free, and come with handy (if small) liner notes, often with art and lyrics. (And unlike many of the MP3s floating in cyberspace, they correctly identify the title and performer of the music.) These qualities assure the mutual nonexclusivity of CDs and MP3s, and are frequently cited by downloaders who continue to buy CDs. Here's how a nineteen-year-old male college student explained it: "Despite the availability of free music online, I will still fork out $12–$17 from my paycheck on the latest Kylie Minogue or Madonna or Britney or Cher. If I support an artist or a film soundtrack I will want to collect the jewel case and cover art. This has to do with respect and the pursuit of authenticity and quality. I will want to hear the highest in quality, and the original, authentic versions." Or as another student suggested, "It's nice to have the real thing."[25]

It is remarkable to hear CDs spoken of as original and authentic. Not long ago they were derided as cold, inhuman, and unattractively small—the antithesis of the LP, with its comforting tactility and oft-cited warmth of sound. Yet LPs were flimsy compared to the thicker, more substantial 78s; and to extend this further, many listeners preferred the "warm" sound of acoustic 78s to those made by the electrical process beginning in 1925. And of course, recording itself can be considered inauthentic compared to live music-making. Authenticity is clearly a moving target. Often something is authentic to the extent that it has been replaced by something newer, less familiar, and more convenient, which is why CDs can now be thought of as "the real thing."

As much as CDs are about sound, they also have visual and tactile qualities that are important to their owners. The tangibility of the CD is part of its charm. A collection is meant to be displayed, and has a visual impact that confers a degree of expertise on its owner. The tall bookcase full of CDs in my home office often impresses visitors who, correctly or not, infer from it a certain breadth and depth of knowledge about music on my part. My MP3 collection, out of sight and intangible, has no such effect. By the same token, collecting loses some of its appeal when the objects of one's search are so easily attainable. A twenty-two-year-old female college student noted that in downloading MP3s, she missed the sense of personal connection she felt with CDs:

> I believe that by utilizing this technology, I lost part of the nostalgia inherent in buying and listening to music. For example, I can listen to my Flaming Lips CD and know that I purchased it the week after my 15th birthday, during my "alternative" stage in high school, but I cannot do this with MP3s. I acquired so many songs at such a fast rate that listening to this music only reminds me of sitting in front of my computer freshman and sophomore years [at college].[26]

Many downloaders treat MP3s not as ends in themselves, but as a means to decide whether to buy a particular CD. The comments of a twenty-one-year-old male student represent the attitudes of many: "While file-sharing may not have increased the number of CDs or LPs that I buy, it also has not decreased the number. What it has changed is how I buy—I have used it as a tool by which to judge and select what I buy."[27]

MP3 and P2P are still young technologies and, assuming they survive, may one day become naturalized to the point that the tangibility of CDs will hold little appeal. For now, however, the intangibility of MP3s means not only that they are free but that, ironically, they will not replace their rivalrous and often costly ancestors.

As I noted in chapter 1, recording made the act of solitary listening practicable and widespread, as everyone with a portable player or a home or car stereo knows firsthand. MP3 has a similar potential to isolate listeners. Yet users of the technology are in fact connecting to one another in great numbers and are forming thriving musical communities. MP3 itself does not make this happen; rather, it is the P2P networks over which digital files circulate and the communication software that these networks feature (bulletin boards, instant messaging, chat rooms, etc.) that bring listeners together. These communities are in some ways radically new, in some ways traditional. Unlike bowling leagues and book clubs, Internet listening communities do not congregate in the same physical space, and members typically never even see or meet one another. Yet members hold common interests, and often feel a close connection with one another. In fact, such communities may address needs that no off-line group could meet. Physical distance collapses, so that the geographically isolated can come together; distinctions of age, class, gender, and race may fade (though not completely), allowing a freedom of interaction unlikely in any other way.

It is worth observing that its practitioners typically call the activity of downloading file-*sharing*. The term is not (or not simply) a coy way to deflect accusations of theft; as used, the term suggests a sense of generosity, selflessness, and mutual concern among the members of a group. As a thirty-nine-year-old female survey respondent from North Carolina wrote, "File sharing is also about community. I have found file-sharers to be amongst the most sharing, friendly, compassionate and helpful, knowledgeable people on the Internet." On most P2P networks, it is possible to download from others without allowing them access to your own files. But many gladly open their computers to network users. A twenty-nine-year-old graduate student from Toronto explained, "sharing (as opposed to merely acquiring) can also have its rewards, and often I feel very compelled to provide others with the music they want, or even the music I feel they ought to get to know."

This sharing can take place with or without verbal communication. As long as you are connected to a P2P network and enable your files to be shared, anyone else on the network can download designated files from your computer without asking or notifying you. It is a strange sensation, having an unknown person silently copying MP3s from your hard drive. (File-sharing programs typically allow users to see when others are accessing their computers.) An ironically intimate—if fleeting—bond is established, for if music helps define and articulate who we are, opening one's computer to others is indeed opening oneself to others. Oftentimes, network users do communicate. Many P2P networks have chat functions, meaning that anyone can send a message and initiate a conversation with anyone else connected at the time. Group discussions can take place on bulletin boards, which provide forums dedicated to particular topics of mutual interest. Discussions might concern hardware or software problems, individual songs, whole genres, favorite groups, and so on.

It is worthwhile to mention a few examples of virtual communities that have arisen around the trading of MP3s. Although they may no longer exist by the time this book is published, they illustrate the wide possibilities available to those with common interests and network access. The Track Exchange describes itself as "an online community of recording collaborators."[28] Using recording software and a P2P network, a group of musicians living hundreds or thousands of miles apart can collectively compose in cyberspace, each member contributing parts, tinkering with the whole, and discussing the results. ZPoc is a P2P network dedicated to Christian music and its fans. As its welcome page explains, it is "a file sharing software for the 'Christian' community to share Jesus, through songs, with your friends. Friendly and helpful people, it's a great community."[29] Network members can chat with one another, read a daily scripture passage, and trade MP3s of their favorite Christian rock artists. Zero Paid and Filetopia, as their names suggest, unite people with strong and idealistic views on the benefits of file-sharing. While neither is dedicated solely to music, much of the trading and discussion center on music. Any number of open and usually angry letters to the Recording Industry Association of America can be found on Zero Paid (the RIAA is a trade group representing the recording industry and heads the effort to stop illegal downloading). When the Audiogalaxy network shut down, Filetopia welcomed former Audiogalaxy members into their community, sponsoring "reunions" of AG "alumni" on its bulletin board. For a final example, consider the Internet opera club that came to light in my survey. Two opera fans using Napster, one in the United States and one in Israel, discovered that they had complementary MP3 collections. The two men decided to trade complete operas by downloading entire works to a separate server to which both had access. (For the most part, they could only collect them piecemeal on Napster.) A third downloader from the Netherlands soon joined in, and he subsequently brought along two Swedish women. As of mid-2002, this private club had seventeen members scattered throughout the. world, and had become much more than a way to trade MP3s. Members posted opera quizzes and debated the merits of recordings, and even became friends outside of music, sharing their personal lives and occasionally visiting each other.[30] Whether convened because of a creative drive, a common religion, commitment to free file-sharing, or an interest in a genre, the members of these communities find meaning in their associations and activities far beyond an interest in free music. They are sharing files, beliefs, ideals, and lifestyles.[31]

Over and again downloaders say that their musical lives have been enriched. They are listening to more and different kinds of music and are connecting to others with similar interests. They also seem to be interested in learning *about* the music they hear. It is possible for one to download MP3s in blissful ignorance of even song titles, but that is not typical. The February 2002 Ipsos study noted that downloaders visit search engines, lyrics servers, and news and entertainment sites in search of information about the music they hear; 84 percent of downloaders reported using the Internet in this way.[32] And as I noted earlier, downloaders are often inspired to see and hear their favorite groups live, demonstrating that the MP3 experience need not replace the concert experience.

In pointing to the benefits of downloading, I may be accused of offering a utopian vision of the technology. I readily admit that I am hardly a disinterested party, for as a scholar, teacher, musician, and music lover, my life and work have been tremendously enriched by my ability to hear and study the broadest array of music with such ease. Yet I am no technological utopian. I do not believe that file-sharing will lead to a more cultured, civilized, and peaceful society (as the early-twentieth-century activists I discussed in chapter 2 predicted of the phonograph). File-sharing cures no ills; on the contrary, it can transform the merely curious into the obsessive, the fan into the fanatic. And as every user knows, file-sharing can be an exercise in frustration—the unpleasant and ever-present realities include an often high failure rate when attempting to download, incomplete and corrupted files, incorrectly labeled songs, and those tantalizing files that come up in a search but never, ever download. Moreover, the intangibility of MP3s and the ease with which they are obtained, disseminated, and deleted may encourage the sense that music is just another disposable commodity, an attitude I personally find worrisome.

There is also, of course, the contentious matter of the legal status of file-sharing, an issue that has driven a wedge between much of the listening public and the recording industry and one that may undermine the potential benefits the technology can offer. I want to devote the remainder of the chapter to this divisive subject.

THE LEGAL DEBATE SURROUNDING MP3 AND P2P

While there is nothing illegal about MP3 and P2P technology per se, it is illegal to download or distribute digital files of copyrighted recordings without the permission of the copyright holder. As the RIAA points out, in the United States there are both civil and criminal penalties for such infringement, the latter including up to $250,000 in fines, six years' imprisonment, or both.[33] And violations are occurring around the clock, throughout the world, in the open, and by the millions.

Individual record companies and the RIAA have sought to stem the tide of illegal file-sharing in a number of ways. The most public avenue has been litigation.[34] Perhaps the best-known case has been *A&M Records et al. v. Napster*, in which nine record companies sued the file-sharing network for copyright infringement. In July 2000, a U.S. district court enjoined Napster from "engaging in, or facilitating others in copying, downloading, uploading, transmitting, or distributing plaintiffs' copyrighted musical compositions and sound recordings."[35] Napster finally lost on appeal in February 2001 and ceased its file-sharing service in July of that year.[36] In June 2002 Audiogalaxy, another centralized service, capitulated to legal pressure brought on by the RIAA and blocked users' access to copyrighted files. The industry then began to file suits against the decentralized file-sharing services, which had largely replaced those based on the Napster model. In April 2003, however, the industry lost an important case against the companies that owned the Morpheus and Grokster services. The presiding judge ruled that the defendants were not responsible for the copyright infringements of their customers because these companies did not store or index the illegal files themselves.[37]

The industry has continued to pursue litigation in other ways, notably by targeting individual users. (Although normally it would have been difficult to identify particular computer users, a U.S. District Court judge—in a decision that was later reversed, much to the industry's dismay—required the Internet service provider Verizon to provide the RIAA with names and addresses of those customers suspected of the illegal activity.) Most notorious were the lawsuits filed in September 2003 against a twelve-year-old girl and a sixty-six-year-old grandmother, a public relations disaster for the industry, which was widely depicted as bullying and vindictive. (The suit against the grandmother was dropped when it was discovered that her computer was incapable of downloading music files, illegal or otherwise.)[38] The industry is clearly—and literally—sending a message to downloaders: before the September lawsuits the RIAA sent millions of electronic missives to users of the Kazaa and Grokster services. "DON'T STEAL MUSIC," the message exhorts. "Distributing or downloading copyrighted music on the Internet without permission from the copyright owner is ILLEGAL. It hurts songwriters who create and musicians who perform the music you love, and all the other people who bring you music."[39]

On a different front, the industry has also engaged in what is collectively known as "denial of service attacks," all intended to disrupt and discourage file-sharing. "Spoofing" is the act of supplying P2Ps with corrupt or bogus MP3s, typically files consisting of silence or of continuous loops of a song's chorus. "Flooding" creates a network traffic jam with phony queries and signals. "Forcing" aims to shut down particularly active network members by sending more queries than their computers can handle. The purpose of the industry's activities is unambiguous. As one record company executive explained, "We're doing this simply because we believe people are stealing our stuff and we want to stymie the stealing."[40] As of this writing, the legality of these attacks is unclear, but that might change. Representative Howard Berman of California has sponsored a bill that would authorize copyright holders to begin "blocking, diverting or otherwise impairing" P2P networks that trade in copyrighted material. Perhaps in protest, in late July 2002 hackers flooded the RIAA website, shutting it down for several days.[41]

The success of the industry's lawsuits and denial-of-service attacks is unclear. In fact, the aggressive tactics and uncompromising stance of the industry have given downloaders a powerful weapon: self-righteousness. File-sharing has come to be seen by many as a political act, a declaration of independence from the heavy hand of big business. The woman from North Carolina quoted earlier, a self-described "office worker/sandwich maker," included this note in her response to my survey: "I feel empowered by file sharing! I feel that we ARE The Revolution and we can change the way the recording industry treats its customers." A forty-two-year-old fellow North Carolinian expanded on this idea in his response: "I regard downloading music as a form of civil disobedience in protest of a monopolistic cartel that wants nothing less than to own and control the distribution of all music. The recording industry . . . would seek to strangle technology to remain profitable, so if P2P file sharing helps to bring about its demise, so much the better." Over and over, on bulletin boards and in survey responses, the same rhetoric recurs. There are even entire websites, such as Boycott RIAA, devoted to giving voice to anti-industry sentiment.[42] It hardly matters whether the arguments are sound or fallacious (there are a good deal of both types); what may have once been simply a way of getting free music has become for many a form of protest, largely in response to the actions of the record industry.[43]

So we find ourselves at an impasse. The industry has the law on its side and fights illegal downloading with every available means, while many of those who share files see nothing wrong with their activities. Although there is a need for understanding and compromise from both sides, I want to argue that file-sharing should actually be opened up even further, not shut down. I believe that the industry could flourish were that to happen.

Given the illegality of much file-sharing, it may seem odd to argue that the downloaders are in the right. In a seminal 1994 article, "The Economy of Ideas," John Perry Barlow, co-founder of the Electronic Frontier Foundation, offers a way to understand this contrarian assertion: "Whenever there is such profound divergence between law and social practice, it is not society that adapts. . . . To assume that systems of law based in the physical world will serve in an environment as fundamentally different as cyberspace is a folly for which everyone doing business in the future will pay."[44]

Barlow makes two important points here. The first is that human laws are typically crafted out of social practice and must be broadly accepted to have any force. Moreover, they have to be enforceable. As Barlow later wrote, "No law can be successfully imposed on a huge population that does not morally support it and possesses easy means for its invisible evasion."[45] Think of Prohibition and the national fifty-five-mile-an-hour speed limit in the United States; both failed spectacularly, despite the fact that both drinking and speeding (especially in combination) are patently unhealthy and cause innumerable deaths every year. Given that file-sharing is (as far as we know) physically harmless, and that the public will to download is strong, stopping it seems a very unlikely prospect. Barlow's second assertion is one I have already stressed, namely, that the physical world and cyberspace are fundamentally different. CDs and MP3s are not the same, and people treat them differently. Thus, Barlow's two points are connected: people feel free to flout copyright law in cyberspace because of the differences between the virtual world and the real world, and they do so whether or not they are conscious of the fact.

The record industry takes great pains to liken downloading to theft and piracy. But downloading is not theft in the traditional sense, precisely because of the fundamental differences between the virtual and the real. Theft involves physically taking property from another without right or permission. But MP3s are nonrivalrous, meaning that when I download something, I am copying, not taking. No one is being deprived of any previously held property. If, as Lawrence Lessig maintains, entities in cyberspace are more like ideas than things, then perhaps downloading is like stealing someone's ideas. But one cannot literally steal another's idea; moreover, ideas are not copyrightable. Figuratively, we say an idea is stolen if someone other than its originator takes credit for it or one profits from it without acknowledging its source. It is highly unlikely, however, that anyone downloading the latest pop song is claiming credit for it, and there is little evidence that downloaders sell MP3s. So if the downloader is taking neither property nor credit, what is being violated?

The answer is control—which, indeed, is the essence of copyright. The copyright holder is given the control to sell a work, to reproduce and authorize others to reproduce it, to generate derivative works from it (translations, remixes, etc.), to perform the work publicly, and to seek legal remedies when these rights are violated.[46] Thus creators are supposedly given incentive to create, for they have some guarantee that they will be allowed to profit from their work and determine to a certain extent how it is used by others. So in theory, when copyright is violated, a creator is being deprived of potential revenue. Isn't this equivalent to theft?

The matter is not so simple, for several reasons. First, practically speaking, it is often *not* the composer or performer but a record or publishing company who holds the rights to a song. Typically, creators transfer copyright (or elements of that right) to a record company in exchange for manufacturing, promoting, and distributing the work. Copyright, therefore, does not necessarily protect creators. As cultural historian Siva Vaidhyanathan argues, the creator is a straw man in copyright debates: "Copyright has in the twentieth century really been about the rights of publishers first, authors second, and the public a distant third."[47]

A second point is that copyright is not simply a means of granting control to copyright holders. In the United States it was originally intended as a means of establishing a *balance* between control and access. As Article I of the U.S. Constitution states, the purpose of copyright is "to promote the progress of science and useful arts, by securing for limited times to authors and inventors the exclusive right to their respective writings and discoveries."[48] Creators were given control of their works as incentive to create—but only for a limited time; after that, the public could have unfettered access to these creations. This was meant to perpetuate the cycle of creativity, since the conception of new works often depends on access to existing ones. But for well over a century, copyright has become increasingly unbalanced. In the early history of the United States a copyright expired after only fourteen years; but owing to numerous revisions over the past two centuries copyrights now hold for the life of the author plus seventy years. In this case, whom exactly is copyright intended to serve? Since copyrighted material can now be protected for 150 years or more, it certainly cannot be the creators who benefit. Typically, it is the long-lived corporations who profit. Indeed, critics of the most recent extension (the 1998 Copyright Term Extension Act) point to corporate influence as the driving force behind the change. As Lawrence Lessig has noted, "Each time, it is said, with only a bit of exaggeration, that Mickey Mouse [owned by the Walt Disney corporation] is about to fall into the public domain, the term of copyright . . . is extended."[49]

My third point is that file-sharing does not necessarily deprive copyright holders of income. If every person who would have downloaded copyrighted music decided instead to buy the CD, copyright holders would indeed stand to make huge sums of money. But that is not the same as saying that downloading is *depriving* copyright holders of that money. It is well established that downloading does not always replace CD purchases. As we have seen, many file-sharers buy CDs of the MP3s they download. Other downloaders interested in just one or two tracks from a CD would not have bought the album in the first place. And yet another portion download MP3s of out-of-print recordings that they could not buy even if they wanted to. The reality of copyright thus blunts the moral force of the industry's argument that downloaders are only hurting their favorite artists, and in turn helps to explain why many who share files feel so strongly about the rightness of what they do.[50]

I must stress that in making these points, I am not claiming that the unauthorized copying of recordings is harmless. Certainly, the industry is losing money to file-sharing. In 2002 economics professor Stan Liebowitz conducted a study of thirty years of record sales and determined that a modest but real percentage of the current downturn in record sales can only be attributed to illegal file-sharing. Significantly, however, he refutes what he calls the "Annihilation Hypothesis"—the idea that file-sharing will destroy the record industry.[51] If the reduction in sales and revenues makes it significantly more expensive to publish recordings, some musicians will surely lose industry support. More directly, musicians, even if they hold no rights to their music or recordings, are denied royalties (however small) when their songs are downloaded instead of purchased. Nevertheless, I maintain that we must question whether copyright as now construed truly serves the public good and, conversely, whether the circulation of copyrighted files on the Internet is quite the plague the industry claims. With this in mind, and given the differences between CDs and MP3s as well as the public will to download, I believe we must shift the focus of the debate over file-sharing. What the file-sharing situation reveals is not the rise of a new criminal class numbering in the hundreds of millions, but the corruption of a system meant to encourage the creativity of exactly those who now find themselves on the wrong side of the law. In other words, we have to figure out not how to make downloaders conform to the system, but how to change the system itself.

"Changing the system" is a quixotic notion, but there is a growing movement to do just that. *Eldred v. Ashcroft*, which challenged the constitutionality of the 1998 copyright extension, included several publishing companies among its plaintiffs; amicus briefs were filed by dozens of law and economics professors, fifteen library associations, and corporate giant Intel. (The challenge, however, failed. In January 2003 the Supreme Court upheld the constitutionality of the 1998 extension.)[52] The Electronic Frontier Foundation and similar organizations are increasingly vocal and active in their campaigns for the freedom of file-trading. Musicians such as Alanis Morissette, Chuck D., Janis Ian, Prince, and the band Negativland also promote file-sharing as good not only for their fans, but for themselves as well.[53]

A NEW FILE-SHARING REGIME

I do not want to go so far as to suggest, as some have, that copyright and even the notion of intellectual property be abolished. Rather, I believe a more attainable goal is the restoration of copyright as a balance between access and control, between public and private rights and interests. In this I am sympathetic with the main argument of Siva Vaidhyanathan's persuasive and reasonable study *Copyrights and Copywrongs,* that "American culture and politics would function better under a system that guarantees 'thin' copyright protection—just enough protection to encourage creativity, yet limited so that emerging artists, scholars, writers, and students can enjoy a rich public domain of 'fair use' of copyrighted material."[54]

How would copyright slim down to become the system Vaidhyanathan proposes? One way is to roll back the extension of copyright, as *Eldred v.*

Ashcroft sought to do. Its failure suggests that this may not be the most successful route, however. Another approach is to expand the application of the fair use doctrine or, more accurately, restore it to its original scope. Fair use places limitations on the exclusive rights of copyright holders, allowing certain uses of material that would otherwise be considered infringements.[55] This is why I can quote Vaidhyanathan's *Copyrights and Copywrongs* without permission of the copyright holder (who, in typical fashion, is not the author but his publisher). It is also why I can photocopy articles for research purposes, tape TV shows to watch at a later date, or "rip" MP3s of my CDs to listen to on my computer. All these uses are fair and do not infringe copyright, even though I have not been granted permission to perform them. I do not need permission because these are private, noncommercial uses that have no effect on the potential market of the material.[56]

How different is file-sharing from these activities? For the most part, downloaders of copyrighted MP3s are engaging in private, noncommercial uses that seem to have relatively little impact on the market of the material. Of course, the industry will dispute this last part, pointing to their success in court against Napster and others to show that there is no established fair use exception for file-sharing. I believe, however, that file-sharing *should* be protected as fair use. The law is intentionally vague, simply providing guidelines for judges (not the industry) to determine fair use on a case-by-case basis. No law needs to be changed, just attitudes. If file-sharing is seen as a public good, and if the industry decided not to litigate, file-sharing would be de facto fair.

Why should the record industry promote file-sharing? For two reasons: money and customer satisfaction, which is to say, also money. I believe that if the recording companies were to give open and easy access to their music via MP3, the public would be willing to pay for that access. This is a simple proposal, and perhaps it sounds simplistic. Why wouldn't listeners just download songs free on P2Ps, as they do now? Wouldn't giving free rein to file-sharing completely destroy the CD market? Why should record companies (practically) give away their music? To answer these questions we have to ask two more basic ones; the answers to these will then explain why this idea could work—and why, in the light of recent initiatives on the part of the industry (more on which later), it is in fact starting to work.

The first question is this: Why pay to download music? Various conditions would in fact provide sound reasons to do so, many of them evident in the responses to my survey and in Internet discussions on the matter.

If it is easy. Paid downloading would be appealing if one could locate any MP3 from a single, powerful search engine and if, once directed to the file, a simple click (or equivalent operation) initiated the download.

If it is fast. Consistently fast downloads would be preferable to the inconsistent (and often slow) download rates on many P2P networks.

If it is reliable. The success of download attempts on P2Ps can be very low. Completion rates much closer to 100 percent might well draw downloaders to legal sites.

If it is legal. While many profess to revel in illegal file-sharing, some would download only if it is legal and many others would rather "do the right thing."

If quality is assured. A guarantee of glitch-free files would have significant drawing power.

If quantity is assured. A consistently wide selection of MP3s would attract many customers.

If it is permanent. Downloaders seem to be unanimous on this point. They do not want self-expiring MP3s or streaming files that are more like broadcasts than CDs (as some early pay systems offered). They want to be able to download files to their computers so that they can control their subsequent use of the music.

If additional resources or services are offered. If downloaders are given exclusive or advance access to new material they will have incentive to pay.

If musicians directly benefit. Some downloaders say they would only pay if they felt the musicians were being fairly compensated.

If even most of these conditions were met, millions of listeners would pay to download. How would listeners pay? It could be on a per-song basis (the most typical suggestion by survey respondents was $1 per download) or as a subscription service paid directly to the record company or the third party that provides access to the MP3s (most suggestions ranged from $5 to $25 a month). One intriguing proposal is to institute a compulsory licensing system whereby the Internet service providers (or ISPs)—the companies such as AOL, Earthlink, and Yahoo! that connect users to the Internet—would pay a flat per-download fee for the songs they make available to customers. In exchange, copyright owners would be required to make their catalogs available to the ISPs.[57] In this scenario the ISPs might or might not pass the costs along to their customers; if they did, they could simply add it onto the existing monthly subscription fee. There would be two advantages of this system over one in which each record company (or small partnerships) provided the content. First, it would provide "one-stop shopping," allowing listeners to find and download MP3s from a single site and search engine. Second, it would be more likely to attract younger customers. Many of the twelve- to seventeen-year-old downloaders (who, according to Ipsos, make up 41 percent of the American file-sharing public) have a difficult time buying goods or services on-line, as few of them have credit cards and some have no regular or independent access to money. The freedom to download without having to make individual transactions would have great appeal to the credit card–less, but would also be more convenient for everyone else. (An alternative, recently offered by some pay services, is for parents to set up prepaid monthly "allowances" that permit children to buy music without requiring access to a credit card.)

Early pay services, such as MusicNet and Pressplay, were unsuccessful for a variety of reasons, whether because they offered a limited range of titles, they used formats that could not be saved on one's computer, or they were expensive. These systems gave downloaders little incentive to forgo free file-sharing.[58] Newer ventures, however, are starting to demonstrate that the industry is discovering why, as I suggested earlier, listeners would be happy to pay to download music given the right circumstances. In April 2003 the computer company Apple—with the cooperation of several major record labels—launched its iTunes Music Store, widely hailed as the model for online music services.[59] From the beginning Music Store delivered much of what listeners could not find elsewhere: fast, reliable, permanent downloads at a reasonable price (99 cents per song, less than

$12 for most albums). While it does not offer the same vast selection of music available through the P2P networks, its popularity—which grew considerably when Apple launched a version for Windows users in late 2003—suggests the possibility of a post-Napster détente between listeners and the recording industry.

Yet even if consumers are willing to pay for online music, there is the lingering objection that making downloading legal, easy, and cheap would drastically depress CD sales. This leads to my second question: Why buy a CD when the same music can be downloaded? Again, many of the answers come from downloaders themselves.

Because of its physicality. Many listeners value the ability to handle their recordings and want the "real thing" as opposed to an MP3.

Because of its permanence. CDs are stable in ways that computer files are not.

Because of its visual aspect. CDs, unlike MP3s, come with something to look at, and thus more to interact with—a mirrorlike disc, cover art, liner notes, and lyrics. Many CDs now come with stickers, posters, and other nondownloadable items to attract listeners of the Internet generation.

Because of its convenience. For someone without access to the Internet or with a slow connection, buying a CD may actually be easier than downloading. Many of my students reported a drop in their file-sharing activities when they moved out of dorms with ultrafast connections and into off-campus housing with much slower modems.

Because of an enhancement. More and more CDs come with an added video component, offering concert footage, music videos, interviews, and the like. Although some of these items may be as easily downloaded as the songs they accompany, the enhanced CD offers all of these features in one convenient package.[60]

Because it supports musicians. Although it is commonly known that recording artists make relatively little on album sales (they tend to make their money on concerts and merchandise), usually at least some portion of the CD price goes to the musicians. And with truly independent labels, buyers can be more certain that their money will find its way into the hands of the artists.

It is sometimes said that we are moving into a post-CD world—that we will be able to receive and hear digital music files anywhere and everywhere we might go, without the need for little plastic discs. I believe, however, that listeners will continue to buy CDs or whatever physical recording medium comes to replace them. To put it bluntly, people like things. And as I have suggested, people will buy recorded things because they have advantages that data files do not.[61]

Why, however, should the record industry change their business practices to serve people they see as criminals? The answer is easy: because these "criminals" are their customers, who continue to buy CDs even as they trade MP3s, and who will pay for MP3s under reasonable conditions. It is these customers from whom they stand to make huge sums of money if only they would stop alienating them. Another reason is that MP3s and their brethren are widely accepted and impossible to ignore. As one ISP executive explained, "It's hard to get the genie back in the bottle."[62] Given this reality, establishing a system of music downloading in which all parties profit is much more sensible than the current antagonistic relationship between listeners and the industry.

Would P2P networks disappear under this scenario? The answer is clear: absolutely not. As long as P2P technology is legal (and even were it outlawed), it will continue to flourish, and networks will continue to traffic in files of all kinds. But *should* they disappear? Certainly not from the listener's standpoint, for no pay service will ever match the breadth of music made accessible by the millions who use P2P networks; and not from the standpoint of many performers, whether unknown musicians in search of an audience, famous ones hoping to whet appetites, or forgotten ones whose work languishes out of print. Yet even the music industry and the various pay services could peacefully coexist with—and yes, profit from—the P2Ps. Using the file-sharing services to provide free market research, the labels can discover which new acts to nurture and which old acts to reissue. Realistically, of course, people will still download music when they could pay for it. Clearly, however, the way to minimize this is to provide listeners with the widest variety of the highest-quality sound files at a reasonable cost. Although I may represent only myself, I found that shortly after signing up for Apple's Music Store I had curtailed my P2P file-sharing considerably. When I want music, I first go to the Music Store, exactly because it provides the quality and convenience P2Ps cannot guarantee; the more Apple offers me, the less I look elsewhere. Never has the truth of the cliché been demonstrated more plainly: if you can't beat 'em, join 'em.

ooo

File-sharing is neither plague nor panacea. MP3 and P2P are influential not because they are good or bad, but because they provide radically new ways to experience and disseminate music. I have sought here to provide a framework for understanding the distinctive traits of these technologies, and for understanding how file-sharing affects the lives of millions of listeners. From a technological standpoint, we live in very interesting times. Given the daily twists and developments in technology, law, and culture, we can expect musical life to get even more interesting. This is not a curse, as the old saying would have it, but a blessing.

CONCLUSION

This book has brought together a wide variety of musical actors, activities, and issues connected perhaps by nothing save recording. To continue this eclectic approach I have enlisted a French poet, an American record producer, and a German music historian—those who provided the epigraphs at the beginning of the book—to help articulate three final thoughts.

RECORDING DOES NOT SIMPLY RECORD

In this book I have claimed for sound recording what Paul Valéry asserted for "great innovations" in general—a role in the transformation of art.[1] Recording has been at the center of far-reaching changes in modern musical life, affecting each facet of artistic endeavor Valéry identified: technique, invention, and aesthetics. In terms of technique, consider the case of violin vibrato, the subject of chapter 4. At the turn of the century, classical violinists treated it as an occasional ornament, yet only a few decades later they had adopted a nearly continuous vibrato. As I argue, this transformation in technique was closely linked to the rise of recording activity among violinists, who adapted their playing to the distinctive traits of the medium. Recording has influenced invention as well, affecting nearly every aspect of musical composition. Composers have found new sources of musical inspiration on recordings; they have discovered novel timbral, rhythmic, and contrapuntal possibilities by treating recorded sound as raw material and playback equipment as musical instruments; and through recordings they have reached otherwise inaccessible listeners. Finally, our very notions of musical beauty and of what constitutes a musical life have changed with the presence of recording. Solitary listening, impracticable without recording, is perhaps now the dominant type of musical experience in most cultures. Musical communities have formed around the trading of MP3 files in cyberspace. The "new" vibrato came to be regarded as integral to beautiful violin playing. Sounds that can only be created by an intentional "abuse" of recording technology have been elevated to the realm of art in the form of turntable scratching. An "amazing change" indeed.

LIVE AND RECORDED MUSIC DIFFER IN FUNDAMENTAL WAYS

John Pfeiffer's Kipling paraphrase, that "a recording is one thing, a concert is another, and never the twain shall meet," identifies the source of all phonograph effects.[2] Every manifestation of recording's influence, whether the act of solitary listening, the length of certain jazz works, or the flare scratch (and turntablism in general, for that matter), may be traced to the traits of recording that distinguish it from live music-making. Recorded music is, among other things, distinctively tangible, portable, repeatable, and manipulable—in other words, it is differently able than live music.

These differences force us to rethink our traditional notions of music. Live performances today so often aspire to the quality of recordings. Repeatability endows recorded performances with the characteristic of fixed compositions. Composers can act like performers, working directly with sound and forgoing notation. Hip-hop samplers eschew live performances for the "authenticity" of recordings. (Recording, perhaps better than anything, proves the flexibility and fluidity of authenticity.) New music masquerades as old with the addition of simulated record static; old music becomes new when sampled in the latest records. The strange and exotic become familiar when repeated endlessly without variation; the familiar becomes strange and exotic when digitally manipulated. And so on and so on. One way to understand this book, then, is as a study of reversals and inversions.

By focusing on the distinctive attributes of recording I hope to have demystified the power of the technology. True, recording commodifies, reifies, politicizes, and fetishizes music. Yet its influence is hardly so abstract, and may be observed in the lives of all who interact with the technology. To understand the source of this influence, we must examine how the actions of users compensate for or exploit the limitations or possibilities of the medium. The process may not always be easy to recognize, but John Pfeiffer's pithy remark provides a starting point.

USERS DETERMINE THE IMPACT AND VALUE OF RECORDING

In declaring that "the machine is neither a god nor a devil," H. H. Stuckenschmidt was not denying that technology may be used for good or for ill.[3] Rather, he was suggesting that the value of any tool depends ultimately on its users, a view I have taken in this book. Consider the repeatability of recorded sound: in itself it is neither boon nor bane, but may be regarded as either depending on its applications. With repeated exposure to recordings, listeners may come to incorporate mistakes or extra-musical noises into their understanding of a work; or they may come to deepen their appreciation for a particular composition, as was the hope of the phonograph partisans discussed in chapter 2. Repeatability may lead performers to mimic the recordings of others, or to study and learn from them. Composers, too, have had varied reactions. Some have said that music dies when repeated without change; others have seen repeatability as the best way for audiences to become familiar with their works. It would be hard to argue that such diverse and even contradictory responses inevitably follow from the nature of repeatability. Rather, while recording prompts users to react to its distinctive attributes, the value of the technology lies in the hands of those users.

Just as the technology shapes the activities of its users, their activities shape the technology. This dynamic is evident throughout the course of recording history. At the turn of the century the phonograph industry, on the verge of collapse, discovered a more lucrative use for the machines initially intended as dictation devices: music. After the 1950s, magnetic tape, originally developed for military purposes in World War II, was embraced by the musical avant-garde and became the basis for a wholly new compositional practice and philosophy, *musique concrète*. By the 1970s, phonograph technology had long been stabilized when some New York DJs found that with a little tweaking it could be transformed into a performing instrument. The industry responded, producing machines to suit their needs. MP3 was initially intended as a compression standard for the film industry, but its embrace by hundreds of millions of listeners globally has made it a hugely influential sound recording medium.

In his famous essay "The Medium Is the Message," Marshall McLuhan opposed the very notion that Stuckenschmidt and I espouse.[4] To him it represented the denial of the harm that technology could wreak and the rejection of its influence in human activity. When I claim that recording is neither good nor evil, however, I am neither ignoring its value (positive or negative) nor denying its impact. Rather, I am attempting to give equal weight to the factors determining recording's influence: the technology itself, the actions of users toward that technology, and the broader cultural and societal forces in which both technology and users are situated. While McLuhan was right to stress technology's shaping role in modern life, the human side of the equation cannot be ignored. Recording is not a mysterious force that compels the actions of its users. Ultimately, they— that is, we—control recording's influence. Recording has been with us for more than a century; it will no doubt remain an important musical force, and users will continue to respond to its possibilities and limitations. A clear view of this relationship will better allow future generations to understand and shape the role of sound recording in the musical life of the world.

Epigraph sources are cited in the notes to the Conclusion.

INTRODUCTION

1. Advertisements for Berliner Gramophone, *Cosmopolitan* 21 (1896): advertising section; Edison-Bettini Micro-Phonograph, 1898, clipping in George H. Clark Collection, Archives Center, National Museum of American History, Washington, DC; Gramophone Zon-o-phone, *Harper's* 97 (1898): advertising section, 68; Columbia Home Grand Graphophone, 1899, clipping in Clark Collection; and Columbia Disc Graphophone, *McClure's* 20 (1902–3): advertising section, 69.

2. *Collier's* 52 (8 November 1913): back cover; concert program, 1927, Jascha Heifetz Collection, Library of Congress, Washington, DC.

3. Oscar Wilde, *The Picture of Dorian Gray* (1890; New York: Random House, 1992), 33.

4. Igor Stravinsky and Robert Craft, *Dialogues and a Diary* (London: Faber & Faber, 1968), 120.

5. Quoted in Anthony Seeger, "The Role of Sound Archives in Ethnomusicology Today," *Ethnomusicology* 30 (spring–summer 1986): 261. For an earlier, concurring view of recordings, see Carl Stumpf, quoted in Edgar Stillman Kelley, "A Library of Living Melody," *Outlook* 99 (30 September 1911): 283–87.

6. Robert Philip, *Early Recordings and Musical Style: Changing Tastes in Instrumental Performance, 1900–1950* (Cambridge: Cambridge University Press, 1992), 1.

7. See, for example, Michael Chanan, *Repeated Takes: A Short History of Recording and Its Effects on Music* (London: Verso, 1995); Timothy Day, *A Century of Recorded Music: Listening to Musical History* (New Haven: Yale University Press, 2000); Evan Eisenberg, *The Recording Angel: Explorations in Phonography* (New York: McGraw-Hill, 1987); and

Glenn Gould, "Music and Technology" and "The Prospects of Record-ing," both in *The Glenn Gould Reader,* ed. Tim Page (New York: Knopf, 1984), 353–68 and 331–53, respectively.

8. I have chosen to name this concept after the phonograph (as opposed to a newer technology) because it is the original mechanism for sound recording and reproduction and, having survived for more than a dozen decades, will be remembered long after others have faded into obscurity.

9. Igor Stravinsky, *An Autobiography* (New York: Norton, 1962), 123–24.

10. For a cogent discussion of the ramifications of technological determin-ism on musical life, see Timothy D. Taylor, *Strange Sounds: Music, Tech-nology, and Culture* (New York: Routledge, 2001), 26–38. For a variety of views on technological determinism, see Merritt Roe Smith and Leo Marx, eds., *Does Technology Drive History? The Dilemma of Technologi-cal Determinism* (Cambridge, MA: MIT Press, 1994).

11. Smith and Marx, eds., *Does Technology Drive History?,* xi.

12. Here I am in general sympathy with historians who espouse the view known as the social construction of technology (SCOT), which exam-ines technology from the standpoint of users and explores their role in technological change. For a fascinating case study on the automobile, which also surveys and refines SCOT, see Ronald Kline and Trevor Pinch, "Users as Agents of Technological Change: The Social Con-struction of the Automobile in the Rural United States," *Technology and Culture* 37 (1996): 763–95.

13. The connection between the car and the American suburb has long been observed in histories of the automobile and in writings on tech-nology in general. See, for example, Ruth Schwartz Cowan, *A Social History of American Technology* (New York: Oxford University Press, 1997), 237–38.

CHAPTER ONE

1. A note on terminology: *phonograph* originally denoted cylinder-playing machines only, while *gramophone* referred to machines that played discs. At the turn of the century these terms were not interchangeable. It was not until the 1920s, when cylinder recording all but disappeared, that both terms referred to disc players. Today, *phonograph* is used in the United States and *gramophone* in Great Britain to describe the record player. In this book, *phonograph* will be used generically. Other terms will be used when dictated by context. For more on the early history of the phono-graph, see Day, *Century of Recorded Music;* Roland Gelatt, *The Fabulous Phonograph,* 2d rev. ed. (New York: Macmillan, 1977); Oliver Read and Walter L. Welch, *From Tin Foil to Stereo: Evolution of the Phonograph,* 2d ed. (Indianapolis: Sams, 1976); and Walter L. Welch and Leah Brodbeck

Stenzel Burt, *From Tinfoil to Stereo: The Acoustic Years of the Recording Industry, 1877–1929* (Gainesville: University Press of Florida, 1994). (The last two are very different editions of the same book.)

2. While this particular scene is of my own invention, it is based on a wide examination of primary documents, including photographs, catalogs, advertisements, and accounts of phonographic listening in the early twentieth century.

3. Quoted in Kurt Blaukopf, *Musical Life in a Changing Society*, trans. David Marinelli (Portland, OR: Amadeus, 1992), 176.

4. Jacques Attali, *Noise: The Political Economy of Music*, trans. Brian Massumi (Minneapolis: University of Minnesota Press, 1985), 101.

5. Eisenberg, *The Recording Angel*, 13.

6. Eric N. Simons, "Gramomania," *Gramophone* 2 (1924): 89–90.

7. *Phonograph Monthly Review* 2 (November 1927): 65–66.

8. Nick Hornby, *High Fidelity* (New York: Riverhead, 1995), 96.

9. Showbiz & A.G., "Diggin' in the Crates," *Showbiz & A.G.*, Polygram compact disc 828309.

10. Pearl Jam, "Spin the Black Circle," *Vitalogy*, Epic compact disc EK 66900.

11. Hornby, *High Fidelity*, 54.

12. For more on record collecting, see Will Straw, "Sizing Up Record Collections: Gender and Connoisseurship in Rock Music Culture," in *Sexing the Groove*, ed. Sheila Whiteley (London: Routledge, 1997), 3–16; Patrick Giles, "Magnificent Obsession—Beyond Pride, Beyond Shame: The Secret World of Record Collectors," *Opera News* 63 (October 1998): 28–33; Jay Hodgson, "Unpacking the CD Library," *Discourses in Music* 3 (spring 2002), www.discourses.ca/v3n3a2.html; and Lise A. Waxer, *The City of Musical Memory: Salsa, Record Grooves, and Popular Music in Cali, Colombia* (Middletown, CT: Wesleyan University Press, 2002), 111–52.

13. Peter Manuel, *Cassette Culture: Popular Music and Technology in North India* (Chicago and London: University of Chicago Press, 1993), 53.

14. Ibid., 63.

15. Ibid., 2.

16. In addition to lower production and manufacturing costs, the Internet has been crucial for the success of these labels by facilitating marketing and sales. See their websites at www.shopsfsymphony.org/home.jsp; www.righteousbabe.com; and www.artistled.com.

17. R. Anderson Sutton, "Commercial Cassette Recordings of Traditional Music in Java," *World of Music* 27, no. 3 (1985): 23–43.

18. My thanks to gamelan performer and scholar Susan Walton for sharing this observation.

19. Walter Benjamin, "The Work of Art in the Age of Mechanical Repro-

duction," in *Illuminations,* ed. Hannah Arendt, trans. Harry Zohn (New York: Harcourt Brace & World, 1968), 222.

20.   Information on the picó comes from Deborah Pacini Hernandez, "Sound Systems, World Beat, and Diasporan Identity in Cartagena, Colombia," *Diaspora: A Journal of Transnational Studies* 5 (1996): 429–66.

21.   The text is undated but was probably written in 1971. Alton A. Adams, "John Philip Sousa as Man and Musician, 1854–1932," in *Culture at the Crossroads: The Memoirs and Writings of Alton Augustus Adams,* ed. Mark Clague (Berkeley and Los Angeles: University of California Press, forthcoming).

22.   "Grâce au gramophone, je vais pouvoir vous faire entendre des disques de musique nègre que j'ai rapportés des Etats-Unis, enregistrés et publiés par des nègres. Il est vraiment bien précieux de pouvoir étudier le folk-lore de tout l'univers grâce à cet instrument" (Darius Milhaud, "Les Ressources nouvelles de la musique," *L'Esprit nouveau,* no. 25 [1924]: [unpaginated; seventh page of the article]).

23.   Carol J. Oja, *Colin McPhee: Composer in Two Worlds* (Washington, DC: Smithsonian Institution Press, 1990), 63.

24.   Steve Reich, "Non-Western Music and the Western Composer," in *Writings On Music, 1965–2000* (New York: Oxford University Press, 2002), 147–51.

25.   Orlo Williams, "Times and Seasons," *Gramophone* 1 (1923): 38–39.

26.   Ibid.

27.   *Disques* 2 (August 1931): 240.

28.   Paul Fahri, "Akito Morita, a Man of Great Import," *Washington Post,* 5 October 1999, C1.

29.   "The Edison Realism Test," broadside, Edison Collection at the Henry Ford Museum and Greenfield Village, Dearborn, MI.

30.   Richard Leppert, *The Sight of Sound: Music, Representation, and the History of the Body* (Berkeley and Los Angeles: University of California Press, 1993), xx–xxi.

31.   Here I am speaking of audio-only recordings (i.e., not music videos) in which traditional performers participate. In certain types of electronic or computer music, there are no performers to see.

32.   Frank Swinnerton, "A Defence of the Gramophone," *Gramophone* 1 (1923): 52–53.

33.   "Illustrated Song Machine," *Talking Machine World* 1 (October 1905): 33. The Stereophone is described in "To Make the Stereophone," *Talking Machine World* 1 (December 1905): 9.

34.   Tableau Vivant, "Gramophone-Opera with a Model Stage," *Gramophone Critic and Society News* 1 (August 1929): 402–3.

35. Stephen G. Rich, "Some Unnoticed Aspects of the School Use of Phonographs," *Journal of Educational Method* 3 (November 1923): 111.

36. Quoted in Leonard B. Meyer, *Emotion and Meaning in Music* (Chicago: University of Chicago Press, 1956), 80.

37. Annalyn Swan, "Itzhak Perlman, Top Fiddle," *Newsweek* 95 (14 April 1980): 65.

38. "Gramophone Celebrities: Jascha Heifetz," *Gramophone* 3 (1925): 278.

39. Harry McGurk and John MacDonald, "Hearing Lips and Seeing Voices," *Nature* 264 (1976): 746–48. My thanks to Richard Lamour for bringing the McGurk Effect to my attention.

40. See Jay Cocks, "Fans, You Know It's True; Milli Vanilli Controversy," *Time* 136 (3 December 1990): 123.

41. Leonard Liebling, "On Preserving Art," *Voice of the Victor* 7 (June 1912): 7.

42. Theodor Adorno, "Opera and the Long-Playing Record," trans. Thomas Y. Levin, in *Essays on Music,* ed. Richard Leppert (Berkeley and Los Angeles: University of California Press, 2002), 284. Adorno's other essays on recording, "The Curves of the Needle" and "The Form of the Phonograph Record," are also in this volume.

43. Nikolaus Harnoncourt, interview with John Harvith and Susan Edwards Harvith, 9 October 1974, in *Edison, Musicians, and the Phonograph: A Century in Retrospect,* ed. John Harvith and Susan Edwards Harvith (Westport, CT: Greenwood, 1987), 198.

44. Janos Starker, interview with John Harvith and Susan Edwards Harvith, 14 March 1977, in Harvith and Harvith, eds., *Edison, Musicians, and the Phonograph,* 185–86. For similar remarks, see Lorin Maazel, interview with James Badal, October 1981, in *Recording the Classics: Maestros, Music, and Technology* (Kent, OH: Kent State University Press, 1996), 18.

45. Eugene Drucker, "Recording with Rostropovich: Learning to Let the Music Speak," *Strings* 8 (July–August 1993): 57.

46. For a detailed account of this trend, see Philip, *Early Recordings and Musical Style,* 6–36.

47. Régine Crespin, *On Stage, Off Stage: A Memoir,* trans. G. S. Bourdain (Boston: Northeastern University Press, 1997), 153.

48. Suman Ghosh, "Impact of the Recording Industry on Hindustani Classical Music in the Last Hundred Years," *IASA Journal,* no. 15 (June 2000): 15.

49. Rotoglow recording session, Springfield, Virginia, 16 December 2001.

50. Yehudi Menuhin, *Unfinished Journey: Twenty Years Later* (London: Fromm International, 1997), 371.

51. What exactly constitutes a musical work is far from a simple matter, one with which philosophers and aestheticians have long struggled. See, for

example, Michael Talbot, ed., *The Musical Work: Reality or Invention?* (Liverpool: Liverpool University Press, 2000). Stephen Davies's *Musical Works and Performances* (Oxford: Clarendon, 2001) is notable here because it expands the scope of the discussion to include performances and recordings.

52. Pablo de Sarasate, *Zigeunerweisen,* Jascha Heifetz, RCA compact disc 7709-2-RG.

53. Thomas G. Porcello, "Sonic Artistry: Music, Discourse, and Technology in the Recording Studio" (Ph.D. diss., University of Texas, 1996), 2.

54. Guarneri String Quartet [Arnold Steinhardt and John Dalley, violins; Michael Tree, viola; David Soyer, cello], interviews with John Harvith and Susan Edwards Harvith, 8 January 1975, 20 February 1977, and 17 April 1977, in Harvith and Harvith, eds., *Edison, Musicians, and the Phonograph,* 255, 258. For an earlier concurring opinion, see Joseph Szigeti, "Josef Szigeti Chats about the Gramophone," *Gramophone* 6 (1929): 525.

55. Joseph Horowitz, *Understanding Toscanini: A Social History of American Concert Life* (Berkeley and Los Angeles: University of California Press, 1987), 414.

56. See, for example, N. J. Corey, "The Place of the Talking Machine in Music Teaching," *Etude* 24 (1906): 672, 680; Maud Powell, "Instructive Possibilities of the Talking Machine for Violin Players," *Musical Observer* 9 (1914): 85, 88; and Sasha Ostrofsky, "The Student and the Phonograph," *American Music Lover* 1 (March 1936): 331–32, 351.

57. Unnamed guitarist quoted in H. Stith Bennett, "The Realities of Practice," in *On Record: Rock, Pop, and the Written Word,* ed. Simon Frith and Andrew Goodwin (New York: Pantheon, 1990), 223.

58. Miha Pogacnik, interview with John Harvith and Susan Edwards Harvith, 14 January 1981, in Harvith and Harvith, eds., *Edison, Musicians, and the Phonograph,* 413.

59. "Ah, mon Dieu!, maintenant je comprends pourquoi je suis Patti! Mon cher, quelle voix! Quelle artiste!" This story was told by the English conductor Landon Ronald but was disputed by Patti biographer Herman Klein. The anecdote and Klein's response are in Herman Klein, *Herman Klein and The Gramophone,* ed. William R. Moran (Portland, OR: Amadeus, 1990), 589.

60. William Bolcom and Joan Morris, interview with John Harvith and Susan Edwards Harvith, 24 June 1977, in Harvith and Harvith, eds., *Edison, Musicians, and the Phonograph,* 302.

61. Most recording artists who have spoken about their listening habits say that they tend to listen to their performances during or soon after recording sessions, but rarely after their recordings have been released.

Many say they find the experience unpleasant. This is frequently reported in the interviews in Harvith and Harvith, eds., *Edison, Musicians, and the Phonograph;* and Badal, *Recording the Classics.*

62. Martina Arroyo, interview with John Harvith and Susan Edwards Harvith, 1 May 1977, in Harvith and Harvith, eds., *Edison, Musicians, and the Phonograph,* 225.

63. Quoted in "The Phonograph as an Aid to Composers," *Phonogram,* no. 3 (July 1900): 67.

64. I make this argument, with particular attention to violin playing, in "The Phonograph Effect: The Influence of Recording on Listener, Performer, Composer, 1900–1940" (Ph.D. diss., University of Michigan, 1999), 138–62.

65. George Gershwin, "The Composer in the Machine Age" (1933), in *The American Composer Speaks,* ed. Gilbert Chase (Baton Rouge: Louisiana State University Press, 1966), 144.

66. Béla Bartók, "Mechanical Music," in *Béla Bartók Essays,* ed. Benjamin Suchoff (London: Faber & Faber, 1976), 298. Copland's comment comes from an undated, unpublished typescript, Aaron Copland Collection, box 201, folder 7, Music Division, Library of Congress, Washington, DC. In 1950, Roger Sessions similarly explained that a recording "ceases to have interest for us . . . the instant we become aware of the fact of literal repetition" (*The Musical Experience of Composer, Performer, Listener* [Princeton: Princeton University Press, 1950], 70).

67. Jonathan D. Kramer, *The Time of Music* (New York: Schirmer, 1986), 69.

68. Arnold Schoenberg, "Mechanical Musical Instruments," trans. Leo Black, in *Style and Idea,* ed. Leonard Stein (New York: St. Martin's Press, 1975), 328.

69. Recording's influence was certainly just as slight on the work of Schoenberg's two most famous pupils. Alban Berg never recorded; the first discs of his music came only in 1936, the year after his death. Anton Webern recorded only his arrangement of some Schubert dances, and few of his original compositions were recorded by others during his lifetime. It would be difficult to see why either man would have been moved to accommodate to a technology with which he had such sparse contact.

70. Steve Reich, "Early Works (1965–68)," in *Writings on Music,* 24.

71. Quoted in Tim Page, "*Einstein on the Beach* by Philip Glass," in *Opera: A History in Documents,* ed. Piero Weiss (New York: Oxford University Press, 2002), 324.

72. Four and one-half minutes was the limit for twelve-inch discs, which were introduced in 1903. Previously, the seven- and ten-inch sizes, which had considerably shorter playing times, were standard. For cylinders, two minutes was the general limit until Edison introduced the

four-minute Amberol in 1908. There were a few exceptions to the four-and-a-half-minute limit before the LP was introduced in 1948, however. Cylinders occasionally exceeded it, and a number of companies produced experimental (and ultimately unsuccessful) longer-playing discs. For more information on playing time, see Guy A. Marco, ed., *Encyclopedia of Recorded Sound in the United States* (New York: Garland, 1993), s.v. *cylinder, disc,* and *long playing record.*

73. Jeff Todd Titon, *Early Downhome Blues: A Musical and Cultural Analysis,* 2d ed. (Chapel Hill: University of North Carolina Press, 1994), 286.

74. Andrew Mead, e-mail message to author, 16 January 1997.

75. Theodor Adorno, "On the Fetish-Character in Music and the Regression of Listening" and "The Radio Symphony," in Leppert, ed., *Essays on Music,* 303, 305, 261–62.

76. For more on Powell's record recital, see Karen A. Shaffer and Neva Gardner Greenwood, *Maud Powell: Pioneer Woman Violinist* (Ames: Iowa State University Press, 1988), 380–82.

77. Ghosh, "Impact of the Recording Industry on Hindustani Classical Music," 12.

78. Marc Schade-Poulsen, *Men and Popular Music in Algeria: The Social Significance of Raï* (Austin: University of Texas Press, 1999), 51.

79. See Mark Katz, "Beethoven in the Age of Mechanical Reproduction: The Violin Concerto on Record," *Beethoven Forum* 10 (2003): 38–55.

80. José Bowen, "Tempo, Duration, and Flexibility: Techniques in the Analysis of Performance," *Journal of Musicological Research* 16 (1996): 116.

81. See Katz, "Phonograph Effect," 149–50.

82. Chopin, Nocturne in E-flat, op. 9, no. 2 (arr. Sarasate), Mischa Elman, Biddulph compact disc, LAB 035.

83. Jerrold Moore, *Elgar on Record: The Composer and the Gramophone* (London: Oxford University Press, 1974), 19. Moore also cites other instances in which Elgar cut his works before recording.

84. Fritz Kreisler Collection, box 1, folder 10, Music Division, Library of Congress.

85. Carl Flesch, *The Memoirs of Carl Flesch,* trans. Hans Keller (London: Rockliff, 1957), 124.

86. Dan Stehman, *Roy Harris: A Bio-Bibliography* (New York: Greenwood, 1991), 79–80.

87. The following lists these works, and the sources that substantiate their origins: d'Indy, *Les Yeux de l'aimeé* (1904, for voice and piano), Vincent d'Indy, *Les Yeux de l'aimeé* (Milan: Gramophone Company, 1904); Fauré, *Le Ramier,* op. 87, no. 2 (1904, for voice and piano), Jean-Michel Nectoux, *Phonographies I: Gabriel Fauré, 1900–1977* (Paris: Bibliothèque Nationale, 1979), 10; Leoncavallo, *Mattinata* (1904, for voice and piano),

New Grove Dictionary of Music and Musicians (London: Macmillan, 1980), s.v. "Leoncavallo, Ruggero"; Elgar, *Carissima* (1914, for orchestra), J. Moore, *Elgar on Record,* 5; Stravinsky, Serenade in A (1925, for piano), Stravinsky, *Autobiography,* 123–24; Harris, *Four Minutes-20 Seconds* (1934, for flute and string quartet), Stehman, *Roy Harris,* 79; Hindemith, *Scherzo* (1934, for viola and piano), Seymour W. Itzkoff, *Emanuel Feuermann, Virtuoso* (Tuscaloosa: University of Alabama Press, 1979), 131–32; Pierné, *Giration* (1935, for orchestra), Gabriel Pierné, *Giration: Divertissement chorégraphique* (Paris: Maurice Senart, 1935); Kreisler, *Dittersdorf Scherzo* (1935, for string quartet), Louis P. Lochner, *Fritz Kreisler* (New York: Macmillan, 1950), 270; and Weill, "Come Up from the Fields, Father" (1947, for voice and piano), David Drew, *Kurt Weill: A Handbook* (London: Faber & Faber, 1987), 357.

88.   Martin Williams, "Recording Limits and Blues Form," in *The Art of Jazz: Essays on the Nature and Development of Jazz* (New York: Oxford University Press, 1959), 93; Gunther Schuller, "Ellington in the Pantheon" (1974), in Mark Tucker, *The Duke Ellington Reader* (New York: Oxford University Press, 1993), 417.

89.   Jazz was one area in which musicians often exploited the extended playing time of LPs.

90.   "The Entertainer," written by Billy Joel © 1974, JoelSongs (ASCAP). All rights reserved. Used by permission. "The Entertainer" has been released on *Streetlife Serenade,* Columbia compact disc 69382.

91.   "Blues Power" was released on *Eric Clapton,* Polydor compact disc 825 093 (studio version) and *Just One Night,* Polydor compact disc 800 093-2 (concert version). "Cocaine" was released on *Slowhand,* Polydor compact disc 823 276 (studio) and *Just One Night* (concert).

92.   The studio and concert versions of "Killing Floor" were released on, respectively, *Radio One,* Rykodisc compact disc RCD 20078; and *Live at Winterland,* Rykodisc compact disc RCD 20038. The studio and concert versions of "Hey Joe" were released on *Are You Experienced?,* Reprise compact disc 6261–2; and *Live at Winterland.*

93.   Lotte Lehmann, interview with John Harvith and Susan Edwards Harvith, 2 January 1975, in Harvith and Harvith, eds., *Edison, Musicians, and the Phonograph,* 71. For another account of studio "pushers," see Yvonne De Treville, "Making a Phonograph Record," *Musician* 21 (November 1916): 658.

94.   De Treville, "Making a Phonograph Record," 658.

95.   Henry Seymour, "The Reproduction of Sound," *Phono Record* 2 (August 1913): 264–65.

96.   For more on the Stroh violin, see Dick Donovan, "The Stroh Violin," *Strand* 23 (January 1902): 89–91; and Cary Clements, "Augustus Stroh

and the Famous Stroh Violin," *Experimental Musical Instruments* 10 (June 1995): 8–15; 11 (September 1995): 38–39.

97. We may take Martin Schwartz's compilation *Early Klezmer Music, 1908–1927* (Arhoolie compact disc 7034) as a representative sample. The selections with tsimbl are exclusively duo ensembles, with the tsimbl acting as accompaniment. None of the larger groups use the tsimbl. For more on the tsimbl, see Mark Slobin, "Fiddler Off the Roof: Klezmer Music as an Ethnic Musical Style," in *The Jews of North America,* ed. Moses Rischin (Detroit: Wayne State University Press, 1987), 98.

98. Arroyo, interview, in Harvith and Harvith, eds., *Edison, Musicians, and the Phonograph,* 225.

99. Jack Douglas, interview with Howard Massey, in *Behind the Glass: Top Record Producers Tell How They Craft the Hits* (San Francisco: Miller Freeman, 2000), 158.

100. Josef Jiránek, *O Smetanových klavíních skladbách a jeho klavírní hře* (Prague: Nákladem Spolecnosti Bedricha Smetany, 1932), 33. I am grateful to Judith Fiehler for bringing this passage to my attention, and to Fiehler and Milada Hornová for making their translation of the Jiránek available to me.

101. For an interesting study of the musical and social dimensions of crooning, see Allison McCracken, "'God's Gift to Us Girls': Crooning, Gender, and the Re-Creation of American Popular Song, 1928–1933," *American Music* 17 (winter 1999): 365–95. The intimacy of crooning is discussed in Timothy D. Taylor, "Music and the Rise of Radio in 1920s America: Technological Imperialism, Socialization, and the Transformation of Intimacy," *Historical Journal of Film, Radio, and Television* 22 (2002): 436–40.

102. See George Martin and Jeremy Hornsby, *All You Need Is Ears* (New York: St. Martin's Press, 1979), 199–201; and Walter Everett, *The Beatles as Musicians: "Revolver" through the Anthology* (New York: Oxford University Press, 1999), 79–80. The album version of "Strawberry Fields Forever" is on *Magical Mystery Tour,* reissued on Capitol compact disc CDP 48062. Take 7, previously unreleased, is available on *The Beatles Anthology,* vol. 2, Capitol compact disc CDP 7243 8 34448 2 3.

103. Gould, "Prospects of Recording," 338, 339. The recording has been reissued on Sony compact disc 52600.

104. J. S. Bach, Concerto in D Minor for Two Violins, Jascha Heifetz, violins, *The Heifetz Collection,* vol. 6, BMG/RCA Victor compact disc 61778.

105. Natalie Cole, "Unforgettable," *Unforgettable, With Love,* Elektra compact disc 61049. For more on this issue, see Fred Goodman, "Duets with the Dead: Homage or Exploitation?" *New York Times,* 16 January 2000, sec. 2, pp. 11, 18.

106. Jimi Hendrix, "Crosstown Traffic," *Are You Experienced,* Reprise compact disc 6261-2; Led Zeppelin, "Whole Lotta Love," *Led Zeppelin II,* Atlantic compact disc 11612; Radiohead, *Pablo Honey,* Capitol compact disc 81409. For a more extensive discussion of the musical and metaphorical uses of the stereo field, see Albin Zak, *The Poetics of Rock: Cutting Tracks, Making Records* (Berkeley and Los Angeles: University of California Press, 2001), 145–51.

107. Chuck Taylor, "Do Vocal Effects Go Too Far? Ability to Perfect Sound via Technology May Affect Drive to Develop Talent," *Billboard* 112 (30 December 2000): 89.

108. *The Simpsons,* episode CABF12, "New Kids on the Blecch," originally broadcast 25 February 2001.

109. Auto-Tune, www.interphase.be/autotune.html (no longer active).

110. C. Taylor, "Do Vocal Effects Go Too Far?" 89.

111. For a thoughtful analysis of Cher's "Believe" and the "role of recording technologies in the construction of female musical corporeality," see Kay Dickinson, "'Believe'? Vocoders, Digitalised Female Identity, and Camp," *Popular Music* 20 (October 2001): 333–48.

112. Some recent works on the role of recordists include Day, *Century of Recorded Music;* Susan Schmidt Horning, "Chasing Sound: The Culture and Technology of Recording Studios in America" (Ph.D. diss., Case Western Reserve University, 2002); James P. Kraft, *Stage to Studio: Musicians and the Sound Revolution, 1890–1950* (Baltimore: Johns Hopkins University Press, 1996); Massey, *Behind the Glass;* and Zak, *Poetics of Rock.*

113. Quoted in Ursula Block and Michael Glasmeier, *Broken Music: Artists' Recordworks* (Berlin: Daadgalerie Berlin, 1989), 73.

114. Christian Marclay, interview with Jason Gross, *Perfect Sound Forever,* March 1998, www.furious.com/perfect/christianmarclay.html. For more on the work of Marclay (who is also a visual artist), see Russell Ferguson, ed., *Christian Marclay* (Los Angeles: UCLA Hammer Museum, 2003).

115. See Schaeffer's *A la recherche d'une musique concrète* (Paris: Editions du Seuil, 1952) and *La Musique concrète* (Paris: Presses universitaires de France, 1967). Schaeffer's works are collected on *Pierre Schaeffer: L'Oeuvre musicale,* INA-GRM compact disc 1006-9.

116. These loops now reside in the Vladimir Ussachevsky Collection in the Recorded Sound section of the Library of Congress.

CHAPTER TWO

1. Robert Haven Schauffler and Sigmund Spaeth, *Music as a Social Force in America* (New York: Caxton Institute, 1927), 1–38. Schauffler's Main

Street is perhaps a response to Sinclair Lewis's pessimistic novel *Main Street* (New York: Harcourt Brace, 1920). Lewis's subject is Gopher Prairie, Minnesota, a small town demographically similar to Schauffler's but whose citizens are largely narrow-minded, unsophisticated, and resistant to reform.

2. Horace Johnson, "Department of Recorded Music: Phonographs in the Home," *Etude* 40 (February 1922): 88.

3. W. Dayton Wegefarth, "The Talking Machine as a Public Educator," *Lippincott's* 37 (1911): 629.

4. May Harbin, in Victor Talking Machine Company, *The Victrola in Rural Schools* (Camden, NJ: Victor Talking Machine Co., 1917), 11. Harbin is referring to Irving Berlin's "Everybody's Doing It" (1911) and "Oh You Beautiful Doll" (1911) by Seymour Brown and Nat Ayer. For further discussion of the differences between European and American musical culture, see, for example, John Sullivan Dwight, "Music as a Means of Culture," *Atlantic* 26 (September 1870): 326; Frédéric Louis Ritter, *Music in America,* new ed. (New York: Charles Scribner's Sons, 1890), 476–78; and Mary Garden, "The American Girl and Music," *Good Housekeeping* 56 (January 1913): 170.

5. *Reading Lessons in Music Appreciation: Aids in Preparation of Students for Music Memory Contest* (Austin: University of Texas, 1922), [iii]. Similar points are made in Peter Christian Lutkin, "Musical Appreciation—How Is It to Be Developed?" *Journal of the Proceedings and Addresses of the National Education Association* 50 (1912): 1013; and Lucy K. Cole, "Music and the Social Problem," *Journal of the Proceedings and Addresses of the National Education Association* 51 (1913): 605.

6. Elsie M. Shawe, "Public-School Music in Relation to the Music of the Community," *Journal of the Proceedings and Addresses of the National Education Association* 49 (1911): 791.

7. Anne Shaw Faulkner, "Does Jazz Put the Sin in Syncopation?" *Ladies' Home Journal* 38 (August 1921): 16, 34; reprinted in *Keeping Time: Readings in Jazz History,* ed. Robert Walser (New York: Oxford University Press, 1999), 32–36.

8. Frances Elliott Clark, in Victor Talking Machine Company, *Music Appreciation for Little Children* (Camden, NJ: Victor Talking Machine Co., 1920), 9. A similar sentiment is expressed in Edith M. Rhetts, "The Development of Music Appreciation in America," *Papers and Proceedings of the Music Teachers' National Association* 16 (1922): 114.

9. Edward Bellamy, *Looking Backward, 2000–1887* (Boston: Ticknor, 1888). Technological utopianism is treated in depth in Howard P. Segal, *Technological Utopianism in American Culture* (Chicago: University of Chicago Press, 1985).

10. Thomas A. Edison, "The Phonograph and Its Future," *North American Review* 126 (May–June 1878): 530–36.

11. See also Bellamy's short story "With the Eyes Shut," *Harper's New Monthly* 79 (1889): 736–45.

12. Lewis H. Galantiere, "Machine-Made Musical Appreciation," *Music Student* 2 (February 1916): 46.

13. "Before We Go to the Opera," *National Music Monthly* 1 (August 1917): 41. The interest in opera was not new, for piano and vocal arrangements of opera excerpts had been popular in American homes for decades. Rather sudden, however, was the possibility of hearing opera performed by the great vocalists of the day at home, rather than at the opera house.

14. J. Hillary Taylor, "Music in the Home," *Negro Music Journal* 1 (September 1902): 10.

15. "Race Artists to Sing for Victrolas," *Chicago Defender*, 8 January 1916, 4.

16. Black Swan Phonograph Company, Inc. advertisement, *Crisis* 25 (January 1922): 139. My thanks to David Suisman for bringing this to my attention.

17. Lawrence Schenbeck, "Music, Gender, and 'Uplift' in the *Chicago Defender*, 1927–1937," *Musical Quarterly* 81 (fall 1997): 350.

18. "Home" phonograph price cited in Timothy C. Fabrizio and George F. Paul, *The Talking Machine: An Illustrated Compendium, 1877–1929* (Atglen, PA: Schiffer, 1997), 37; graphophone price cited in Joyce H. Cauthen, *With Fiddle and Well-Rosined Bow: Old-Time Fiddling in Alabama* (Tuscaloosa: University of Alabama Press, 1989), 19.

19. Edward Harrolds, "The Indefatigable Harrolds on Record Prices," *Phonograph Monthly Review* 3 (October 1928): 23–24.

20. Adolph Schmuck, "The Case for Mere Listening," *Disques* 2 (May 1931): 108.

21. A. R. Gilliland and H. T. Moore, "The Immediate and Long-Time Effects of Classical and Popular Phonograph Selections," *Journal of Applied Psychology* 8 (September 1924): 309–23; and Margaret Floy Washburn, Margaret S. Child, and Theodora Mead Abel, "The Effect of Immediate Repetition on the Pleasantness or Unpleasantness of Music," in *The Effects of Music*, ed. Max Schoen (London: Kegan Paul, Trench, Trubner; New York: Harcourt, Brace, 1927), 199–210.

22. Karleton Hackett, "Is 'Canned Music' Worthwhile?" *Ladies' Home Journal* 29 (November 1912): 56. Similar statements may be found in Robert Haven Schauffler, "The Mission of Mechanical Music," *Century* 89 (1914): 293–98; and Moses Smith, "From Jazz to Symphony: Self-Education by Means of the Phonograph," *Phonograph Monthly Review* 1 (November 1926): 16–17.

23.   S. K., "Open Forum," *Phonograph Monthly Review* 1 (February 1927): 213.

24.   S. K., "Stradella and Schubert, but Not Strawinski—Yet," *Phonograph Monthly Review* 3 (December 1928): 95.

25.   Lutkin, "Musical Appreciation," 1010, 1011.

26.   Liebling, "On Preserving Art," 7; Pauline Partridge, "The Home Set to Music," *Sunset* 53 (November 1924): 68.

27.   See "The Phonograph as a Decorative Element in the Home," *Country Life* 33 (March 1918): 108–9; and Eleanor Hayden, "Phonographs as Art Furniture," *International Studio* 78 (1923): 249–57.

28.   See, for example, Hackett, "Is 'Canned Music' Worthwhile?" 56; Anne Shaw Faulkner, *Music in the Home: An Aid to Parents and Teachers in the Cause of Better Listening* (Chicago: Seymour, 1917); "Before We Go to the Opera"; and R. D. Darrell, "Are American Homes Musical?" *Phonograph Monthly Review* 1 (November 1926): 13–14, 16.

29.   George Ruhlen, response to Thomas A. Edison, Inc., questionnaire, 18 February 1921, collection of the University of Michigan Libraries, Ann Arbor. The questionnaire was sent to Edison phonograph owners throughout the country in 1921, with the following request: "Will you do this? It will take, perhaps, fifteen minutes of your time. We want to learn the favorite tunes of twenty thousand representative people, who own New Edisons. Please tell us your real honest to goodness favorites. I want to record them for you, if they have not already been recorded. Tell us just what tunes you like best, and if possible, tell us why. There are spaces below for twenty tunes. Give us your favorites in the order of your preference. A stamped and addressed envelope is enclosed for your reply. May I not hear from you promptly? THOMAS A. EDISON." Respondents often included notes, providing valuable insights into their experiences with recorded music. I am grateful to Bill Kenney for introducing me to this valuable resource. For further discussion of the questionnaire, see William Howland Kenney, *Recorded Music in American Life: The Phonograph and Popular Memory, 1890–1945* (New York: Oxford University Press, 1999), 5–12.

30.   Dorothy B. Fisher, "Women and the Phonograph," *Phonograph Monthly Review* 1 (October 1926): 31.

31.   Johnson, "Department of Recorded Music," 88.

32.   *Phonograph Monthly Review* 1 (1927): 507.

33.   George Grenfell, "Well Worth Reading: How the Victor Helped Two Trappers in the Wilds of the Far North," *Voice of the Victor* 6 (May–June 1911): 5; Florence Barrett Willoughby, "The Phonograph in Alaska," *Phonograph* 1 (26 July 1916): 13, 16; and V. W. Benedict, response to Thomas A. Edison, Inc., questionnaire, 11 January 1921, collection of the University of Michigan Libraries.

34. Fisher, "Women and the Phonograph," 31.
35. Phillip S. Gibbons, response to Thomas A. Edison, Inc., questionnaire, 21 February 1921, collection of the University of Michigan Libraries.
36. Albertus, quoted in "Phonographic Propaganda," *Phonograph Monthly Review* 4 (May 1930): 259.
37. Robert Haven Schauffler, "Canned Music—The Phonograph Fan," *Collier's* 67 (23 April 1921): 23.
38. *Collier's* 52 (4 October 1913): back cover.
39. "Who Buys Phonographs?" *Sonora Bell* 2 (October 1919): 1–6. Women also played an important role in the retail side of the phonograph trade. See Kenney, *Recorded Music in American Life,* 95–100.
40. Harold Randolph, "The Feminization of Music," *Papers and Proceedings of the Musical Teachers' National Association* 17 (1923): 196, 197.
41. Richard J. Magruder, "Manufacturing Music Lovers," *Disques* 2 (March 1931): 17.
42. "Phonograph Society Reports: Minneapolis Phonograph Society," *Phonograph Monthly Review* 1 (October 1926): 33.
43. Richard Crawford, quoted in *The Phonograph and Our Musical Life: Proceedings of a Centennial Conference, 7–10 December 1977,* ed. H. Wiley Hitchcock (Brooklyn, NY: ISAM, 1980), 71.
44. Aeolian Company, "The Aeolian Vocalion: The Phonograph of Richer Tone That You Can Play" (brochure, 1915), [16]. Similar devices were also available at this time, such as the one attached to the curiously named Manophone. See Andre Millard, *America on Record: A History of Recorded Sound* (Cambridge: Cambridge University Press, 1995), 145–46.
45. This is a condensed version of the original ad copy, which appeared in *Vanity Fair* 6 (May 1916): 115. The italics are original to the ad.
46. For an engaging discussion of recording, gender, and the American home of a later era, see Keir Keightley, "'Turn it down!' she shrieked: Gender, Domestic Space, and High Fidelity, 1948–59," *Popular Music* 15 (1996): 149–77.
47. Early-twentieth-century discussions of the changing priorities of American music education include Waldo S. Pratt, "New Ideals in Musical Education," *Atlantic* 86 (December 1900): 826–30; Lutkin, "Musical Appreciation," 1009–13; and Edward Bailey Birge, "Music Appreciation—The Education of the Listener," *Papers and Proceedings of the Music Teachers' National Association* 17 (1923): 189–93. More recent surveys of nineteenth- and early-twentieth-century American music education include James A. Keene, *A History of Music Education in the United States* (Hanover, NH: University Press of New England, 1982); and Joseph A. Labuta and Deborah A. Smith, *Music Education: Historical Contexts and Perspectives* (Upper Saddle River, NJ: Prentice Hall, 1997).

48. Constantin von Sternberg, "Are You Musical?" *Musician* 17 (1912): 91.

49. Anne Shaw Faulkner, "Phonographs and Player Instruments," *National Music Monthly* 1 (August 1917): 28. For similar usage of the term, see Agnes Moore Fryberger, *Listening Lessons in Music, Graded for Schools* (Boston: Silver, Burdett, 1916), 1–2; and Robert Haven Schauffler, "Handing You a Musical Ear Opener," *Collier's* 72 (1 December 1923): 13.

50. Birge, "Music Appreciation," 189.

51. Frances Elliott Clark, "What School Facilities Should be Provided for Instruction by Means of Motion-Picture Machines, Stereo-opticon Lanterns, Phonographs, Player-Pianos, etc. Part B," *Journal of the Proceedings and Addresses of the National Education Association* 50 (1912): 1235.

52. James Humphris, "How the Talking Machine Gives Reality to Musical History," *Musician* 24 (September 1919): 39.

53. See Corey, "Place of the Talking Machine in Music Teaching," 680; and Humphris, "How the Talking Machine Gives Reality to Musical History," 9.

54. Harbin, in Victor Talking Machine Co., *Victrola in Rural Schools,* 12.

55. Annie Pike Greenwood, "The Victor in the Rural School," *Journal of Education* 79 (26 February 1914): 235.

56. Henry Doughty Tovey, "Bringing Music to the Rural Districts," *Musician* 24 (February 1919): 14.

57. Greenwood, "Victor in the Rural School," 235.

58. Tovey, "Bringing Music to the Rural Districts," 14.

59. Victor Talking Machine Co., *Victrola in Rural Schools,* [106–7].

60. A. E. Winship, "The Mission of School Music," *Journal of Education* 84 (21 September 1916): 260. See also W. Arthur B. Clementson, "The Sound Reproducing Machine in the Country School," *Etude* 46 (November 1928): 840.

61. C. M. Tremaine, "The Music Memory Contest, etc.," *Proceedings of the Music Supervisors' National Conference* 11 (1919): 102.

62. C. M. Tremaine, "Music Memory Contests," *Journal of the National Education Association* 15 (February 1926): 43–44. Another source put the number of participating cities in 1926 at 1,083; see Edward Bailey Birge, *History of Public School Music in the United States,* rev. ed. (Boston: Ditson, 1939; repr. Reston, VA: Music Educators National Conference, 1988), 214–15.

63. Robert S. Lynd and Helen Merrell Lynd, *Middletown: A Study in American Culture* (New York: Harcourt, Brace & World, 1929), 202.

64. Quoted in Will H. Mayes, "How to Conduct a Music Memory Contest," *Etude* 41 (March 1923): 153.

65. In early contests player pianos were often used in conjunction with

phonographs and live performances, but as their popularity began to fade in the early 1920s, so did their role in music memory contests. In the mid-1920s radio began to be used in some contests; stations participated by scheduling performances of certain works on the contest lists.

66. Robert J. Coleman, *The Victrola in Music Memory Contests* (Camden, NJ: Victor Talking Machine Co., 1922).

67. J. C. Seegers, "Teaching Music Appreciation by Means of the Music-Memory Contest," *Elementary School Journal* 26 (November 1925): 219; "Organize a Music Memory Contest," *Talking Machine Journal* 6 (March 1919): 8.

68. Pratt, "New Ideals in Musical Education," 827, 828.

69. Richard Lee Dunham, "Music Appreciation in the Public Schools" (Ph.D. diss., University of Michigan, 1961), 76.

70. James Humphris, "Study Music Structure by Phonograph," *Musician* 24 (May 1919): 10. A photograph shows a phonograph in an NYU classroom in 1916.

71. Anne Shaw Faulkner, *What We Hear In Music* (Camden, NJ: Victor Talking Machine Co., 1913). See also Columbia Graphophone Company, *The Grafonola in the Classroom* (New York: Columbia Graphophone Co., 1920).

72. Thaddeus P. Giddings, et al., *Music Appreciation in the Schoolroom* (Boston: Ginn, 1926).

73. Agnes Hollister Winslow, *An Appreciation and History of Music* (Camden, NJ: Victor Talking Machine Co., 1928).

74. Faulkner, "Phonographs and Player Instruments," 29.

75. A 1920 article in *Musician* explained, "Ask any dealer in phonographs and he will tell you that he sells about ten 'jazz' records to one of what we call 'Classical' music" ("A Great Force Needs Your Guidance," *Musician* 25 [May 1920]: 5). My own informal survey of early record catalogs suggests a similar ratio.

76. Joseph N. Weber, president of the American Federation of Musicians, led the campaign against mechanical music. See his articles "Will Real Music Survive?" *Metronome* 45 (March 1930): 16, 44; "Canned Music," *American Federationist* 38 (1931): 1063–70; and "Mechanics and Music," *Papers and Proceedings of the Musical Teachers' National Conference* 25 (1931): 208–17.

77. Even before the decline of the phonograph industry, radio was seen as a way to provide a cultural service. See, for example, Mabel Travis Wood, "Becoming Familiar with Great Music," *Radio Broadcast* 2 (March 1923): 406; and Charles Orchard, Jr., "Is Radio Making America Musical?" *Radio Broadcast* 3 (October 1924): 454–55. I am grateful to Tim Taylor for providing me with these citations.

78. Gelatt, *Fabulous Phonograph,* 255.

79. Dane Yorke, "The Rise and Fall of the Phonograph," *American Mercury* 27 (September 1932): 12.

80. John Philip Sousa, "The Menace of Mechanical Music," *Appleton's* 8 (1906): 280. Sousa, however, eventually came to appreciate the phonograph. "Only a few years ago," he explained in 1923, "it was impossible for the public to hear more than a few of the world's great artists. Now, thanks to [the phonograph], these artists can be heard in the humblest homes" (quoted in "A Momentous Musical Meeting: Thomas A. Edison and Lt. Comm. John Philip Sousa Meet for the First Time and Talk upon Music," *Etude* 41 [October 1923]: 663–64).

81. "The Effect of Mechanical Instruments upon Musical Education," *Etude* 34 (July 1916): 484.

82. Philip G. Hubert, Jr., "What the Phonograph Will Do for Music and Music Lovers," *Century* 46 (May 1893): 153.

83. Liebling, "On Preserving Art," 7.

84. Ella Wheeler Wilcox, "Wail of an Old-Timer," in *Poems of Sentiment* (Chicago: W. B. Conkey, 1906), 125.

85. Sinclair Lewis, *Babbitt* (New York: Harcourt, Brace & World, 1922; repr. New York: Signet Classics, 1961), 150.

86. United States Bureau of the Census, *Census of Manufactures, 1914* (Washington, DC: Government Printing Office, 1918), 13, 21; Lynd and Lynd, *Middletown,* 244 n. 35.

87. *How We Gave a Phonograph Party* (New York: National Phonograph Co., 1899).

88. This recording has been reissued on *I'm Making You a Record: Home and Amateur Recordings on Wax Cylinder, 1902–1920,* Phonozoic compact disc 001. Patrick Feaster, producer of this CD, is writing a dissertation on home recordings: "By the Round: Early Phonography and the Performance Event" (Ph.D. diss., Indiana University, forthcoming).

89. Albert E. Wier, *Grand Opera with a Victrola* (New York: D. Appleton, 1915).

90. Marie K. Chaffee, response to Thomas A. Edison, Inc., questionnaire, 27 February 1921, University of Michigan Music Library.

91. "Effect of Mechanical Instruments upon Musical Education," 483–84. Similar testimony may be found in George Cecil, "The Phonograph as an Aid to Students of Singing," *Etude* 21 (1903): 482; and in "The Use of the Sound Reproducing Machine in Vocal Instruction and Musical Education," *Etude* 27 (1909): 195–96, 340.

92. Oscar Saenger, *The Oscar Saenger Course in Vocal Training: A Complete Course of Vocal Study for the Soprano Voice on Victor Records* (Camden, NJ: Victor Talking Machine Co., 1916); Hazel Gertrude Kinscella, "The

Subtle Lure of Duet-Playing," *Musician* 29 (January 1924): 8, 15; and Gustave Langenus, *The Langenus Clarinet Correspondence School with Talking Machine Records* (New York: n.p., 1915).

93. On the phonograph's surgical uses, see Dale B. Taylor, "Music in General Hospital Treatment from 1900 to 1950," *Journal of Music Therapy* 18 (1981): 62–73. For its use in language study, see G. P. Fougeray, *A Student's Manual for the Mastery of French Pronunciation to Accompany the Iroquois Phonograph Records* (Syracuse, NY: Iroquois Publishing Co., 1924); or John Tarver Willett, *Spanish Phonograph* (El Paso, TX: Tip. Latino Americano, 1917). In connection with exercise, see Victor Talking Machine Company, *Victor Records for Health Exercises* (Camden, NJ: Victor Talking Machine Co., 1922). On deafness, see George A. Leech, *The New Method of Curing Deafness by Special Adaptation of the Edison Phonograph* (New York: Knickerbocker, 1893).

CHAPTER THREE

1. There has been some confusion about the identity of the first jazz recording. Some sources have reported that the ODJB's first Columbia disc, containing "Darktown Strutters Ball" and "Indiana," was made during the band's January visit to Columbia's studios, and was thus the first jazz recording. Evidence suggests, however, that the Columbia recordings were made on 31 May 1917, more than three months after the Victor sessions. Columbia files give the May date for the session, and the disc's matrix numbers—the numbers that identify the disc's place in the sequence of a company's issues—also date from May. It would seem, then, that the band did not record any numbers for Columbia in January, but simply auditioned. The case for the primacy of the Victor discs is made in Tim Gracyk and Frank W. Hoffmann, *Popular American Recording Pioneers, 1895–1925* (Binghamton, NY: Haworth, 2000): 255–57. The ODJB's early Victor recordings have been reissued on *The Original Dixieland Jazz Band, 1917–1921,* Timeless compact disc CBC 1-009.

2. See, for example, Gunther Schuller, *Early Jazz: Its Roots and Early Development* (New York: Oxford University Press, 1968), 179–81.

3. Although the focus here is on recording, the impact of radio and the phonograph on the dissemination of jazz often overlap. Many of the phonograph effects identified in this discussion of portability may also be considered "radio effects." Film, too, influenced the reception of jazz, beginning in 1927 with *The Jazz Singer,* the first "talkie."

4. Richard M. Sudhalter and Philip R. Evans, *Bix: Man and Legend* (New Rochelle, NY: Arlington House, 1974), 35–36.

5. Jimmy Maxwell, interview with Milt Hinton, Jazz Oral History Project,

Smithsonian Institution, 16 April 1979, 13; transcript on deposit at the Institute of Jazz Studies, Rutgers University.

6.   Quoted in Jed Rasula, "The Media of Memory: The Seductive Menace of Records in Jazz History," in *Jazz among the Discourses*, ed. Krin Gabbard (Durham, NC: Duke University Press, 1995), 143.

7.   Quoted in Burton Peretti, *The Creation of Jazz: Music, Race, and Culture in Urban America* (Urbana: University of Illinois Press, 1992), 152–53.

8.   As the reader will find, a good deal of evidence I cite in this chapter is anecdotal, typically coming from the jazz musicians themselves. Jazz scholars know that such reminiscences are not equally reliable, given the vagaries of memory and motive. However, I have not cited (as far as I know) any widely discredited or generally presumed apocryphal stories. Moreover, for each point I make about recording's influence on jazz, I usually cite multiple independent accounts as supporting evidence and, whenever possible, further corroborating evidence based on recordings, scores, or the judgments of other scholars. To say this, however, is not to diminish the crucial importance of first-hand accounts to the understanding of jazz generally or its relationship with recording specifically.

9.   Quoted in David Chevan, "The Double Bass as a Solo Instrument in Early Jazz," *Black Perspective in Music* 17 (1989): 81.

10.   Baby Dodds, *The Baby Dodds Story,* rev. ed. (Baton Rouge: Louisiana State University Press, 1992), 71.

11.   Ralph Berton, *Remembering Bix: A Memoir of the Jazz Age* (New York: Harper & Row, 1974), 162.

12.   This performance of "Diminuendo in Blue and Crescendo in Blue" was captured on disc at a time when recordings were no longer limited to just a few minutes. It has been reissued on *Ellington at Newport 1956,* Columbia compact disc CK-40587.

13.   Occasionally, pieces had to be augmented to fit a record side. Ellington's 1926 recording of "Animal Crackers," for example, takes longer to play than the printed arrangement. Mark Tucker observed that the "insertion of two hot solo choruses before the full ensemble reprise brings the arrangement up to the required recording length" (Mark Tucker, *Ellington: The Early Years* [Urbana: University of Illinois Press, 1991], 161).

14.   Hardwick's emphasis on the offbeats in the second take, however, gives the solo a more propulsive, off-balance feel. These have been reissued on *Early Ellington: The Complete Brunswick and Vocalion Recordings of Duke Ellington, 1926–1931,* Decca compact disc, GRD-3-640.

15.   Schuller, *Early Jazz,* 330. As Schuller remarked about a later Ellington work, "Reminiscing in Tempo," the lack of improvisation need not be considered a fault. "The decision to eschew improvisation was one

which he did not regard as a serious failing. Indeed, why *must* there be improvisation—even in a jazz piece—as certain critics were suggesting (and still are apt to do)" (Gunther Schuller, *The Swing Era: The Development of Jazz, 1930–1945* [New York: Oxford University Press, 1989], 78).

16. Jeffrey Magee, "The Music of Fletcher Henderson and His Orchestra in the 1920s" (Ph.D. diss., University of Michigan, 1992), 326.

17. David Chevan, "Written Music in Early Jazz" (Ph.D. diss., City University of New York, 1997), 299–302.

18. Richard Crawford, *The American Musical Landscape* (Berkeley and Los Angeles: University of California Press, 1993), 197.

19. "Reminiscing" spans four sides, the others two. Ellington was not alone in experimenting with multisided jazz works. For example, Troy Floyd's band recorded "Shadowland Blues" and "Dreamland Blues," both two-side works, in 1928 and 1929. These pieces are discussed briefly in Schuller, *Early Jazz,* 292–93. "Boogie Woogie Prayer" (1938) by Albert Ammons, Pete Johnson, and Meade Lux Lewis also spanned two sides. See Jürgen Hunkemöller, "Die Rolle der Schallplatte im Jazz," *Jazzforschung* 12 (1980): 107.

20. Schuller, *Early Jazz,* 346. Two takes of "Tiger Rag" have been reissued on *Early Ellington,* Decca compact disc GRD-3-640.

21. Schuller, *Swing Era,* 91.

22. "Diminuendo and Crescendo in Blue" has been reissued on the *Smithsonian Collection of Classic Jazz,* Smithsonian Collection of Recordings compact disc RD 033–3. The work is treated in greater depth in Schuller, *Swing Era,* 90–93; and Crawford, *American Musical Landscape,* 199–209.

23. Quoted in Neil Leonard, *Jazz and the White Americans: The Acceptance of a New Art Form* (Chicago: University of Chicago Press, 1962), 96.

24. Maxwell example cited in Maxwell, interview, 15. Freeman example cited in Bud Freeman, interview with Ms. Dance, Jazz Oral History Project, Smithsonian Institution, 1977, 23; transcript on deposit at the Institute of Jazz Studies, Rutgers University. The Parker-Young-Trumbauer connection is cited in Ted Gioia, *The Imperfect Art: Reflections on Jazz and Modern Culture* (New York: Oxford University Press, 1988), 65; and Rasula, "Media of Memory," 142. Marsalis example cited in Paul F. Berliner, *Thinking in Jazz: The Infinite Art of Improvisation* (Chicago: University of Chicago Press, 1994), 98. (Parker, an alto saxophonist, had to adjust the speed of his phonograph so he could match the pitch of Young's tenor solos.) Further examples are given in Kathy J. Ogren, *The Jazz Revolution: Twenties America and the Meaning of Jazz* (New York: Oxford University Press, 1989), 151–52; Berliner, *Thinking in Jazz,* 92–

107; and Ingrid Monson, *Saying Something: Jazz Improvisation and Interaction* (Chicago: University of Chicago Press, 1996), 126. The study of jazz recordings may also be more formalized than the individual approach just described. Composer and jazz pedagogue David Baker, for example, has long assigned his students at Indiana University to transcribe and perform recorded jazz solos; see David Baker, "The Phonograph in Jazz History and its Influence on the Emergent Jazz Performer," in *The Phonograph and Our Musical Life: Proceedings of a Centennial Conference,* ed. H. Wiley Hitchcock (Brooklyn, NY: ISAM, 1980), 48–50.

25. Berliner, *Thinking in Jazz,* 98.

26. Quoted ibid., 106.

27. Ibid., 106–7. The visuality of jazz performance also has an important influence on the way audiences understand the music of particular performers. David Ake persuasively argues that, for example, the hunched posture and withdrawn demeanor of pianist Bill Evans contributed to the reception of his music as "intellectual," while fellow pianist Keith Jarrett's music is often heard as "sensual" or "mystical," in part from the striking visual impact of his amatory gyrations at the keyboard. See David Ake, *Jazz Cultures* (Berkeley and Los Angeles: University of California Press, 2002), 83–111.

28. Dodds, *Baby Dodds Story,* 69–70. Note that Dodds remarks, "I forgot my part," suggesting that he had worked out his solo in advance.

29. Berton, *Remembering Bix,* 352. "Goosepimples" has been reissued on *Bix Beiderbecke, 1927–1930,* Classics compact disc 788.

30. Mark Tucker, e-mail message to author, 11 October 1997.

31. " . . . il n'est pas un instrument du jazz qui ne soit 'phonogénique'" (Roland-Manuel, "Musique et mécanique," *Le Menestrel* 85 [25 May 1923]: 234).

32. *New Grove Dictionary of Jazz,* 2d ed., ed. Barry Kernfeld (London: Macmillan, 2002), s.v. "recording," 3:371.

33. Dodds, *Baby Dodds Story,* 70–71.

34. Quoted in Ogren, *Jazz Revolution,* 94.

35. R. Raven-Hart, "Composing for Radio," *Musical Quarterly* 16 (January 1930): 135.

36. Quoted in Bill Crow, ed., *Jazz Anecdotes* (New York: Oxford University Press, 1990), 110.

37. Raven-Hart, "Composing for Radio," 135.

38. For more on the slap style, see Chevan, "Double Bass as a Solo Instrument," 77.

39. Quoted in Crow, ed., *Jazz Anecdotes,* 107–8.

40. Such cramped seating is mentioned in Dodds, *Baby Dodds Story,* 70;

and *New Grove Dictionary of Jazz,* 2d ed., ed. Barry Kernfeld, s.v. "recording," 358.

41. Duke Ellington, "My Hunt for Song Titles," in Tucker, ed., *Duke Ellington Reader,* 89. "Mood Indigo" has been reissued on *Early Ellington: The Complete Brunswick and Vocalion Recordings of Duke Ellington, 1926–1931,* Decca compact disc, GRD-3-640.

42. Quoted in Gama Gilbert, "'Hot Damn!' Says Ellington When Ranked with Bach," in Tucker, ed., *Duke Ellington Reader,* 113.

43. Quoted in Jack Cullen, interview with Duke Ellington, ibid., 339–40.

44. Mark Tucker questioned Ellington's claims: "The 'Mood Indigo' story always struck me as a bit suspicious—he tended to give pat descriptions about the composing process since people asked him such questions so often" (Tucker, e-mail message to author).

CHAPTER FOUR

1. There is little debate on this point. For concurring observations, see, for example, Scott N. Reger, "Historical Survey of the String Instrument Vibrato," in *Studies in the Psychology of Music,* vol. 1: *The Vibrato,* ed. Carl Seashore (Iowa City: University of Iowa Press, 1932), 289–304; Frederick Neumann, *Violin Left Hand Technique: A Survey of the Related Literature* (Urbana, IL: American String Teachers Association, 1969), 111–26; Ottó Szende, *Unterweisung im Vibrato auf der Geige* (Vienna: Universal Edition, 1985), 10–12; Clive Brown, "Bowing Styles, Vibrato, and Portamento in Nineteenth-Century Violin Playing," *Journal of the Royal Musical Association* 113 (1988): 97–128; and Philip, *Early Recordings and Musical Style,* 97–108.

2. Such remarks can be found from as early as 1677 and as late as 1916. See Bartolomeo Bismantova, quoted in David Boyden with Sonya Monosoff, "Violin Technique," in *The New Grove Violin Family* (New York: Norton, 1989), 72; and Lucien Capet, *La Technique supérieure de l'archet* (Paris: Maurice Senart, 1916), 24.

3. Quoted in *New Grove Dictionary of Music,* s.v. *vibrato,* 19:697.

4. Pierre Marie François de Baillot, *The Art of the Violin,* ed. and trans. Louise Goldberg (Evanston, IL: Northwestern University Press, 1991), 240–41. The excerpt is from a work by Giovanni Battista Viotti and indicates vibrato as Viotti used it. For the Bériot, see the violinist's *Méthode de violon* (Mainz, [1858]), 242. The cited musical example is also reproduced in Brown, "Bowing Styles, Vibrato, and Portamento," 115.

5. Quoted in Brown, "Bowing Styles, Vibrato, and Portamento," 114.

6. Archibald Saunders, *A Practical Course in Vibrato for Violinists* (London: Lavender, n.d.), 7.

7. For example, a review of an 1881 performance in London by an English

violinist complained of the performer's "constant *tremolo* [i.e., vibrato] which we have frequently to note in violinists of the French school" (*Athenaeum,* no. 2779 [29 January 1881]: 173).

8. The Strolling Player, "The Everlasting 'Vibrato,'" *Strad* 17 (January 1908): 305.

9. James Winram, *Violin Playing and Violin Adjustment* (Edinburgh: Blackwood & Sons, 1908), 34.

10. Siegfried Eberhardt, *Violin Vibrato,* trans. Melzar Chaffee (New York: Carl Fischer, 1911), 14; Percival Hodgson, "Vibrato," *Strad* 27 (September 1916): 148. See similar comments in Petrowitch Bissing, *Cultivation of the Violin Vibrato Tone* (Chicago: Central States Music, 1914), 8; Pavel L. Bytovetski, *How to Master the Violin* (Boston: Ditson, 1917), 77; and Samuel B. Grimson and Cecil Forsyth, *Modern Violin-Playing* (New York: Gray, 1920), 5.

11. Carl Flesch, *The Art of Violin Playing,* vol. 1, trans. Frederick H. Martens (New York: Carl Fischer, 1924), 40.

12. Frederick Hahn, *Practical Violin Study* (Philadelphia: Theodore Presser, 1929), 137.

13. I am focusing here on solo violin playing (i.e., of unaccompanied works and works with piano or orchestral accompaniment) as opposed to chamber or orchestral playing, and am doing so for two reasons. First, it is difficult to analyze vibrato or distinguish one player's use of it from another's when many violinists are playing simultaneously; and second, soloists led the vibrato trend, with ensemble players following behind.

14. Carl Flesch, *The Memoirs of Carl Flesch,* trans. Hans Keller (London: Rockliff, 1957), 79.

15. Joseph Joachim, performing J. S. Bach, Adagio from Sonata in G Minor, BWV 1001, on *Great Virtuosi of the Golden Age, Volume I,* Pearl compact disc GEMM CD 9101.

16. Listeners may notice that the recording is pitched quite a bit lower than is typical (this is particularly obvious when comparing it to the Heifetz and Seidel performances included on the CD). It is very unlikely that Joachim tuned his violin flat for this recording; the change in pitch almost certainly occurred in the recording or remastering process.

17. When studying Joachim's recordings we must allow for the possibility that his advanced age at the time (seventy-two) affected his vibrato. I believe the recordings are generally representative of his practice, however, for his use of vibrato reflects his written statements on the matter and seems too purposeful to be the result of the ravages of old age.

18. Pablo de Sarasate, performing Pablo de Sarasate, *Zigeunerweisen,* on *Great Virtuosi of the Golden Age, Volume I,* Pearl compact disc GEMM CD 9101.

19. Flesch, *Art of Violin Playing*, 40.

20. Eugène Ysaÿe performing Henri Vieuxtemps, *Rondino,* on *Eugène Ysaÿe, Violinist and Conductor: The Complete Violin Recordings,* Sony compact disc MHK 62337.

21. Flesch, *Art of Violin Playing*, 40.

22. Fritz Kreisler performing Fritz Kreisler, *Liebesleid,* on *The Kreisler Collection: The Complete Acoustic HMV Recordings,* Biddulph compact disc LAB 009-10.

23. Three of Hall's recordings have been reissued on *Great Virtuosi of the Golden Age, Volume II,* Pearl compact disc GEMM CD 9102. Many of Kubelik's discs have been compiled on *Jan Kubelik, the Acoustic Recordings (1902–1913),* Biddulph compact disc LAB 033-34.

24. Joseph Szigeti performing J. S. Bach, Adagio from Sonata in G Minor, BWV 1001, on *Joseph Szigeti: A Golden Treasury of His Best English Columbia 78s,* Music and Arts compact disc CD 813; Jascha Heifetz performing J. S. Bach, Adagio from Sonata in G Minor, BWV 1001, on *The Heifetz Collection,* vol. 3, BMG Classics compact disc 09026-61734-2.

25. Jascha Heifetz performing Johannes Brahms, Hungarian Dance no. 1 (arr. Joachim), on *The Heifetz Collection: The Acoustic Recordings, 1917–1924,* BMG compact disc 0942-2-RG; Toscha Seidel performing Johannes Brahms, Hungarian Dance no. 1 (arr. Joachim), on *The Auer Legacy, Volume Two,* Appian compact disc CDAPR 7016.

     A note on vibrato measurement: This example indicates only the presence of vibrato, not the frequency or pitch extent. Computer software is available for measuring these aspects of vibrato, but is not used here because such programs reliably analyze only unaccompanied performance. All observations in this chapter about particular violinists' vibrato thus arise from close listening to recordings. While this approach has its limitations, conclusions drawn from this method of listening are based on human perception, not on possibly imperceptible differences measurable only by computer.

26. Leopold Auer, *Violin Playing as I Teach It* (New York: Stokes, 1921), 62.

27. Zino Francescatti performing Pablo de Sarasate, *Zigeunerweisen,* on *Zino Francescatti: The Complete HMV Recordings,* Biddulph compact disc LAB 030.

28. For further comparisons, see Robert Philip's survey of recorded string vibrato, *Early Recordings and Musical Style,* 97–108, which complements and corroborates the present one.

29. See, for example, Henri Vercheval, *Dictionnaire du violoniste* (Paris: Fischbacher, 1923), 129; and Ferruccio Bonavia, "On Vibrato," *Musical Times* 68 (1 December 1927): 1077–78.

30. Adila Fachiri, "Trends in Violin Playing," *Music and Letters* 31 (Octo-

ber 1950): 282; Hans Keller, "Violin Technique: Its Modern Development and Musical Decline," in *The Book of the Violin,* ed. Dominic Gill (New York: Rizzoli, 1984), 149–50.

31. Werner Hauck, *Vibrato on the Violin,* trans. Kitty Rokos (London: Bosworth, 1975), 23–24.

32. Robin Stowell, "Technique and Performing Practice," in *The Cambridge Companion to the Violin,* ed. Robin Stowell (Cambridge: Cambridge University Press, 1992), 130.

33. Fritz Kreisler's earliest recordings have been reissued on *The Kreisler Collection: The Complete Acoustic HMV Recordings,* Biddulph compact disc LAB 009-10. Examples of Powell's playing from 1909 to 1917 may be heard on *Maud Powell,* Biddulph compact disc LAB 094. Powell noted in an interview given around 1918 that she had been using a steel E-string for twelve years, so these recordings were all presumably made with the steel E; see Maud Powell, interview with Frederick Martens, in *Violin Mastery* (New York: Stokes, 1919), 194–95.

34. Flesch, *Art of Violin Playing,* 40. See also Ferruccio Bonavia, "Violin Playing during the Past Fifty Years," *Strad* 50 (May 1939): 7; Henry Roth, *Master Violinists in Performance* (Neptune City, NJ: Paganiniana, 1982), 26; Keller, "Violin Technique," 149; Boyden with Monosoff, "Violin Technique," 102; Stowell, "Technique and Performing Practice," 131; and Philip, *Early Recordings and Musical Style,* 106.

35. Arcadie Birkenholtz, interview with John Harvith and Susan Edwards Harvith, 11 December 1974, in Harvith and Harvith, eds., *Edison, Musicians, and the Phonograph,* 65–67.

36. Louis Kaufman, interviews with John Harvith and Susan Edwards Harvith, 20–21 December 1974 and 1 September 1975, ibid., 116.

37. For a discussion of the "intensity vibrato," see Scott N. Reger, "The String Instrument Vibrato," in *Vibrato,* 322–23 and 330–31.

38. The difference in the audibility of the two E-flats probably has little to do with improvements in recording technology between 1910 and 1918. Both recordings were made with acoustic recording horns, and other than the very high notes, the sound on both recordings is comparably clear.

39. Kaufman, interview, 116; italics added.

40. Lilit Yoo, Stephan Moore, David Sullivan, and Ichiro Fujinaga, "The Effect of Vibrato on Response Time in Determining the Pitch Relationship of Violin Tones," *Proceedings of the International Conference on Music Perception and Cognition,* 1998, 477–81.

41. Edmund Severn, interview with Frederick Martens, in *Violin Mastery,* 237; Auer, *Violin Playing as I Teach It,* 59; Flesch, *Art of Violin Playing,* 20.

42. Quoted in Jane W. Davidson, "Visual Perception of Performance

Manner in the Movements of Solo Musicians," *Psychology of Music* 21 (1993): 103.

43. Ibid., 112.

44. Hans Wessely, *A Practical Guide to Violin-Playing* (London: Joseph Williams, 1913), 90; Maximilian Plilzer, interview with Frederick Martens, in *Violin Mastery*, 179; and Hahn, *Practical Violin Study*, 137.

45. Eberhardt, *Violin Vibrato*, 14.

46. Flesch, *Art of Violin Playing*, 35.

CHAPTER FIVE

1. Hindemith's recordings and their fate are discussed in Martin Elste, "Hindemiths Versuche 'grammophonplatten-eigene Stücke' im Kontext einer Ideengeschichte der Mechanische Musik im 20. Jahrhundert," *Hindemith Jahrbuch* 25 (1996): 195–221; and idem, "Hindemith's Experiments with the Gramophone: Long Lost Recordings Rediscovered" (paper presented at the conference of the Association for Recorded Sound Collections, Syracuse, NY, May 1998).

2. For more on these festivals, see Josef Häusler, *Spiegel der neuen Musik: Donaueschingen* (Kassel: Bärenreiter, 1996).

3. The program for the Neue Musik Berlin 1930 festival is reprinted in ibid., 430.

4. Martin Elste has tested this possibility by overdubbing two recordings of the work eight beats apart. I have heard Elste's canonic recording and find it effective, though it is only speculation that Hindemith played the recordings in this way.

5. "Arie mit Klavierbegleitung schreibt, in der sich die menschliche Stimme in einem Umfang von ungefähr 3½ Oktaven ergeht" (Willi Schuh, "Neue Musik Berlin 1930," *Schweizerische Musikzeitung* 70 [1 August 1930]: 550).

6. "Über meinen Beitrag zur Original-Grammophon-Musik möchte ich sagen: dem Versuch liegt der Gedanke zugrunde, die Maschine, die bisher der möglichst getreuen Reproduktion von original ausgeführter Musik galt, erweiternd dahin auszunützen, daß sie durch die Besonderheit ihrer Funktion und durch die Auswertung jener Abfall-Zone ihrer Möglichkeiten, welche für ihren eigentlichen Zweck (eben die getreue Reproduktion) wertlos, weil verändernd ist, eine ihr typische, arteigene Musik hervorbringe" (Toch, "Über meine Kantate 'Das Wasser' und meine Grammophonmusik," *Melos* 9 [May–June 1930]: 221–22).

7. "Ich wählte dazu das gesprochene Wort und ließ einen vierstimmigen gemischten Kammerchor genau festgelegte Rhythmen, Vokale, Konsonanten, Silben, und Worte so sprechen, daß unter Einschaltung der

mechanischen Möglichkeiten bei der Aufnahme (Vervielfachung des Tempos und die damit verbundene Ton-Erhöhung), eine Art Instrumentalmusik enstand, die es wohl fast vergessen machen mag, daß ihrer Hervorbringung nur ein Sprechen zugrunde liegt. (Nur in einem Punkte täuschte mich die Maschine leider: sie veränderte die Vokale in einer nicht von mir beabsichtigten Weise mit). In zwei bewegten Sätzchen und einer 'Fuge aus der Geographie' versuchte ich, das Problem von mehreren Seiten anzupacken" (ibid.).

8. "Wenn etwa Vokale gesungen und in der Tonhöhe gesteigert werden, so erklingen merkwürdig fremde Klanglaute; und wenn sie nun noch mit Konsonanten verbunden sind, in der Art der Singsilben, so kommen schon beinahe instrumental-geräuschartige Klänge zustande. Die Stücke wirkten geradezu verblüffend, kaum ein Musiker konnte sagen, wie diese ungewohnten Klänge entstanden sind, niemand wußte, ob Musikinstrumente, Stimmen oder gar Geräusche kombiniert waren. Und doch war alles kompositorisch logisch und klanglich genau entworfen" (Georg Schünemann, "Produktive Kräfte der mechanischen Musik," *Die Musik* 24 [January 1932]: 246–47). For a similar but less awestricken response, see László Moholy-Nagy's comments quoted in Douglas Kahn, *Noise, Water, Meat: A History of Sound in the Arts* (Cambridge, MA: MIT Press, 1999), 127.

9. Lilly Toch, "The Orchestration of a Composer's Life," an oral history conducted by Bernard Galm, Oral History Program, University of California, Los Angeles, 1978, 298; transcript on deposit at Bancroft Library, University of California, Berkeley.

10. "Es ist doch etwas Seltsames um diese rätselvolle Gravierung der schwarzen Platte vor uns. Gravierung: Ja, das ist's, wenn auch niemals ein Graveur diese Schallwellengravierung wird nachmachen können. Wirklich niemals? Ein toller Gedanke: Warum sollen wir denselben Weg, den wir vorwärts geschritten sind, nicht auch rückwärts gehen können? Durch die Eindrücke der Schallwellen ist dem warmen Wachs eine Form gegeben worden, die sich durch den Apparat und seine Schalldose in tönendes Leben übersetzt. Die Stimme ist 'materialisiert' worden. Wir können ihr Bild mit dem Mikroskop sehen, so gut wie etwas anderes, was Menschenkunst geschaffen hat. Was bisher ungreifbar im Raume schwebte, hat Form gewonnen. Wie, wenn wir dieselbe oder eine ähnliche Form, ohne Schallwellen, auf rein mechanischem Wege, erzielten? Wäre dann nicht die Möglichkeit erschlossen, auf solcher Platte einen Sänger von einem unbegrenzten Stimmumfang mit beliebigem Timbre zu konstruieren?" (Alexander Dillmann, "Das Grammophon," *Die Stimme* 1 [March 1910]: 11).

11. Rainer Maria Rilke, "Ur-Geräusch," *Das Inselschiff* 1 (October 1919): 14–

20; quoted in Friedrich A. Kittler, *Gramophone, Film, Typewriter,* trans. Geoffrey Winthrop-Young and Michael Wutz (Stanford: Stanford University Press, 1999), 39–40.

12. László Moholy-Nagy, "Produktion—Reproduktion," *De Stijl,* no. 7 (1922); translation in *Moholy-Nagy,* ed. and trans. Krisztina Passuth (London: Thames & Hudson, 1985), 290.

13. László Moholy-Nagy, "Neue Gestaltung in der Musik: Möglichkeiten des Grammophons," *Der Sturm,* no. 14 (July 1923); translation ibid., 291.

14. "Die Mannigfaltigkeit der Klänge wird das alte Orchester ganz primitiv erscheinen lassen . . . Die Rolle des Interpreten gehört der Vergangenheit an" (H. H. Stuckenschmidt, "Die Mechanisierung der Musik," *Pult und Taktstock* 2 [1925]: 8).

15. "Der vorliegende Aufsatz wird allgemeines Kopfschütteln hervorrufen. Namentlich bei den Dirigenten" (ibid., 1).

16. H. H. Stuckenschmidt, "Machines—A Vision of the Future," *Modern Music* 4 (March–April 1927): 9, 11.

17. Ibid.

18. Ernst Křenek, *Music Here and Now,* trans. Barthold Fles (New York: Norton, 1939), 238.

19. The idea of indexical notation was taken up by Theodor Adorno in the mid-1930s. See Thomas Y. Levin, "For the Record: Adorno on Music in the Age of Its Technological Reproducibility," *October* 5 (winter 1990): 32–38.

20. "Konzert für Grammophon mit Begleitung einiger 'realer' Instrumente" (Hansjörg Dammert, "Grammophon-Konzerte," *Musikblätter des Anbruch* 8 [October–November 1926]: 406).

21. "Welche Möglichkeiten hat ein Komponist, den Solopart zu nuancieren, was Klang sowohl wie auch Farben anbelangt! Wie eigenartig und wechselvoll kann man die Unterhaltung der beiden Klanggruppen gestalten, als Gegeneinanderbewegung und auch als Folge von Solo und Tutti! (Man denke sich zum Beispiel zu einer matten Farbe des Begleitungsensembles, sagen wir Flöte, sordinierte Violine, Klavier in höherer Lage, den sonoren Klang eines vom Blech gestützten Streichorchesters in Phonographen.) Also: die Mittel diese Art zu musizieren, sind fast unbegrenzt, von Einfachsten bis zum Raffiniertesten" (ibid., 407).

22. Hugh Davies, "A History of Sampling," *Organised Sound* 1 (April 1996): 9.

23. On Hoérée, see Richard S. James, "Expansion of Sound Resources in France, 1913–1940, and its Relationship to Electronic Music" (Ph.D. diss., University of Michigan, 1981), 250. Antheil's work is cited (but not

described) in Stuckenschmidt, "Mechanisierung der Musik," 7–8. Milhaud's experiments are mentioned in Lowell Cross, "Electronic Music, 1948–1953," *Perspectives of New Music* 7 (fall–winter 1968): 35.

24. Ottorino Respighi, *Pini di Roma* (Milan: Ricordi, 1925).

25. Kurt Weill, *Der Zar lässt sich photographieren* (Vienna: Universal Edition, 1927). Weill's use of the phonograph is discussed in Susan Cook, *Opera for a New Republic: The Zeitopern of Křenek, Weill, and Hindemith* (Ann Arbor, MI: UMI Research Press, 1988), 139–40.

26. Carol-Bérard, "Recorded Noises—Tomorrow's Instrumentation," *Modern Music* 6 (January–February 1929): 29.

27. Raymond Lyon, "Le Phonographe d'avant garde," *Le Joie musicale*, no. 3 (1930): 34.

28. "Von größtem Interesse wäre es aber, spezifische Musik für die phonographische Wiedergabe zu schaffen, eine Musik, die erst ihr wahres Bild, den Originalklang, durch die mechanische Wiedergabe erhielte. Dies wäre wohl das Endziel des eigens für die Schallplatte schaffenden Komponisten der Zukunft" (Igor Stravinsky, "Meine Stellung zur Schallplatte," *Kultur und Schallplatte* 1 [March 1930]: 65).

29. Stravinsky, *Autobiography*, 101.

30. Schünemann, "Produktive Kräfte der Mechanischen Musik," 247.

31. "Ein interessanter akustischer Versuch . . . ein musikalischer Scherz wohl auch" (Toch, "Über meine Kantate 'Das Wasser,'" 222).

32. Alfred Einstein, "Berlin's New Music Festival," *New York Times,* 17 August 1930, sec. 8, p. 5; Hans Gutman, "The Festivals as Music Barometers," *Modern Music* 8 (November–December 1930): 30.

33. Křenek, *Music Here and Now,* 238–39.

34. See Richard S. James, "Avant-garde Sound-on-Film Techniques and Their Relationship to Electro-Acoustic Music," *Musical Quarterly* 72 (1986): 74–89; and idem, "Expansion of Sound Resources in France," 203ff.

35. See Rex Lawson, "Stravinsky and the Pianola," in *Confronting Stravinsky,* ed. Jann Pasler (Berkeley and Los Angeles: University of California Press, 1986), 284–301.

36. The program is reprinted in Häusler, *Spiegel der neuen Musik,* 427.

37. For more on the Theremin, see Albert Glinsky, *Theremin: Ether Music and Espionage* (Urbana: University of Illinois Press, 2000).

38. "Nichts unterläuft, was nicht durch Tonhöhe, Metrum, Rhythmus, Tempo, Dynamik in den *Noten* fixiert ist; jede Spur einer Spontaneität, eines Sentimentes, eines Impulses ist hinausgedrängt" (Ernst Toch, "Musik für mechanische Instrumente," *Neue Musikzeitung* 47 [July 1926]: 433).

39. "Möglichkeit der absoluten Festlegung des Willens des Komponisten

... Erweiterung der technischen und klanglichen Möglichkeiten" (Paul Hindemith, "Zur mechanischen Musik," *Musikanten Gilde* 5 [15 November 1927]: 156).

40. John Cage, *Imaginary Landscape No. 1* (New York: Peters, 1960). Cage used turntables in later works as well, including *Credo in Us* (1942), *Imaginary Landscape no. 5* (1952), and *33⅓* (1969).

41. Lawrence Weschler, "My Grandfather's Last Tale," *Atlantic* 278 (December 1996): 95.

CHAPTER SIX

1. Babu explains how he came up with the term in the 2001 documentary film *Scratch* (Palm digital videodisc 3046-2). *Scratch,* as well as the 1997 documentary *Battle Sounds* (videotape, no label number, available through www.battlesounds.com), is required viewing for anyone interested in the world of the hip-hop DJ.

2. Turntablists are not the only DJs who do more than play records. Those who spin records at dance clubs often manipulate and combine songs in a variety of creative ways. See Sarah Thornton, *Club Cultures: Music, Media, and Subcultural Capital* (Hanover, NH: Wesleyan University Press, 1996), 63–66; and Kai Fikentscher, *"You Better Work!": Underground Dance Music in New York City* (Hanover, NH: Wesleyan University Press, 2000), 33–56.

3. This story has been recounted in a number of sources. Livingston himself retells it in *Battle Sounds* and *Scratch.* See also Bill Brewster and Frank Broughton, *Last Night a DJ Saved My Life* (New York: Grove Press, 2000), 224–25; and Jim Fricke and Charlie Ahearn, *Yes Yes Y'all: The Experience Music Project Oral History of Hip-Hop's First Decade* (Cambridge, MA: Da Capo, 2002), 63.

4. Although the birth of turntablism is usually traced to the Bronx of the 1970s, DJs in Jamaica, where Kool Herc and others had roots, had earlier practiced similar forms of sound manipulation. See Dick Hebdige, *Cut 'n' Mix: Culture, Identity, and Caribbean Music* (London: Comedia, 1987), 136–48. An even earlier, though unrelated, type of phonographic manipulation was, as discussed in chapter 5, practiced by Paul Hindemith, Ernst Toch, John Cage, and others starting in the 1920s.

5. Fricke and Ahearn, *Yes Yes Y'all,* 63.

6. There is an analogous practice using reel-to-reel tape recorders known as scrubbing. The tape is manually moved back and forth against the playback head in order to locate a specific point on the tape for editing purposes. The sound it produces is similar to that of scratching. Although scrubbing predates scratching, no similar musical practice arose from it, and it seems to have no connection to turntablism. I am

grateful to Susan Schmidt Horning for bringing scrubbing to my attention.

7. Of course, these categories are porous: more or less all DJs start out in the bedroom, and many would fall into multiple categories simultaneously. A 2002 poll at the Scratch DJ website asked readers to identify themselves with one of these four DJ types. As of 24 October 2003 the results were as follows: production (6.48 percent); club (9.03 percent); performance—that is, turntablist (18.46 percent); and bedroom (66.03 percent). It is unclear how closely this sample of respondents matches the total DJ population. (To see up-to-date statistics, go to www .scratchdj.com/cgi-bin/poll/prev_poll.cgi?start and click on Question 4 results.)

8. Many DJs perform with rappers; Mixmaster Mike's work with the Beastie Boys is just one of innumerable examples. DJs are also members of rock groups such as Incubus, Limp Bizkit, and Sugar Ray, and play with jazz musicians, such as Medeski Martin & Wood and Courtney Pine. The Invisibl Skratch Piklz, the Beat Junkies, and the X-Ecutioners are a few of the DJ crews. Solo artists, like DJ Shadow and DJ Spooky, have ties to turntablism but blur the line between DJing and electronic music composition. DJ Radar is one of the small but apparently growing number of hip-hop DJs who have performed with classical orchestras.

9. Although generically, *turntable, record player,* and *phonograph* are interchangeable, *turntable* is the preferred term in DJ circles. More colloquial terms include tables, decks, 1s and 2s (referring to the two turntables usually used by DJs), wheels of steel, and techs or 1200s (from the popular Technics 1200 model of turntable).

10. For an extensive discussion of digging, see Joseph Schloss, "Making Beats: The Art of Sample-Based Hip Hop" (Ph.D. diss., University of Washington, 2000), 93–119. This dissertation, in revised form, was published under the same title in 2004 by Wesleyan University Press.

11. For an appreciation of *Ultimate Breaks and Beats* and a complete listing of its contents, see Andrew Mason, "Building Blocks," *Wax Poetics,* no. 1 (winter 2002): 44–50.

12. For a review of Final Scratch, see Jason Blum, "Stanton Final Scratch: Digital Vinyl for PC," *Remix* 4 (December 2002): 72–74.

13. DJ A-Trak, e-mail message to author, 26 August 2002. See also Michael Endelman, "Scratching without Vinyl: A Hip-Hop Revolution," *New York Times,* 3 December 2002, E4, online at www.nytimes.com/2002/12/03/arts/03SCRA.html.

14. Christie Z-Pabon, e-mail message to author, 16 November 2002.

15. Rob Swift, interview with author, Roslyn, Virginia, 6 July 2001.

16. See Oliver Wang, "Legions of Boom: Filipino American Disc Jockeys in the San Francisco Bay Area, 1970s–1990s" (Ph.D. diss., University of California, Berkeley, 2004).

17. DJ A-Trak, e-mail message to author, 26 August 2002.

18. Routine by DJ Dexta, on *Technics World DJ Championship 1999* (1999), DMC videocassette VWF 99.

19. This routine is included on *The Allies Present: Allstar Beatdown July 20, 2001,* Turntable Thugs videocassette, 2001.

20. Roli Rho, quoted in *Scratch Academy Semester 1,* ScratchVideo Productions DVD, 2003.

21. Supa Dave, conversation with author, Baltimore, 25 April 2002.

22. Christine Z-Pabon, e-mail announcement for the 2001 Zulu Nation DJ Battle, 29 October 2001.

23. Z-Pabon, e-mail message to author, 16 November 2002.

24. Rob Swift, quoted in Chris Macias, "X-tra Strength Funk," *Heckler Magazine,* online at www.heckler.com/old_heckler/5.6/music/xecutioners .html (viewed 31 March 2002; now defunct).

25. For more detailed explanations of these terms, interested readers may consult the wide variety of DJ tutorials, available in many forms. Videos include *Turntable Wizardry Stage 1* (Up Above videocassette, no label number, n.d.); *Shure Turntablism 101* (Shure videocassette TT101, 2000); and *DJ QBerts Complete Do-It-Yourself,* Vol. 1: *Skratching* (Thud-Rumble DVD, DIY001-DVD, n.d.). Stephen Webber's *Turntable Technique: The Art of the DJ* (Boston: Berklee Press, 2000) consists of a book and two LPs. A number of Internet tutorials have come and gone in recent years, a good one (as of mid-2003) being The Ever, billed as "The Most Comprehensive Scratch Tutorial Ever," at www.asisphonics.net/ theever.html. My thanks to Felicia Miyakawa for telling me of this site.

26. Hebdige, *Cut 'n' Mix,* 142.

27. Sugarcuts, conversation with author, New York City, 5 June 2002.

28. Swift, interview with author. The lack of improvisation distinguishes DJ battles from MC (rap) battles, in which contestants are expected to improvise to a certain extent. Part of the difference between battles stems from the fact that in DJ battles, the records determine the material of the routine, while MCs have more flexibility. MC battles have become more popular of late, due in part to the success of the 2002 film *8 Mile,* starring rapper Eminem. The raucous battle scenes in the film nicely capture the atmosphere of both MC and DJ battles, though battles of both types tend to be more racially and ethnically diverse than depicted in the film.

29. I.Emerge is a New York–based turntablist whose crew affiliations include the 5th Platoon, the Zulu Kings New York, and the Fader Bal-

listix Crew. This routine appears on the CD through the kind permission of its composer. The World Series Turntable Championship is an unusual battle in that it is conducted entirely on the Internet, with routines submitted online by DJs around the world. The other routines by I.Emerge and his competitors may be heard at http://bionicstylus.com/final2003.html.

30. I.Emerge, telephone conversation with author, 23 June 2003. My analysis of this routine is greatly indebted to this discussion.

31. The intent of this message is clearly to intimidate, though in its original context—the animated children's movie *Shrek*—the effect is somewhat less menacing.

32. Robert Walser, *Running with the Devil: Power, Gender, and Madness in Heavy Metal Music* (Hanover, NH: Wesleyan University Press, 1993), 109.

33. DJ Babu, on *Turntable Wizardry Stage 1* videocassette. Anecdotally, it is said that turntablism, and hip-hop in general, emerged in New York at a time when funding for school music programs was being drastically cut. It may be that rapping and DJing emerged as alternatives.

34. See Clyde Haberman, "New Vandals Scratching Up the Subways," *New York Times,* 26 January 1999, B1. The link between the two forms of scratching is made explicit on the cover of the X-Ecutioners 1997 album *X-pressions* (Asphodel compact disc 0977), which features a photograph of the group's name scratched into a subway car window.

35. For scholarly discussions of signifying, see Claudia Mitchell-Kernan, "Signifying, in *Mother Wit from the Laughing Barrel: Readings in the Interpretation of Afro-American Folklore,* ed. Alan Dundes (Englewood Cliffs, NJ: Prentice-Hall, 1973), 310–28; and Henry Louis Gates Jr., *The Signifying Monkey: A Theory of African-American Literary Criticism* (New York, Oxford University Press, 1988).

36. Several examples of cutting contests are described in Crow, ed., *Jazz Anecdotes,* 89–100.

37. Thurmon Garner, "Playing the Dozens: Folklore as Strategies for Living," *Quarterly Journal of Speech* 69 (1983): 47–57; Robin D. G. Kelley, *Yo' Mama's Disfunktional! Fighting the Culture Wars in Urban America* (Boston: Beacon, 1997), 32–35.

38. John Dollard, "The Dozens: Dialectic of Insult," *American Imago* 1 (1939): 3–25; Roger D. Abrahams, "Playing the Dozens," *Journal of American Folklore* 75 (1962): 209–20. These essays are reprinted in Dundes, ed., *Mother Wit from the Laughing Barrel,* 277–94 and 295–309, respectively.

39. Peretti, *Creation of Jazz,* 27, 114–15.

40. Ibid., 27.

41. *Turntable Wizardry Stage 1* videocassette.
42. Z-Pabon, e-mail message to author.
43. Deborah Tannen, *Talking from 9 to 5* (New York: Morrow, 1994), 236. See also Walter J. Ong, *Fighting for Life: Contest, Sexuality, and Consciousness* (Ithaca, NY: Cornell University Press, 1981).
44. Tricia Rose, *Black Noise: Rap Music and Black Culture in Contemporary Culture* (Hanover, N.H.: Wesleyan University Press, 1994), 57.
45. According to John Carluccio, director of the *Battle Sounds* documentary, battles are sometimes described as "almanacs," for battle videos circulate widely within the DJ community and are closely studied by turntablists (telephone conversation with author, 16 October 2001).

CHAPTER SEVEN

1. "Funky Drummer" was originally released as an LP on King 6290 in 1970. It has been reissued on *Star Time,* Polydor compact disc 849 108.
2. Many more examples of "Funky Drummer" borrowings are cited at the Sample FAQ, a generally reliable resource for identifying samples in popular music, www.the-breaks.com/perl/search.pl?term=Funky+Drummer&type=4.
3. Examples include Beastie Boys, "So Wat'cha Want" (1992); Fugees, "Fugee-La" (1996); Beck, "Where It's At" (1997); Whiskeytown, "What the Devil Wanted" (2001); Wagon Christ, "Perkission" (2001); and Oasis, "Hindu Times" (2002). For more examples and an interesting discussion of the purposeful addition of "transduction noise" in recent pop music, see Stan Link, "The Work of Reproduction in the Mechanical Aging of an Art: Listening to Noise," *Computer Music Journal* 25 (spring 2001): 34–47.
4. F. Richard Moore, *Elements of Computer Music* (Englewood Cliffs, NJ: Prentice-Hall, 1990), 27.
5. Paul Lansky, *Notjustmoreidlechatter,* on *More Than Idle Chatter* (Bridge compact disc BCD 9050). Lansky's other "chatter works" are *Idle Chatter* (1985), *just_more_idle_chatter* (1987), and *Idle Chatter Junior* (1999). The first two are included on *More Than Idle Chatter;* the most recent was released in 2000 on Paul Lansky, *Ride* (Bridge compact disc BCD 9103). Lansky also manipulates speech, though in different ways, in several works on *Conversation Pieces* (Bridge compact disc BCD 9083).
6. Paul Lansky, e-mail message to author, 28 June 2001.
7. Paul Lansky, e-mail message to author, 7 April 2003.
8. www.cdemusic.org/artists/lansky.html.
9. "Praise You" was released on *You've Come a Long Way, Baby* (Skint compact disc BRASSIC11CD 66247–2); "Take Yo' Praise" has been re-released on *The Iron Pot Cooker* (Vanguard compact disc 79356-2).

10.   Norman Cook, telephone interview with author, 10 August 2003.

11.   Michael Gelfand, "Private Lesson: The Art of the Gag—Reflections on Sampling from Fat Boy Slim," *Musician* 234 (May 1998): 18–19.

12.   Camille Yarbrough, telephone interview with author, 15 July 2001. Unless otherwise noted, all following quotations of Yarbrough come from this source as well.

13.   Review posted 17 April 2000 at www.epinions.com/musc-review-7CEE -132C3929-38FBF273-prod5. I did find one review that actually interpreted the lyrics. The reviewer, who wanted to have the song played at his wedding, explained: "To me these words pretty much sum up every couple in the world. Two people that love and care for one another through thick and thin" (www.epinions.com/musc-review-646 -3A14354C-3A1AEE0D-prod6, posted 21 November 2000).

14.   I base this assessment on the reactions I have gotten to the song when presenting it to students and acquaintances.

15.   Cook, telephone interview with author.

16.   Dickinson, "'Believe'?" 343.

17.   Cook, telephone interview with author.

18.   Ibid.

19.   Brian O'Connor, "The Funk Soul Brother: As Fatboy Slim, UK DJ Norman Cook Leads the BigBeat Parade—And Laughs All the Way to the Bank," *DJ Times* 11 (November 1998): 26.

20.   Camille Yarbrough, conversation with author, Baltimore, 2 April 2002.

21.   See, for example, Juan Carlos Thom, note in the *Loyola Entertainment Law Journal* 8 (1988): 181, cited in Siva Vaidhyanathan, *Copyrights and Copywrongs: The Rise of Intellectual Property and How It Threatens Creativity* (New York: New York University Press, 2001), 134; J. D. Considine, "Larcenous Art?" *Rolling Stone,* no. 580 (14 June 1990): 107–8; Paul Myers, "Art or Theft? Sampling Opinions on Copyright," *Electronic Musician* 14 (November 1998): 44.

22.   Robert Walser offers a transcription of this groove in his analysis of "Fight the Power" in "Rhythm, Rhyme, and Rhetoric in the Music of Public Enemy," *Ethnomusicology* 39 (spring–summer 1995): 201.

23.   In hip-hop, there is typically a division of labor between the rappers, who write and perform the vocal part of a song, and the producer(s), who compose the accompaniment—referred to as the rhythm track or the beats—but do not perform. The opening section of "Fight the Power" and the rhythm track for the whole song were created by the Bomb Squad, Public Enemy's production team. Published interviews of the rappers and the production team make it clear, however, that there was a close collaboration in the creation of the tracks and the lyrics in *Fear of a Black Planet,* the album on which "Fight the Power" appears.

See Mark Dery, "Public Enemy: Confrontation," *Keyboard* 16 (September 1990): 81–96.

24. Ibid., 92.

25. For more on the relationship between DJing and producing, see Schloss, "Making Beats," 65–74.

26. Dery, "Public Enemy," 92.

27. Olly Wilson, "The Heterogeneous Sound Ideal in African-American Music," in *Signifyin(g), Sanctifyin', and Slam Dunking: A Reader in African American Expressive Culture,* ed. Gena Dagel Caponi (Amherst: University of Massachusetts Press, 1999), 159.

28. Chuck D. proves prescient here, for Elvis Presley, who is derided earlier in the song as "straight up racist," was put on a United States postage stamp to great fanfare in 1992, not long after the release of the song.

29. Bobby McFerrin's "Don't Worry, Be Happy" is also cited, though this sunny song is held up for derision.

30. Rose, *Black Noise,* 71.

31. Jake One, quoted in Schloss, "Making Beats," 79.

32. Stetsasonic, "Talkin' All that Jazz" (1988), on *In Full Gear* (Tommy Boy compact disc 1459).

33. Gates, *Signifying Monkey,* 51.

34. For a discussion of the way that music problematizes this distinction, see Vaidhyanathan, *Copyrights and Copywrongs,* 117–18.

35. Dery, "Public Enemy," 92.

CHAPTER EIGHT

1. All Music Guide, www.allmusic.com/cg/amg.dll?p=amg&uid=UIDSUB 040401021529162800&sql=Absuw6j7271y0.

2. T. Taylor, *Strange Sounds,* 3.

3. There are other file-compression formats, such as Windows Media Audio (WMA), Real Audio, Ogg Vorbis, and AAC. However, I will be focusing on MP3, as it is the current de facto standard for file-sharing.

4. Charles C. Mann, "The Heavenly Jukebox," *Atlantic Monthly* 286 (September 2000): 53, online at www.theatlantic.com/issues/2000/09/mann .htm.

5. My thanks to Christopher Burns for clarifying the concept of perceptual coding to me. For a very lucid explanation of perceptual coding and, more generally, the process of creating MP3 files, see Paul Sellars, "Behind the Mask—Perceptual Coding: How MP3 Compression Works," *Sound on Sound* (May 2000), www.sospubs.co.uk/sos/may00/ articles/mp3.htm.

It should also be noted that not all MP3s have the same sound quality. The sound quality depends on the bit rate—the average number of bits (1s or 0s in binary code) used to represent one second of sound. For MP3s, a rate of 128 kilobits (128,000 bits) produces near CD-quality sound but generates only about one-twelfth the amount of data as a CD. Lower bit rates produce lower-quality sound but allow greater compression, while higher bit rates more closely approximate the sound quality of the original CD but at the expense of compression.

6. For more on the workings of P2P networks, see Andy Oram, ed., *Peer-to-Peer: Harnessing the Power of Disruptive Technologies* (Sebastopol, CA: O'Reilly, 2001); Hassan Fattah, *P2P: How Peer-to-Peer Technology Is Revolutionizing the Way We Do Business* (Chicago: Dearborn, 2002); Dejan S. Milojicic, et al., "Peer-to-Peer Computing," technical report, Hewlett-Packard Co., 8 March 2002, www.hpl.hp.com/techreports/2002/HPL-2002-57.pdf, viewed 29 July 2002.

7. For Napster usage statistics, see "Jupiter Media Metrix Reports Multi-Country Napster Usage Statistics for February 2001," *Jupiter Research,* 5 April 2001, http://www.jupiterresearch.com/xp/jmm/press/2001/pr_040501.html (now defunct). For more on the Napster phenomenon, see Spencer E. Ante, "Inside Napster," *Business Week* (14 August 2000): 112–20, online at www.businessweek.com/2000/00_33/b3694001.htm; and Trevor Merriden, *Irresistible Forces: The Business Legacy of Napster and the Growth of the Underground Internet* (Oxford: Capstone, 2001).

8. For more on Gnutella and Kazaa, see Ariana Eunjung Cha, "E-Power to the People: New Software Bypasses Internet Service Providers," *Washington Post,* 18 May 2000, p. A1; and Ariana Eunjung Cha, "File Swapper Eluding Pursuers," *Washington Post,* 20 December 2002, A1, online at www.washingtonpost.com/wp-dyn/articles/A19821-2002Dec20.html.

9. Quoted in John Perry Barlow, "The Economy of Ideas," *Wired* 2 (March 1994): 85, online at www.wired.com/wired/archive/2.03/economy.ideas.html.

10. Lawrence Lessig, *The Future of Ideas: The Fate of the Commons in a Connected World* (New York: Random House, 2001), 116. For more on the nature of rivalrous and nonrivalrous resources, see esp. pp. 21–22, 94–97, and 115–16.

11. Ipsos-Insight, "File-Sharing and CD Burning Remain Steady in 2002," 20 February 2003, www.ipsos-pa.com/dsp_displaypr_us.cfm?id_to _view=1743. Since new research is conducted and published regularly, interested readers are encouraged to consult the latest studies (easily accessible on the Internet) to find the most recent data.

12. Ipsos-Reid, "The Digital Music Landscape, and Research on It," www.ipsos-reid.com/us/services/syndicated/dsp_TEMPO_charts .cfm#globalMusic (viewed 17 June 2002; now defunct).

13. "The African Internet—A Status Report," http://demiurge.wn.apc.org/africa/afstat.htm.

14. *Arab Human Development Report 2002* (New York: United Nations Development Programme, Regional Bureau for Arab States, 2002), 73–84 and 156, online at www.undp.org/rbas/ahdr/english2002.html.

15. The survey, which I posted on the Internet in the summer of 2002 and advertised on a variety of Internet bulletin boards, asked for basic demographic information (age, gender, race, location) and file-sharing habits (programs used, numbers of MP3s collected, types of music downloaded, etc.). The main purpose of the survey was not to generate statistics on the prevalence of file-sharing but to solicit prose statements explaining respondents' attitudes toward file-sharing and its impact on their listening habits. I received more than one hundred responses to my questionnaire from downloaders aged thirteen to sixty living throughout North America and Europe. Although it was an unscientific survey, nearly all of the statements I quote in this chapter were echoed by many other respondents, suggesting that the sentiments I cite are widely shared.

16. Electric Boys Tribute site, http://electricboys.com/bonus.html.

17. VietnameseClick, www.soundclick.com/bands/vietnameseclick_music.htm.

18. I should note that I found these MP3s on the World Wide Web and not through a P2P network. Although I could also find them on P2Ps, it is difficult to target such quirky genres, especially without performers' names or song titles, on most file-sharing search engines.

19. Ipsos-Reid, "File Sharing and CD Burners Proliferate," 12 June 2002, www.ipsos-na.com/news/pressrelease.cfm?id=1542.

20. Claire Kim, unpublished paper, 23 April 2002.

21. Amy Chernuchin, unpublished paper, 23 April 2002.

22. Ipsos-Reid, "Fee-Based Online Music Faces Uphill Battle," 25 February 2002, www.ipsos-reid.com/media/dsp_displaypr_us.cfm?id_to_view=1439.

23. John Borland, "Study: File Sharing Boosts Music Sales," *C/Net News*, 3 May 2002, http://news.com.com/2100-1023-898813.html?tag=rn.

24. Irene Hsu, unpublished paper, 23 April 2002.

25. Jonathan Groce, unpublished paper, 23 April 2002; Rachel Gallico, unpublished paper, 23 April 2002. An interesting opposing view came from a fifteen-year-old female survey respondent who wrote that file-sharing allowed her to get recordings that her parents wouldn't buy for her on CD because of objectionable cover art (and perhaps parental advisory stickers as well). "My parents are the kind that judge a book by its cover," she explained.

26. Emily Le, unpublished paper, 23 April 2002.

27. Aidan Smith, unpublished paper, 23 April 2002.

28. www.musicplayer.com/thetrackexchange/ (viewed 14 July 2002; site defunct).

29. www.zpoc.com/index.php.

30. Information on the Internet opera club was provided to me by two of its members who responded to my survey and answered follow-up questions via e-mail. Bill Burkhart, e-mail to author, 15 July 2002; Eva Noren, e-mail to author, 18 July 2002.

31. Community in cyberspace (musical and otherwise) has been the subject of a good deal of scholarly attention. See, for example, Howard Rheingold, *Virtual Community: Homesteading on the Electronic Frontier* (Reading, MA: Addison Wesley, 1993); Arthur Lizie Jr., "Community and Identity in Cyberspace: Popular Music and the International Flow of Information" (Ph.D. diss., Temple University, 2000); and Marc Smith and Peter Kollock, eds., *Communities in Cyberspace* (London: Routledge, 2001).

32. Ipsos-Reid, "Fee-Based Online Music Faces Uphill Battle."

33. Recording Industry Association of America, Frequently Asked Questions—Downloading and Uploading, www.riaa.com/issues/music/downup_faq.asp.

34. Links to many of the notable rulings on online music in 1999 and 2000 may be found at http://www.cnn.com/LAW/library/documents/index.html#copyright.

35. From opinion on *A&M Records, Inc., v. Napster, Inc.*, U.S. Court of Appeals for the Ninth Circuit, No. 00-16401, argued and submitted 2 October 2000, filed 12 February 2001, online at http://i.cnn.net/cnn/LAW/library/documents/napster/napsterop0212.pdf.

36. See Brad King, "The Day the Napster Died," *Wired News,* 15 May 2002, www.wired.com/news/mp3/0,1285,52540,00.html.

37. *Metro-Goldwyn-Mayer (MGM) Studios, Inc., v. Grokster, Ltd.;* see Frank Ahrens, "File-Swap Sites Not Infringing, Judge Says: Firms Held Blameless for Copyright Violations," *Washington Post,* 26 April 2003, E1, online at www.washingtonpost.com/wp-dyn/articles/A39322-2003.html.

38. Jay Lyman, "RIAA Tactics in Question after Dismissal of Suit," *TechNewsWorld,* 25 September 2003, www.technewsworld.com/perl/story/31675.html.

39. Quoted in Scott Carlson, "Record Industry Will Send Warnings to Millions of Users of 2 File-Sharing Services," *Chronicle of Higher Education,* 30 April 2003, A36, online at http://chronicle.com/free/2003/04/2003043001t.htm.

40. Anonymous executive quoted in Dawn C. Chmielewski, "Music Industry Swamps Swap Networks with Phony Files," *Silicon Valley,* 27 June 2002, www.siliconvalley.com/mld/siliconvalley/3560365.htm. See also David Segal, "A New Tactic in the Download War," *Washington Post,* 20 August 2002, A1, A8.

41. Declan McCullagh, "Attack Disables Music Industry Web Site," *C/NET News,* 29 July 2002, http://news.com.com/2100-1023-947072.html.

42. www.boycott-riaa.com/ See also the Electronic Frontier Foundation, www.eff.org.

43. Not everyone who downloads MP3s feels this sense of righteousness. A handful of respondents to my survey expressed reservations about their actions. One stopped downloading altogether once the Napster decision was announced; another called file-sharing immoral.

44. Barlow, "Economy of Ideas," 88.

45. John Perry Barlow, "The Next Economy of Ideas," *Wired* 8 (October 2000): 240, online at www.wired.com/wired/archive/8.10/download .html.

46. The scope and definition of copyright is admirably explained in Vaidhyanathan, *Copyrights and Copywrongs,* 20–26.

47. Ibid., 11.

48. U.S. Constitution, art. I, sec. 8, clause 8. The Supreme Court reaffirmed the purpose of copyright in 1984, asserting that copyright law seeks a balance between "the interests of authors . . . in the control and exploitation of their writings . . . on the one hand, and society's competing interests in the flow of ideas . . . on the other hand" (*Sony Corp. of America v. Universal Studios,* 464 U.S. 429 [1984]; cited in Jon O. Newman, "New Lyrics for an Old Melody: The Idea/Expression Dichotomy in the Computer Age," *Cardozo Arts and Entertainment Law Journal* 17 [2000]: 981–93; online at www.cardozo.yu.edu/news_events/papers/4.pdf).

49. Lessig, *Future of Ideas,* 116.

50. Indeed, due to industry practices, recording musicians often fail to make money (and may even lose money) even on highly successful albums that generate huge sums for the record companies. For two insiders' perspectives on this issue, see Steve Albini, "The Problem with Music," www.negativland.com/albini.html; and Courtney Love, "Courtney Love Does the Math," *Salon,* 14 June 2000, www.salon.com/tech/feature/ 2000/06/14/love/.

51. Stan Liebowitz, "Will MP3 Downloads Annihilate the Record Industry? The Evidence So Far," June 2003, www.utdallas.edu/~liebowit/ intprop/records.pdf.

52. The full opinion can be found at http://laws.findlaw.com/us/000/01-618 .html.

53.   See "Alanis: Major Label System 'Not Working,'" *Billboard,* 23 June 2001, www.billboard.com/billboard/daily/article_display.jsp?vnu_content_id=964592; Chuck D., " . . . And Just What Exactly Do We Do This For?" *Public Enemy,* 12 July 2002, www.publicenemy.com/index .php?page=page3&item=58; Janis Ian, "The Internet Debacle—An Alternative View," http://janisian.com/article-internet_debacle.html; "Prince Voices Support for Napster," *Reuters,* 9 August 2000, http://news.com .com/2100-1023-244282.html (now defunct); and "Negativland Statement in Support of Peer-to-Peer File Sharing," 21 July 2002, www.eff.org/ IP/P2P/MGM_v_Grokster/20020121_negativland_essay.html.

54.   Vaidhyanathan, *Copyrights and Copywrongs,* 15–16.

55.   The "fair use clause" may be found in the United States Code, USC Title 17, chap. 1, sec. 107.

56.   One practice *not* treated as fair by the music industry is the quotation of song lyrics, though it is the threat of financially devastating lawsuits, not legal precedent, that has established this as an "exception" to fair use. For example, it cost me $150 to quote the four lines of Billy Joel's "The Entertainer" in chapter 1. I am told I got off easy.

57.   For a variety of compulsory licensing proposals, see Matthew Montfort, "An Open Letter Offering a Solution Allowing Music File Sharing on the Internet," 14 March 2001, www.ancient-future.com/cogressletter1 .html; "House Subcommittee Holds Hearing on Compulsory Licensing of Music on the Internet," *Tech Law Journal,* 17 May 2001, www .techlawjournal.com/intelpro/20010517.asp; and Jefferson Graham, "Kazaa, Verizon Propose to Pay Artists Directly," *USA Today,* 13 May 2002, online at www.usatoday.com/life/cyber/tech/2002/05/14/music-kazaa .htm.

58.   See Graham, "Kazaa, Verizon Propose to Pay Artists Directly"; and Anna Wilde Mathews et al., "The Music Industry Is Finally Online, but Few Listen," *Wall Street Journal,* 7 May 2002, A1, A20.

59.   For more on the iTunes Music Store, see its website, www.apple.com/ music/store/; and Neil Strauss, "Apple Finds the Future for Online Music Sales," *New York Times,* 29 May 2003, B1, B8. Another promising early service, Listen.com's Rhapsody, is profiled in Leslie Walker, "Online Music Sites Seek Paying Customers," *Washington Post,* 16 February 2003, H7, online at www.washingtonpost.com/wp-dyn/articles/ A10727-2003Feb14.html.

60.   See Jenny Eliscu, "New CD Bait: Record Labels Hope Album Extras Bring Buyers Back to Stores," *Rolling Stone,* no. 908 (31 October 2002): 32.

61.   This may also help explain why electronic books, or e-books, pose little threat to their paper counterparts. See Linton Weeks, "E-Books Not

Exactly Flying Off the Shelves," *Washington Post*, 6 July 2002, C1, online at www.washingtonpost.com/wp-dyn/articles/A30379-2002Jul5 .html.

62.   Sarah Deutsch, quoted in Graham, "Kazaa, Verizon Propose to Pay Artists Directly."

CONCLUSION

1.   Paul Valéry, "The Conquest of Ubiquity," [1929], quoted in Walter Benjamin, "The Work of Art in the Age of Mechanical Reproduction," in *Illuminations* (New York: Harcourt Brace & World, 1968), 219.

2.   John Pfeiffer, interview with Mark Katz, New York City, 15 June 1995. Pfeiffer worked as an engineer and then producer for RCA Victor (later BMG) from the late 1940s until his death in 1996, collaborating with many of the great classical musicians of the twentieth century.

3.   "Die Maschine ist weder ein Gott noch ein Teufel." H. H. Stuckenschmidt, "Mechanisierung," *Musikblätter des Anbruch* 8 (October–November 1926): 346.

4.   Marshall McLuhan, "The Medium Is the Message" (1964), in *Understanding Media: The Extensions of Man* (Cambridge: MIT Press, 1994), 7–21.

REFERENCES

BOOKS, ARTICLES, AND WEBSITES

Abrahams, Roger D. "Playing the Dozens." *Journal of American Folklore* 75 (1962): 209–20. Reprinted in *Mother Wit from the Laughing Barrel: Readings in the Interpretation of Afro-American Folklore,* ed. Alan Dundes, 295–309. Englewood Cliffs, NJ: Prentice Hall, 1973.

Adams, Alton A. "John Philip Sousa as Man and Musician, 1854–1932." In *Culture at the Crossroads: The Memoirs and Writings of Alton Augustus Adams,* ed. Mark Clague. Berkeley and Los Angeles: University of California Press, forthcoming.

Adorno, Theodor. "On the Fetish Character in Music and the Regression of Listening." In *Essays on Music,* ed. Richard Leppert, 283–87. Berkeley and Los Angeles: University of California Press, 2002.

———"Opera and the Long-Playing Record." Trans. Thomas Y. Levin. In *Essays on Music,* ed. Richard Leppert, 288–317. Berkeley and Los Angeles: University of California Press, 2002.

———. "The Radio Symphony." In *Essays on Music,* ed. Richard Leppert, 251–69. Berkeley and Los Angeles: University of California Press, 2002.

Aeolian Company. "The Aeolian Vocalion: The Phonograph of Richer Tone That You Can Play." Brochure, 1915.

"The African Internet—A Status Report." http://demiurge.wn.apc.org/africa/afstat.htm.

Ahrens, Frank. "File-Swap Sites Not Infringing, Judge Says: Firms Held Blameless for Copyright Violations." *Washington Post,* 26 April 2003, E1. Online at www.washingtonpost.com/wp-dyn/articles/A39322-2003Apr25.html.

Ake, David. *Jazz Cultures.* Berkeley and Los Angeles: University of California Press, 2002.

Albini, Steve. "The Problem with Music." www.negativland.com/albini.html.

Ante, Spencer E. "Inside Napster." *Business Week*, 14 August 2000, 112–20. Online at www.businessweek.com/2000/00_33/b3694001.htm.

Arab Human Development Report 2002. New York: United Nations Development Programme, Regional Bureau for Arab States, 2002. Online at www.undp.org/rbas/ahdr/english2002.html.

ArtistLed. www.artistled.com.

Attali, Jacques. *Noise: The Political Economy of Music*. Trans. Brian Massumi. Minneapolis: University of Minnesota Press, 1985.

Auer, Leopold. *Violin Playing as I Teach It*. New York: Stokes, 1921.

Badal, James. *Recording the Classics: Maestros, Music, and Technology*. Kent, OH: Kent State University Press, 1996.

Baillot, Pierre Marie François de Sales. *The Art of the Violin*. Ed. and trans. Louise Goldberg. Evanston, IL: Northwestern University Press, 1991.

Baker, David. "The Phonograph in Jazz History and its Influence on the Emergent Jazz Performer." In *The Phonograph and Our Musical Life: Proceedings of a Centennial Conference*, ed. H. Wiley Hitchcock, 45–50. Brooklyn, NY: ISAM, 1980.

Barlow, John Perry. "The Economy of Ideas." *Wired* 2 (March 1994): 84–90, 126–29. Online at www.wired.com/wired/archive/2.03/economy.ideas.html.

———. "The Next Economy of Ideas." *Wired* 8 (October 2000): 238–52. Online at www.wired.com/wired/archive/8.10/download.html.

Bartók, Béla. "Mechanical Music." In *Béla Bartók Essays*, ed. Benjamin Suchoff, 289–98. London: Faber & Faber, 1976.

"Before We Go to the Opera." *National Music Monthly* 1 (August 1917): 41.

Bellamy, Edward. *Looking Backward, 2000–1887*. Boston: Ticknor, 1888.

———. "With the Eyes Shut." *Harper's New Monthly* 79 (1889): 736–45.

Benjamin, Walter. "The Work of Art in the Age of Mechanical Reproduction." In *Illuminations*, ed. Hannah Arendt, trans. Harry Zohn, 219–53. New York: Harcourt Brace & World, 1968.

Bennett, H. Stith. "The Realities of Practice." In *On Record: Rock, Pop, and the Written Word*, ed. Simon Frith and Andrew Goodwin, 221–37. New York: Pantheon, 1990.

Bériot, Charles de. *Méthode de violon*. Mainz, [1858]. Translated as *Ch. De Beriot's Celebrated Method for the Violin*. New York: Carl Fischer, 1892.

Berliner, Paul F. *Thinking in Jazz: The Infinite Art of Improvisation*. Chicago: University of Chicago Press, 1994.

Berton, Ralph. *Remembering Bix: A Memoir of the Jazz Age*. New York: Harper & Row, 1974.

Bescoby-Chambers, John. *The Archives of Sound*. Lingfield, Eng.: Oakwood, 1966.

Birge, Edward Bailey. *History of Public School Music in the United States.* Rev. ed. Boston: Oliver Ditson, 1939; repr. Reston, VA: Music Educators National Conference, 1988.

———. "Music Appreciation—The Education of the Listener." *Papers and Proceedings of the Music Teachers' National Association* 17 (1923): 189–93.

Bissing, Petrowitch. *Cultivation of the Violin Vibrato Tone.* Chicago: Central States Music, 1914.

Blaukopf, Kurt. *Musical Life in a Changing Society.* Trans. David Marinelli. Portland, OR: Amadeus, 1992.

Block, Ursula, and Michael Glasmeier. *Broken Music: Artists' Recordworks.* Berlin: Daadgalerie Berlin, 1989.

Blum, Jason. "Stanton Final Scratch: Digital Vinyl for PC." *Remix* 4 (December 2002): 72–74.

Bonavia, Ferruccio. "On Vibrato." *Musical Times* 68 (1 December 1927): 1077–78.

———. "Violin Playing during the Past Fifty Years." *Strad* 50 (May 1939): 7–9.

Borland, John. "Study: File Sharing Boosts Music Sales." *C/Net News,* 3 May 2002. http://news.com.com/2100-1023-898813.html.

Bowen, José Antonio. "Tempo, Duration, and Flexibility: Techniques in the Analysis of Performance." *Journal of Musicological Research* 15 (1996): 111–56.

Boyden, David D., with Sonya Monosoff. "Violin Technique." In *The New Grove Violin Family,* 36–103. New York: Norton, 1989.

The-Breaks. www.the-breaks.com

Brewster, Bill, and Frank Broughton. *Last Night a DJ Saved My Life.* New York: Grove Press, 2000.

Brown, Clive. "Bowing Styles, Vibrato, and Portamento in Nineteenth-Century Violin Playing." *Journal of the Royal Musical Association* 113 (1988): 97–128.

Bytovetski, Pavel L. *How to Master the Violin.* Boston: Oliver Ditson, 1917.

Cage, John. *Imaginary Landscape No. 1.* New York: Peters, 1960.

Capet, Lucien. *La Technique supériere de l'archet.* Paris: Maurice Senart, 1916.

Carlson, Scott. "Record Industry Will Send Warnings to Millions of Users of Two File-Sharing Services." *Chronicle of Higher Education,* 30 April 2003, A36. Online at http://chronicle.com/free/2003/04/2003043001t.htm.

Carol-Bérard. "Recorded Noises—Tomorrow's Instrumentation." *Modern Music* 6 (January–February 1929): 26–29.

Cauthen, Joyce H. *With Fiddle and Well-Rosined Bow: Old-Time Fiddling in Alabama.* Tuscaloosa: University of Alabama Press, 1989.

Cecil, George. "The Phonograph as an Aid to Students of Singing." *Etude* 21 (1903): 482.

Cha, Ariana Eunjung. "E-Power to the People: New Software Bypasses Internet Service Providers." *Washington Post,* 18 May 2000, A1.

———. "File Swapper Eluding Pursuers." *Washington Post,* 20 December 2002, A1. Online at www.washingtonpost.com/wp-dyn/articles/ A19821-2002Dec20 .html.

Chanan, Michael. *Repeated Takes: A Short History of Recording and Its Effects on Music.* London: Verso, 1995.

Chevan, David. "The Double Bass as a Solo Instrument in Early Jazz." *Black Perspective in Music* 17 (1989): 73–92.

———. "Written Music in Early Jazz." Ph.D. diss., City University of New York, 1997.

Chmielewski, Dawn C. "Music Industry Swamps Swap Networks with Phony Files." *SiliconValley.com,* 27 June 2002. www.siliconvalley.com/mld/siliconvalley/ 3560365.htm.

Chuck D. " . . . And Just What Exactly Do We Do This For?" *Public Enemy,* 12 July 2002. www.publicenemy.com/index.php?page=page8&item=58.

Clark, Frances Elliott. "What School Facilities Should be Provided for Instruction by Means of Motion-Picture Machines, Stereo-opticon Lanterns, Phonographs, Player-Pianos, etc. Part B." *Journal of the Proceedings and Addresses of the National Education Association* 50 (1912): 1234–37.

Clements, Cary. "Augustus Stroh and the Famous Stroh Violin." *Experimental Musical Instruments* 10 (June 1995): 8–15; 11 (September 1995): 38–39.

Clementson, W. Arthur B. "The Sound Reproducing Machine in the Country School." *Etude* 46 (November 1928): 840.

Cocks, Jay. "Fans, You Know It's True; Milli Vanilli Controversy." *Time* 136 (3 December 1990): 123.

Cole, Lucy K. "Music and the Social Problem." *Journal of the Proceedings and Addresses of the National Education Association* 51 (1913): 604–9.

Coleman, Robert J. *The Victrola in Music Memory Contests.* Camden, NJ: Victor Talking Machine Co., 1922.

Columbia Graphophone Company. *The Grafonola in the Classroom.* New York: Columbia Graphophone Co., 1920.

Considine, J. D. "Larcenous Art?" *Rolling Stone,* no. 580 (14 June 1990): 107–8.

Cook, Susan. *Opera for a New Republic: The Zeitopern of Křenek, Weill, and Hindemith.* Ann Arbor, MI: UMI Research Press, 1988.

Copland, Aaron. "The World of the Phonograph." *American Scholar* 6 (1937): 27–38.

Corey, N. J. "The Place of the Talking Machine in Music Teaching." *Etude* 24 (1906): 672, 680.

Cowan, Ruth Schwartz. *A Social History of American Technology.* New York: Oxford University Press, 1997.

Crawford, Richard. *The American Musical Landscape.* Berkeley and Los Angeles: University of California Press, 1993.

Crespin, Régine. *On Stage, Off Stage: A Memoir.* Trans. G. S. Bourdain. Boston: Northeastern University Press, 1997.

Cross, Lowell. "Electronic Music, 1948–1953." *Perspectives of New Music* 7 (fall–winter 1968): 32–65.

Crow, Bill, ed. *Jazz Anecdotes.* New York: Oxford University Press, 1990.

Crutchfield, Will. "Historical Playing Styles: Myth and Reality." *New York Times,* 12 August 1990, H25, H30.

Dammert, Hansjörg. "Grammophon-Konzerte." *Musikblätter des Anbruch* 8 (October–November 1926): 406–7.

Darrell, R. D. "Are American Homes Musical?" *Phonograph Monthly Review* 1 (November 1926): 13–14, 16.

Davidson, Jane W. "Visual Perception of Performance Manner in the Movements of Solo Musicians." *Psychology of Music* 21 (1993): 103–13.

Davies, Hugh. "A History of Sampling." *Organised Sound* 1 (April 1996): 3–11.

Davies, Stephen. *Musical Works and Performances.* Oxford: Clarendon, 2001.

Day, Timothy. *A Century of Recorded Music: Listening to Musical History.* New Haven: Yale University Press, 2000.

Dery, Mark. "Public Enemy: Confrontation." *Keyboard* 16 (September 1990): 81–96.

De Treville, Yvonne. "Making a Phonograph Record." *Musician* 21 (November 1916): 658.

Dickinson, Kay. "'Believe'? Vocoders, Digitalised Female Identity, and Camp." *Popular Music* 20 (October 2001): 333–48.

Dillmann, Alexander. "Das Grammophon." *Die Stimme* 1 (March 1910): 10–11.

Dodds, Baby. *The Baby Dodds Story.* Rev. ed. Baton Rouge: Louisiana State University Press, 1992.

Dollard, John. "The Dozens: Dialectic of Insult." *American Imago* 1 (1939): 3–25. Reprinted in *Mother Wit from the Laughing Barrel: Readings in the Interpretation of Afro-American Folklore,* ed. Alan Dundes, 277–94. Englewood Cliffs, NJ: Prentice Hall, 1973.

Donovan, Dick. "The Stroh Violin." *Strand* 23 (January 1902): 89–91.

Drew, David. *Kurt Weill: A Handbook.* London: Faber & Faber, 1987.

Drucker, Eugene. "Recording with Rostropovich: Learning to Let the Music Speak." *Strings* 8 (July–August 1993): 56–58.

Dunham, Richard Lee. "Music Appreciation in the Public Schools." Ph.D. diss., University of Michigan, 1961.

Dwight, John Sullivan. "Music as a Means of Culture." *Atlantic* 26 (September 1870): 321–31.

Eberhardt, Siegfried. *Violin Vibrato.* Trans. Melzar Chaffee. New York: Carl Fischer, 1911.

Edison, Thomas A. "The Phonograph and Its Future." *North American Review* 126 (May–June 1878): 530–36.

Edwards, Eddie. "Once Upon a Time." In *Selections from the Gutter: Jazz Portraits from "The Jazz Record,"* ed. Art Hodes and Chadwick Hansen. Berkeley and Los Angeles: University of California Press, 1977.

"The Effect of Mechanical Instruments upon Musical Education." *Etude* 34 (1916): 483–84.

Einstein, Alfred. "Berlin's New Music Festival." *New York Times,* 17 August 1930, sec. 8, p. 5.

Eisenberg, Evan. *The Recording Angel: Explorations in Phonography.* New York: McGraw-Hill, 1987.

Eliscu, Jenny. "New CD Bait: Record Labels Hope Album Extras Bring Buyers Back to Stores." *Rolling Stone,* no. 908 (31 October 2002): 32.

Elste, Martin. "Hindemith's Experiments with the Gramophone: Long Lost Recordings Rediscovered." Paper presented at the conference for the Association for Recorded Sound Collections, Syracuse, NY, May 1998.

———. "Hindemiths Versuche 'grammophonplatten-eigene Stücke' im Kontext einer Ideengeschichte der Mechanische Musik im 20. Jahrhundert." *Hindemith Jahrbuch* 25 (1996): 195–221.

Endelman, Michael. "Scratching without Vinyl: A Hip-Hop Revolution." *New York Times,* 3 December 2002, E4.

Everett, Walter. *The Beatles as Musicians: "Revolver" through the Anthology.* New York: Oxford University Press, 1999.

Fabrizio, Timothy C., and George F. Paul. *The Talking Machine: An Illustrated Compendium, 1877–1929.* Atglen, PA: Schiffer, 1997.

Fachiri, Adila. "Trends in Violin Playing." *Music and Letters* 31 (October 1950): 282–84.

Fahri, Paul. "Akito Morita, a Man of Great Import." *Washington Post,* 5 October 1999, C1, C14.

Fattah, Hassan. *P2P: How Peer-to-Peer Technology Is Revolutionizing the Way We Do Business.* Chicago: Dearborn, 2002.

Faulkner, Anne Shaw. "Does Jazz Put the Sin in Syncopation?" *Ladies' Home Journal* 38 (August 1921): 16, 34.

————. *Music in the Home: An Aid to Parents and Teachers in the Cause of Better Listening*. Chicago: Ralph Fletcher Seymour, 1917.

————. "Phonographs and Player Instruments." *National Music Monthly* 1 (August 1917): 27–29.

————. *What We Hear in Music*. Camden, NJ: Victor Talking Machine Co., 1913.

Feaster, Patrick. "By the Round: Early Phonography and the Performance Event." Ph.D. diss., Indiana University, forthcoming.

Ferguson, Russell, ed. *Christian Marclay*. Los Angeles: UCLA Hammer Museum, 2003.

Fikentscher, Kai. *"You Better Work!": Underground Dance Music in New York City*. Hanover, NH: Wesleyan University Press, 2000.

Fisher, Dorothy B. "Women and the Phonograph." *Phonograph Monthly Review* 1 (October 1926): 30–31.

Flesch, Carl. *The Art of Violin Playing*. Vol. 1. Trans. Frederick H. Martens. New York: Carl Fischer, 1924.

————. *The Memoirs of Carl Flesch*. Trans. Hans Keller. London: Rockliff, 1957.

Fougeray, G. P. *A Student's Manual for the Mastery of French Pronunciation to Accompany the Iroquois Phonograph Records*. Syracuse, NY: Iroquois Publishing Co., 1924.

Freeman, Bud. Interview with Ms. Dance. Jazz Oral History Project, Smithsonian Institution, 1977. Transcript on deposit at the Institute of Jazz Studies, Rutgers University.

Fricke, Jim, and Charlie Ahearn. *Yes Yes Y'all: The Experience Music Project Oral History of Hip-Hop's First Decade*. Cambridge, MA: Da Capo, 2002.

Fryberger, Agnes Moore. *Listening Lessons in Music: Graded for Schools*. Boston: Silver, Burdett, 1916.

Gaisberg, Fred W. *The Music Goes Round*. New York: Macmillan, 1942.

Galantiere, Lewis H. "Machine-Made Musical Appreciation." *Music Student* 2 (February 1916): 42–47.

Garden, Mary. "The American Girl and Music." *Good Housekeeping* 56 (January 1913): 168–74.

Garner, Thurmon. "Playing the Dozens: Folklore as Strategies for Living." *Quarterly Journal of Speech* 69 (1983): 47–57.

Gates, Henry Louis, Jr. *The Signifying Monkey: A Theory of African-American Literary Criticism*. New York: Oxford University Press, 1988.

Gelatt, Roland. *The Fabulous Phonograph*. 2d rev. ed. New York: Macmillan, 1977.

Gelfand, Michael. "Private Lesson: The Art of the Gag—Reflections on Sampling from Fat Boy Slim." *Musician* 234 (May 1998): 18–19.

Gershwin, George. "The Composer in the Machine Age." In *The American Com-*

poser Speaks, ed. Gilbert Chase, 140–45. Baton Rouge: Louisiana State University Press, 1966.

Ghosh, Suman. "Impact of the Recording Industry on Hindustani Classical Music in the Last Hundred Years." *IASA Journal,* no. 15 (June 2000): 12–16.

Giddings, Thaddeus P., et al. *Music Appreciation in the Schoolroom.* Boston: Ginn, 1926.

Giles, Patrick. "Magnificent Obsession—Beyond Pride, Beyond Shame: The Secret World of Record Collectors." *Opera News* 63 (October 1998): 28–33.

Gilliland, A. R., and H. T. Moore. "The Immediate and Long-Time Effects of Classical and Popular Phonograph Selections." *Journal of Applied Psychology* 8 (September 1924): 309–23.

Gioia, Ted. *The Imperfect Art: Reflections on Jazz and Modern Culture.* New York: Oxford University Press, 1988.

Glinsky, Albert. *Theremin: Ether Music and Espionage.* Urbana: University of Illinois Press, 2000.

Goodman, Fred. "Duets with the Dead: Homage or Exploitation?" *New York Times,* 16 January 2000, sec. 2, pp. 11, 18.

Gould, Glenn. "Music and Technology." In *The Glenn Gould Reader,* ed. Tim Page, 353–68. New York: Knopf, 1984.

———. "The Prospects of Recording." In *The Glenn Gould Reader,* ed. Tim Page, 331–53. New York: Knopf, 1984.

Gracyk, Theodore. "Listening to Music: Performances and Recordings." *Journal of Aesthetics and Art Criticism* 55 (spring 1997): 139–50.

Gracyk, Tim, and Frank Hoffmann. *Popular American Recording Pioneers, 1895–1925.* Binghamton, NY: Haworth, 2000.

Graham, Jefferson. "Kazaa, Verizon Propose to Pay Artists Directly." *USAToday,* 13 May 2002. Online at www.usatoday.com/life/cyber/tech/2002/05/14/music-kazaa.htm.

"Gramophone Celebrities: Jascha Heifetz." *Gramophone* 3 (1925): 278.

"A Great Force Needs Your Guidance." *Musician* 25 (May 1920): 5, 40.

Greenwood, Annie Pike. "The Victor in the Rural School." *Journal of Education* 79 (26 February 1914): 235.

Grenfell, George. "Well Worth Reading: How the Victor Helped Two Trappers in the Wilds of the Far North." *Voice of the Victor* 6 (May–June 1911): 5.

Grimson, Samuel B., and Cecil Forsyth. *Modern Violin-Playing.* New York: Gray, 1920.

Gutman, Hans. "The Festivals as Music Barometers." *Modern Music* 8 (November–December 1930): 30.

Haberman, Clyde. "New Vandals Scratching Up the Subways." *New York Times*, 26 January 1999, B1.

Hackett, Karleton. "Is 'Canned Music' Worthwhile?" *Ladies' Home Journal* 29 (November 1912): 56.

Hahn, Frederick. *Practical Violin Study.* Philadelphia: Theodore Presser, 1929.

Harrolds, Edward. "The Indefatigable Harrolds on Record Prices." *Phonograph Monthly Review* 3 (October 1928): 23–24.

Harvith, John, and Susan Edwards Harvith, eds. *Edison, Musicians, and the Phonograph: A Century in Retrospect.* Westport, CT: Greenwood, 1987.

Hauck, Werner. *Vibrato on the Violin.* Trans. Kitty Rokos. London: Bosworth, 1975.

Häusler, Josef. *Spiegel der neuen Musik: Donaueschingen.* Kassel: Bärenreiter, 1996.

Hayden, Eleanor. "Phonographs as Art Furniture." *International Studio* 78 (December 1923): 249–57.

Hebdige, Dick. *Cut 'n' Mix: Culture, Identity, and Caribbean Music.* London: Comedia, 1987.

Hernandez, Deborah Pacini. "Sound Systems, World Beat, and Diasporan Identity in Cartagena, Colombia." *Diaspora: A Journal of Transnational Studies* 5 (1996): 429–66.

Hindemith, Paul. "Zur mechanischen Musik." *Musikanten Gilde* 5 (15 November 1927): 155–59.

Hitchcock, H. Wiley, ed. *The Phonograph and Our Musical Life: Proceedings of a Centennial Conference, 7–10 December 1977.* Brooklyn: ISAM, 1980.

Hodgson, Jay. "Unpacking the CD Library." *Discourses in Music* 3 (spring 2002). www.discourses.ca/v3n3a2.html.

Hodgson, Percival. "Vibrato." *Strad* 17 (September 1916): 146–48.

Hornby, Nick. *High Fidelity.* New York: Riverhead, 1995.

Horning, Susan Schmidt. "Chasing Sound: The Culture and Technology of Recording Studios in America." Ph.D. diss., Case Western Reserve University, 2002.

Horowitz, Joseph. *Understanding Toscanini: A Social History of American Concert Life.* Berkeley and Los Angeles: University of California Press, 1987.

"House Subcommittee Holds Hearing on Compulsory Licensing of Music on the Internet." *Tech Law Journal,* 17 May 2001. www.techlawjournal.com/intelpro/20010517.asp.

How We Gave a Phonograph Party. New York: National Phonograph Co., 1899.

Hubert, Philip G., Jr. "What the Phonograph Will Do for Music and Music Lovers." *Century* 46 (May 1893): 152–54.

Humphris, James. "How the Talking Machine Gives Reality to Musical History." *Musician* 24 (September 1919): 8–9, 39.

———. "Study Music Structure by Phonograph." *Musician* 24 (May 1919): 10–11, 37.

Hunkemöller, Jürgen. "Die Rolle der Schallplatte im Jazz." *Jazzforschung* 12 (1980): 87–113.

Ian, Janis. "The Internet Debacle—An Alternative View." http://janisian.com/article-internet_debacle.html.

"Illustrated Song Machine." *Talking Machine World* 1 (October 1905): 33.

Indy, Vincent d'. *Les Yeux de l'aimeé*. Milan: Gramophone Co., Ltd., 1904.

Ipsos-Reid. "Fee-Based Online Music Faces Uphill Battle." 25 February 2002. www.ipsos-reid.com/media/dsp_displaypr_us.cfm?id_to_view=1439.

———. "File Sharing and CD Burners Proliferate." 12 June 2002. www.ipsos-na.com/news/pressrelease.cfm?id=1542.

Itzkoff, Seymour W. *Emanuel Feuermann, Virtuoso*. Tuscaloosa: University of Alabama Press, 1979.

James, Richard S. "Avant-garde Sound-on-Film Techniques and Their Relationship to Electro-Acoustic Music." *Musical Quarterly* 72 (1986): 74–89.

———. "Expansion of Sound Resources in France, 1913–1940, and Its Relationship to Electronic Music." Ph.D. diss., University of Michigan, 1981.

Jiránek, Josef. *O Smetanových klavíních skladbách a jeho klavírní hře*. Prague: Nákladem Spolecnosti Bedricha Smetany, 1932.

Johnson, Horace. "Department of Recorded Music: Phonographs in the Home." *Etude* 40 (February 1922): 88.

"Jupiter Media Metrix Reports Multi-Country Napster Usage Statistics for February 2001." *Jupiter Research*, 5 April 2001. http://www.jupiterresearch.com/xp/jmm/press/2001/pr_040501.html (now defunct).

Kahn, Douglas. *Noise, Water, Meat: A History of Sound in the Arts*. Cambridge, MA: MIT Press, 1999.

Katz, Mark. "Beethoven in the Age of Mechanical Reproduction: The Violin Concerto on Record." *Beethoven Forum* 10 (2003): 38–55.

———. "The Phonograph Effect: The Influence of Recording on Listener, Performer, Composer, 1900–1940." Ph.D. diss., University of Michigan, 1999.

Keene, James A. *A History of Music Education in the United States*. Hanover, NH: University Press of New England, 1982.

Keightley, Keir. "'Turn it down!' she shrieked: Gender, Domestic Space, and High Fidelity, 1948–59." *Popular Music* 15 (1996): 149–77.

Keil, Charles, and Steven Feld. *Music Grooves*. Chicago: University of Chicago Press, 1994.

Keller, Hans. "Violin Technique: Its Modern Development and Musical Decline." In *The Book of the Violin*, ed. Dominic Gill, 145–57. New York: Rizzoli, 1984.

Kelley, Edgar Stillman. "A Library of Living Melody." *Outlook* 99 (30 September 1911): 283–87.

Kelley, Robin D. G. *Yo' Mama's Disfunktional! Fighting the Culture Wars in Urban America*. Boston: Beacon, 1997.

Kenney, William Howland. *Recorded Music in American Life: The Phonograph and Popular Memory, 1890–1945*. New York: Oxford University Press, 1999.

Kernfeld, Barry, ed. *New Grove Dictionary of Jazz*. 2d ed. London: Macmillan, 2002.

King, Brad. "The Day the Napster Died." *Wired News*, 15 May 2002. www.wired.com/news/mp3/0,1285,52540,00.html.

Kinscella, Hazel Gertrude. "The Subtle Lure of Duet-Playing." *Musician* 29 (January 1924): 8, 15.

Kittler, Friedrich A. *Gramophone, Film, Typewriter*. Trans. Geoffrey Winthrop-Young and Michael Wutz. Stanford: Stanford University Press, 1999.

Klein, Herman. *Herman Klein and the Gramophone*. Ed. William R. Moran. Portland, OR: Amadeus, 1990.

Kline, Ronald, and Trevor Pinch. "Users as Agents of Technological Change: The Social Construction of the Automobile in the Rural United States." *Technology and Culture* 37 (1996): 763–95.

Kraft, James P. *Stage to Studio: Musicians and the Sound Revolution, 1890–1950*. Baltimore: Johns Hopkins University Press, 1996.

Kramer, Jonathan D. *The Time of Music*. New York: Schirmer, 1986.

Křenek, Ernst. *Music Here and Now*. Trans. Barthold Fles. New York: Norton, 1939.

Labuta, Joseph A., and Deborah A. Smith. *Music Education: Historical Contexts and Perspectives*. Upper Saddle River, NJ: Prentice Hall, 1997.

Langenus, Gustave. *The Langenus Clarinet Correspondence School with Talking Machine Records*. New York: n.p., 1915.

Lawson, Rex. "Stravinsky and the Pianola." In *Confronting Stravinsky*, ed. Jann Pasler, 284–301. Berkeley and Los Angeles: University of California Press, 1986.

Leech, George A. *The New Method of Curing Deafness by Special Adaptation of the Edison Phonograph*. New York: Knickerbocker, 1893.

Leonard, Neil. *Jazz and the White Americans: The Acceptance of a New Art Form*. Chicago: University of Chicago Press, 1962.

Leppert, Richard. *The Sight of Sound: Music, Representation, and the History of the Body*. Berkeley and Los Angeles: University of California Press, 1993.

Lessig, Lawrence. *The Future of Ideas: The Fate of the Commons in a Connected World*. New York: Random House, 2001.

Levin, Thomas Y. "For the Record: Adorno on Music in the Age of Its Technological Reproducibility." *October* 55 (winter 1990): 23–47.

Lewis, Sinclair. *Babbitt*. New York: Harcourt, Brace & World, 1922.

———. *Main Street*. New York: Harcourt, Brace & World, 1920.

Liebling, Leonard. "On Preserving Art." *Voice of the Victor* 7 (June 1912): 7.

Liebowitz, Stan. "Will MP3 Downloads Annihilate the Record Industry? The Evidence So Far." June 2003. http://www.utdallas.edu/~liebowit/intprop/records.pdf.

Link, Stan. "The Work of Reproduction in the Mechanical Aging of an Art: Listening to Noise." *Computer Music Journal* 25 (spring 2001): 34–47.

Lizie, Arthur, Jr. "Community and Identity in Cyberspace: Popular Music and the International Flow of Information." Ph.D. diss., Temple University, 2000.

Lochner, Louis P. *Fritz Kreisler*. New York: Macmillan, 1950.

Love, Courtney. "Courtney Love Does the Math." *Salon,* 14 June 2000. www.salon.com/tech/feature/2000/06/14/love/.

Lutkin, Peter Christian. "Musical Appreciation—How Is It to Be Developed?" *Journal of the Proceedings and Addresses of the National Education Association* 50 (1912): 1009–13.

Lyman, Jay. "RIAA Tactics in Question after Dismissal of Suit." *TechNewsWorld,* 25 September 2003. www.technewsworld.com/perl/story/31675.html.

Lynd, Robert S., and Helen Merrell Lynd. *Middletown: A Study in American Culture*. New York: Harcourt, Brace & World, 1929.

Lyon, Raymond. "Le Phonographe d'avant garde." *Le Joie musicale,* no. 3 (1930): 34.

Magee, Jeffrey. "The Music of Fletcher Henderson and His Orchestra in the 1920s." Ph.D. diss., University of Michigan, 1992.

Magruder, Richard J. "Manufacturing Music Lovers." *Disques* 2 (March 1931): 14–18.

Mann, Charles C. "The Heavenly Jukebox." *Atlantic Monthly* 286 (September 2000): 39–59.

Manuel, Peter. *Cassette Culture: Popular Music and Technology in North India*. Chicago: University of Chicago Press, 1993.

Marclay, Christian. Interview with Jason Gross. *Perfect Sound Forever,* March 1998. www.furious.com/perfect/christianmarclay.html.

Marco, Guy A., ed. *Encyclopedia of Recorded Sound in the United States*. New York: Garland, 1993.

Martens, Frederick. *Violin Mastery*. New York: Stokes, 1919.

Martin, George, and Jeremy Hornsby. *All You Need Is Ears*. New York: St. Martin's Press, 1979.

Mason, Andrew. "Building Blocks." *Wax Poetics,* no. 1 (winter 2002): 44–50.

Massey, Howard. *Behind the Glass: Top Record Producers Tell How They Craft the Hits.* San Francisco: Miller Freeman, 2000.

Mathews, Anna Wilde, et al. "The Music Industry Is Finally Online, but Few Listen." *Wall Street Journal,* 7 May 2002, A1, A20.

Maxwell, Jimmy. Interview with Milt Hinton. Jazz Oral History Project, Smithsonian Institution, 16 April 1979. Transcript on deposit at the Institute of Jazz Studies, Rutgers University.

Mayes, Will H. "How to Conduct a Music Memory Contest." *Etude* 41 (March 1923): 153.

McCracken, Allison. "'God's Gift to Us Girls': Crooning, Gender, and the Re-Creation of American Popular Song, 1928–1933." *American Music* 17 (winter 1999): 365–95.

McCullagh, Declan. "Attack Disables Music Industry Web Site." *C|NET News,* 29 July 2002. http://news.com.com/2100-1023-947072.html.

McGurk, Harry, and John MacDonald. "Hearing Lips and Seeing Voices." *Nature* 264 (1976): 746–48.

McLuhan, Marshall. "The Medium Is the Message." In *Understanding Media: The Extensions of Man,* 7–21. Cambridge, MA: MIT Press, 1994.

Menuhin, Yehudi. *Unfinished Journey: Twenty Years Later.* London: Fromm International, 1997.

Merriden, Trevor. *Irresistible Forces: The Business Legacy of Napster and the Growth of the Underground Internet.* Oxford: Capstone, 2001.

Meyer, Leonard B. *Emotion and Meaning in Music.* Chicago: University of Chicago Press, 1956.

Milhaud, Darius. "Les Ressources nouvelles de la musique." *L'Esprit nouveau,* no. 25 (1924): n.p.

Millard, Andre. *America on Record: A History of Recorded Sound.* Cambridge: Cambridge University Press, 1995.

Milojicic, Dejan S., et al. "Peer-to-Peer Computing." Technical report, Hewlett-Packard Co., 8 March 2002. www.hpl.hp.com/techreports/2002/HPL-2002-57.pdf.

Mitchell-Kernan, Claudia. "Signifying." In *Mother Wit from the Laughing Barrel: Readings in the Interpretation of Afro-American Folklore,* ed. Alan Dundes, 310–28. Englewood Cliffs, NJ: Prentice-Hall, 1973.

Moholy-Nagy, László. "New Form in Music: Potentialities of the Phonograph." In *Moholy-Nagy,* ed. and trans. Krisztina Passuth, 291–92. London: Thames & Hudson, 1985.

———. "Production—Reproduction." In *Moholy-Nagy,* ed. and trans. Krisztina Passuth, 289–90. London: Thames & Hudson, 1985.

"A Momentous Musical Meeting: Thomas A. Edison and Lt. Comm. John Philip Sousa Meet for the First Time and Talk upon Music." *Etude* 41 (October 1923): 663–64.

Monson, Ingrid. *Saying Something: Jazz Improvisation and Interaction.* Chicago: University of Chicago Press, 1996.

Montfort, Matthew. "An Open Letter Offering a Solution Allowing Music File Sharing on the Internet." 14 March 2001. www.ancient-future.com/cogressletter1.html.

Moore, F. Richard. *Elements of Computer Music.* Englewood Cliffs, NJ: Prentice-Hall, 1990.

Moore, Jerrold. *Elgar on Record: The Composer and the Gramophone.* London: Oxford University Press, 1974.

Morissette, Alanis. "Alanis: Major Label System 'Not Working.'" *Billboard,* 23 June 2001. www.billboard.com/billboard/daily/article_display.jsp?vnu_content_id=964592.

Myers, Paul. "Art or Theft? Sampling Opinions on Copyright." *Electronic Musician* 14 (November 1998): 38–39, 42, 44, 46, 48, 50, 52.

Nectoux, Jean-Michel. *Phonographies I: Gabriel Fauré, 1900–1977.* Paris: Bibliothèque Nationale, 1979.

"Negativland Statement in Support of Peer-to-Peer File Sharing." 21 January 2002. www.eff.org/IP/P2P/MGM_v_Grokster/20020121_negativland_essay.html.

Neumann, Frederick. *Violin Left Hand Technique: A Survey of the Related Literature.* Urbana, IL: American String Teachers Association, 1969.

New Grove Dictionary of Music and Musicians. London: Macmillan, 1980.

Newman, Jon O. "New Lyrics for an Old Melody: The Idea/Expression Dichotomy in the Computer Age." *Cardozo Arts and Entertainment Law Journal* 17 (1999). www.cardozo.yu.edu/news_events/papers/4.pdf.

O'Connor, Brian. "The Funk Soul Brother: As Fatboy Slim, UK DJ Norman Cook Leads the Big Beat Parade—And Laughs All the Way to the Bank." *DJ Times* 11 (November 1998): 22–24, 26, 28–30.

Ogren, Kathy J. *The Jazz Revolution: Twenties America and the Meaning of Jazz.* New York: Oxford University Press, 1989.

Oja, Carol J. *Colin McPhee: Composer in Two Worlds.* Washington, DC: Smithsonian Institution Press, 1990.

Ong, Walter J. *Fighting for Life: Contest, Sexuality, and Consciousness.* Ithaca, NY: Cornell University Press, 1981.

Oram, Andy, ed. *Peer-to-Peer: Harnessing the Power of Disruptive Technologies.* Sebastopol, CA: O'Reilly, 2001.

Orchard, Charles, Jr. "Is Radio Making America Musical?" *Radio Broadcast* 3 (October 1924): 454–55.

"Organize a Music Memory Contest." *Talking Machine Journal* 6 (March 1919): 8.

Ostrofsky, Sasha. "The Student and the Phonograph." *American Music Lover* 1 (March 1936): 331–32, 351.

Page, Tim. "*Einstein on the Beach* by Philip Glass." In *Opera: A History in Documents,* ed. Piero Weiss, 322–27. New York: Oxford University Press, 2002.

Partridge, Pauline. "The Home Set to Music." *Sunset* 53 (November 1924): 68, 75–76.

Peretti, Burton. *The Creation of Jazz: Music, Race, and Culture in Urban America.* Urbana: University of Illinois Press, 1992.

Philip, Robert. *Early Recordings and Musical Style: Changing Tastes in Instrumental Performance, 1900–1950.* Cambridge: Cambridge University Press, 1992.

"The Phonograph as a Decorative Element in the Home." *Country Life* 33 (March 1918): 108–9.

"The Phonograph as an Aid to Composers." *Phonogram,* no. 3 (July 1900): 67.

"Phonograph Society Reports: Minneapolis Phonograph Society." *Phonograph Monthly Review* 1 (October 1926): 33.

"Phonographic Propaganda." *Phonograph Monthly Review* 4 (May 1930): 259.

Pierné, Gabriel. *Giration: Divertissement chorégraphique.* Paris: Maurice Senart, 1935.

Porcello, Thomas. "Sonic Artistry: Music, Discourse, and Technology in the Recording Studio." Ph.D. diss., University of Texas, 1996.

Powell, Maud. "Instructive Possibilities of the Talking Machine for Violin Players." *Musical Observer* 9 (1914): 85, 88.

Pratt, Waldo S. "New Ideals in Musical Education." *Atlantic* 86 (December 1900): 826–30.

"Prince Voices Support for Napster." *Reuters,* 9 August 2000. http://news.com .com/2100-1023-244282.html (now defunct).

"Race Artists to Sing for Victrolas." *Chicago Defender,* 8 January 1916, 4.

Randolph, Harold. "The Feminization of Music." *Papers and Proceedings of the Musical Teachers' National Association* 17 (1923): 194–200.

Rasula, Jed. "The Media of Memory: The Seductive Menace of Records in Jazz History." In *Jazz among the Discourses,* ed. Krin Gabbard, 134–62. Durham, NC: Duke University Press, 1995.

Raven-Hart, R. "Composing for Radio." *Musical Quarterly* 16 (January 1930): 133–39.

Read, Oliver, and Walter L. Welch. *From Tin Foil to Stereo: Evolution of the Phonograph.* 2d ed. Indianapolis: Sams, 1976.

Reading Lessons in Music Appreciation: Aids in Preparation of Students for Music Memory Contest. Austin: University of Texas, 1922.

Recording Industry Association of America, Frequently Asked Questions—Downloading and Uploading. www.riaa.com/issues/music/downup_faq.asp.

Reger, Scott N. "Historical Survey of the String Instrument Vibrato." In *Studies in the Psychology of Music*, vol. 1: *The Vibrato*, ed. Carl Seashore, 289–304. Iowa City: University of Iowa Press, 1932.

———. "The String Instrument Vibrato." In *Studies in the Psychology of Music*, vol. 1: *The Vibrato*, ed. Carl Seashore, 305–43. Iowa City: University of Iowa Press, 1932.

Reich, Steve. *Writings on Music, 1965–2000.* New York: Oxford University Press, 2002.

Respighi, Ottorino. *Pina di Roma.* Milan: Ricordi, 1925.

Rheingold, Howard. *Virtual Community: Homesteading on the Electronic Frontier.* Reading, MA: Addison Wesley, 1993.

Rhetts, Edith M. "The Development of Music Appreciation in America." *Papers and Proceedings of the Music Teachers' National Association* 16 (1922): 112–20.

Rich, Stephen G. "Some Unnoticed Aspects of the School Use of Phonographs." *Journal of Educational Method* 3 (November 1923): 108–14.

Ritter, Frédéric Louis. *Music in America.* New ed. New York: Charles Scribner's Sons, 1890.

Roland-Manuel. "Musique et mécanique." *Le Menestrel* 85 (25 May 1923): 233–34.

Rose, Tricia. *Black Noise: Rap Music and Black Culture in Contemporary Culture.* Hanover, NH: Wesleyan University Press, 1994.

Roth, Henry. *Master Violinists in Performance.* Neptune City, NJ: Paganiniana, 1982.

Saenger, Oscar. *The Oscar Saenger Course in Vocal Training: A Complete Course of Vocal Study for the Soprano Voice on Victor Records.* Camden, NJ: Victor Talking Machine Co., 1916.

Saunders, Archibald. *A Practical Course in Vibrato for Violinists.* London: Lavender, 1900.

Schade-Poulsen, Marc. *Men and Popular Music in Algeria: The Social Significance of Raï.* Austin: University of Texas Press, 1999.

Schaeffer, Pierre. *A la recherche d'une musique concrète.* Paris: Editions du Seuil, 1952.

———. *La Musique concrète.* Paris: Presses universitaires de France, 1967.

Schauffler, Robert Haven. "Canned Music—The Phonograph Fan." *Collier's* 67 (23 April 1921): 10–11, 23–24.

———. "Handing You a Musical Ear Opener." *Collier's* 72 (1 December 1923): 13.

———. "The Mission of Mechanical Music." *Century* 89 (December 1914): 293–98.

Schauffler, Robert Haven, and Sigmund Spaeth. *Music as a Social Force in America.* New York: Caxton Institute, 1927.

Schenbeck, Lawrence. "Music, Gender, and 'Uplift' in the *Chicago Defender,* 1927–1937." *Musical Quarterly* 81 (fall 1997): 344–70.

Schloss, Joseph. "Making Beats: The Art of Sample-Based Hip Hop." Ph.D. diss., University of Washington, 2000.

Schmuck, Adolph. "The Case for Mere Listening." *Disques* 2 (May 1931): 106–10.

Schoenberg, Arnold. "Mechanical Musical Instruments." Trans. Leo Black. In *Style and Idea,* ed. Leonard Stein, 326–30. New York: St. Martin's Press, 1975.

Schuh, Willi. "Neue Musik Berlin 1930." *Schweizerische Musikzeitung* 70 (1 August 1930): 547–52.

Schuller, Gunther. *Early Jazz: Its Roots and Musical Development.* New York: Oxford University Press, 1968.

———. "Ellington in the Pantheon" (1974). In *The Duke Ellington Reader,* ed. Mark Tucker, 414–17. New York: Oxford University Press, 1993.

———. *The Swing Era: The Development of Jazz, 1930–1945.* New York: Oxford University Press, 1989.

Schünemann, Georg. "Produktive Kräfte der mechanischen Musik." *Die Musik* 24 (January 1932): 246–49.

Scratchdj. www.scratchdj.com.

Seeger, Anthony. "The Role of Sound Archives in Ethnomusicology Today." *Ethnomusicology* 30 (spring–summer 1986): 261–76.

Seegers, J. C. "Teaching Music Appreciation by Means of the Music-Memory Contest." *Elementary School Journal* 26 (November 1925): 215–23.

Segal, David. "A New Tactic in the Download War." *Washington Post,* 20 August 2002, A1, A8.

Segal, Howard P. *Technological Utopianism in American Culture.* Chicago: University of Chicago Press, 1985.

Sellars, Paul. "Behind the Mask—Perceptual Coding: How MP3 Compression Works." *Sound on Sound,* May 2000. www.sospubs.co.uk/sos/may00/articles/mp3.htm.

Sessions, Roger. *The Musical Experience of Composer, Performer, Listener.* Princeton: Princeton University Press, 1950.

Seymour, Henry. "The Reproduction of Sound." *Phono Record* 2 (August 1913): 264–65.

Shaffer, Karen A., and Neva Gardner Greenwood. *Maud Powell: Pioneer Woman Violinist.* Ames: Iowa State University Press, 1988.

Shawe, Elsie M. "Public-School Music in Relation to the Music of the Community." *Journal of the Proceedings and Addresses of the National Education Association* 49 (1911): 790–94.

Simons, Eric N. "Gramomania." *Gramophone* 2 (1924): 89–90.

S. K. "Open Forum." *Phonograph Monthly Review* 1 (February 1927): 213.

———. "Stradella and Schubert, but Not Strawinski—Yet." *Phonograph Monthly Review* 3 (December 1928): 95.

Slobin, Mark. "Fiddler Off the Roof: Klezmer Music as an Ethnic Musical Style." In *The Jews of North America,* ed. Moses Rischin, 95–104. Detroit: Wayne State University Press, 1987.

Smith, Marc, and Peter Kollock, eds. *Communities in Cyberspace.* London: Routledge, 2001.

Smith, Merritt Roe, and Leo Marx, eds. *Does Technology Drive History? The Dilemma of Technological Determinism.* Cambridge, MA: MIT Press, 1994.

Smith, Moses. "From Jazz to Symphony: Self-Education by Means of the Phonograph." *Phonograph Monthly Review* 1 (November 1926): 16–17.

Sousa, John Philip. "The Menace of Mechanical Music." *Appleton's* 8 (1906): 278–84.

Stehman, Dan. *Roy Harris: A Bio-Bibliography.* New York: Greenwood, 1991.

Sternberg, Constantin von. "Are You Musical?" *Musician* 17 (1912): 91.

Stowell, Robin. "Technique and Performing Practice." In *The Cambridge Companion to the Violin,* ed. Robin Stowell, 122–42. Cambridge: Cambridge University Press, 1992.

Strauss, Neil. "Apple Finds the Future for Online Music Sales." *New York Times,* 29 May 2003, B1, B8.

Stravinsky, Igor. *An Autobiography.* New York: Norton, 1962.

———. "Meine Stellung zur Schallplatte." *Kultur und Schallplatte* 1 (March 1930): 65.

Stravinsky, Igor, and Robert Craft. *Dialogues and a Diary.* London: Faber & Faber, 1968.

Straw, Will. "Sizing Up Record Collections: Gender and Connoisseurship in Rock Music Culture." In *Sexing the Groove,* ed. Sheila Whiteley, 3–16. London: Routledge, 1997.

The Strolling Player. "The Everlasting 'Vibrato.'" *Strad* 17 (January 1908): 305–7.

Stuckenschmidt, H. H. "Machines—A Vision of the Future." *Modern Music* 4 (March–April 1927): 8–14.

———. "Mechanisierung." *Musikblätter des Anbruch* 8 (October–November 1926): 345–46.

———. "Die Mechanisierung der Musik." *Pult und Taktstock* 2 (1925): 1–8.

Sudhalter, Richard M., and Philip R. Evans. *Bix: Man and Legend.* New Rochelle, NY: Arlington House, 1974.

Sutton, R. Anderson. "Commercial Cassette Recordings of Traditional Music in Java." *World of Music* 27, no. 3 (1985): 23–43.

Swan, Annalyn. "Itzhak Perlman, Top Fiddle." *Newsweek* 95 (14 April 1980): 62–71.

Swinnerton, Frank. "A Defence of the Gramophone." *Gramophone* 1 (1923): 52–53.

Szende, Ottó. *Unterweisung im Vibrato auf der Geige.* Vienna: Universal Edition, 1985.

Szigeti, Joseph. "Josef Szigeti Chats about the Gramophone." *Gramophone* 6 (1929): 525.

Tableau Vivant. "Gramophone-Opera with a Model Stage." *Gramophone Critic and Society News* 1 (August 1929): 402–3.

Talbot, Michael, ed. *The Musical Work: Reality or Invention?* Liverpool: Liverpool University Press, 2000.

Tannen, Deborah. *Talking from 9 to 5.* New York: Morrow, 1994.

Taylor, Chuck. "Do Vocal Effects Go Too Far? Ability to Perfect Sound via Technology May Affect Drive to Develop Talent." *Billboard* 112 (30 December 2000): 1, 88–89.

Taylor, Dale B. "Music in General Hospital Treatment from 1900 to 1950." *Journal of Music Therapy* 18 (1981): 62–73.

Taylor, J. Hillary. "Music in the Home." *Negro Music Journal* 1 (September 1902): 10.

Taylor, Timothy D. "Music and the Rise of Radio in 1920s America: Technological Imperialism, Socialization, and the Transformation of Intimacy." *Historical Journal of Film, Radio, and Television* 22 (2002): 425–43.

———. *Strange Sounds: Music, Technology, and Culture.* New York: Routledge, 2001.

Théberge, Paul. *Any Sound You Can Imagine: Making Music/Consuming Technology.* Hanover, NH: Wesleyan University Press, 1997.

Thornton, Sarah. *Club Cultures: Music, Media, and Subcultural Capital.* Hanover, NH: Wesleyan University Press, 1996.

Titon, Jeff Todd. *Early Downhome Blues: A Musical and Cultural Analysis.* 2d ed. Chapel Hill: University of North Carolina Press, 1994.

"To Make the Stereophone." *Talking Machine World* 1 (December 1905): 9.

Toch, Ernst. "Musik für mechanische Instrumente." *Neue Musikzeitung* 47 (July 1926): 431–34.

———. "Über meine Kantate 'Das Wasser' und meine Grammophonmusik." *Melos* 9 (May–June 1930): 221–22.

Toch, Lilly. "The Orchestration of a Composer's Life." Oral history conducted by Bernard Galm, Oral History Program, University of California, Los Angeles, 1978. Transcript on deposit at Bancroft Library, University of California, Berkeley.

Tovey, Henry Doughty. "Bringing Music to the Rural Districts." *Musician* 24 (February 1919): 14.

Tremaine, C. M. "The Music Memory Contest, etc." *Proceedings of the Music Supervisors' National Conference* 11 (1919): 99–107.

———. "Music Memory Contests." *Journal of the National Education Association* 15 (February 1926): 43–44.

Tucker, Mark. *Ellington: The Early Years.* Urbana: University of Illinois Press, 1991.

———, ed. *The Duke Ellington Reader.* New York: Oxford University Press, 1993.

United States Bureau of the Census. *Census of Manufactures, 1914.* Washington, DC: Government Printing Office, 1918.

"The Use of the Sound Reproducing Machine in Vocal Instruction and Musical Education." *Etude* 27 (1909): 195–96, 340.

Vaidhyanathan, Siva. *Copyrights and Copywrongs: The Rise of Intellectual Property and How It Threatens Creativity.* New York: New York University Press, 2001.

Vercheval, Henri. *Dictionnaire du violoniste.* Paris: Fischbacher, 1923.

Victor Talking Machine Company. *Music Appreciation for Little Children.* Camden, NJ: Victor Talking Machine Co., 1920.

———. *Victor Records for Health Exercises.* Camden, NJ: Victor Talking Machine Co., 1922.

———. *The Victrola in Rural Schools.* Camden, NJ: Victor Talking Machine Co., 1917.

Walker, Leslie. "Online Music Sites Seek Paying Customers." *Washington Post,* 16 February 2003, H7. Online at www.washingtonpost.com/wp-dyn/articles/A10727-2003Feb14.html.

Walser, Robert. "Rhythm, Rhyme, and Rhetoric in the Music of Public Enemy." *Ethnomusicology* 39 (spring–summer 1995): 193–218.

———. *Running with the Devil: Power, Gender, and Madness in Heavy Metal Music.* Hanover, NH: Wesleyan University Press, 1993.

———, ed. *Keeping Time: Readings in Jazz History.* New York: Oxford University Press, 1999.

Wang, Oliver. "Legions of Boom: Filipino American Disc Jockeys in the San Francisco Bay Area, 1970s–1990s." Ph.D. diss., University of California, Berkeley, 2004.

Washburn, Margaret Floy, Margaret S. Child, and Theodora Mead Abel. "The Effect of Immediate Repetition on the Pleasantness or Unpleasantness of Music." In *The Effects of Music*, ed. Max Schoen, 199–210. London: Kegan Paul, Trench, Trubner; New York: Harcourt, Brace, 1927.

Watkins, Glenn. *Pyramids at the Louvre*. Cambridge, MA: Harvard University Press, 1994.

Waxer, Lise A. *The City of Musical Memory: Salsa, Record Grooves, and Popular Music in Cali, Colombia*. Middletown, CT: Wesleyan University Press, 2002.

Webber, Stephen. *Turntable Technique: The Art of the DJ*. Boston: Berklee Press, 2000.

Weber, Joseph N. "Canned Music." *American Federationist* 38 (1931): 1063–70.

———. "Mechanics and Music." *Papers and Proceedings of the Musical Teachers' National Conference* 25 (1931): 208–17.

———. "Will Real Music Survive?" *Metronome* 45 (March 1930): 16, 44.

Weeks, Linton. "E-Books Not Exactly Flying Off the Shelves." *Washington Post*, 6 July 2002, C1. Online at www.washingtonpost.com/wp-dyn/articles/A30379 -2002Jul5.html.

Wegefarth, W. Dayton. "The Talking Machine as a Public Educator." *Lippincott's* 37 (1911): 628–30.

Welch, Walter L., and Leah Brodbeck Stenzel Burt. *From Tinfoil to Stereo: The Acoustic Years of the Recording Industry, 1877–1929*. Gainesville: University Press of Florida, 1994.

Weschler, Lawrence. "My Grandfather's Last Tale." *Atlantic Monthly* 278 (December 1996): 86–106.

Wessely, Hans. *A Practical Guide to Violin-Playing*. London: Joseph Williams, 1913.

"Who Buys Phonographs?" *Sonora Bell* 2 (October 1919): 1–6.

Wier, Albert E. *Grand Opera with a Victrola*. New York: D. Appleton, 1915.

Wilcox, Ella Wheeler. "Wail of an Old-Timer." In *Poems of Sentiment*, 125–26. Chicago: Conkey, 1906.

Wilde, Oscar. *The Picture of Dorian Gray*. 1890; New York: Random House, 1992.

Willett, John Tarver. *Spanish Phonograph*. El Paso, TX: Tip. Latino Americano, 1917.

Williams, Martin. "Recording Limits and Blues Form." In *The Art of Jazz: Essays on the Nature and Development of Jazz*, 91–93. New York: Oxford University Press, 1959.

Williams, Orlo. "Times and Seasons." *Gramophone* 1 (1923): 38–39.

Willoughby, Florence Barrett. "The Phonograph in Alaska." *Phonograph* 1 (26 July 1916): 13, 16.

Wilson, Olly. "The Heterogenous Sound Ideal in African-American Music." In *Signifyin(g), Sanctifyin', and Slam Dunking: A Reader in African American Expressive Culture,* ed. Gena Dagel Caponi, 157–71. Amherst: University of Massachusetts Press, 1999.

Winram, James. *Violin Playing and Violin Adjustment.* Edinburgh: Blackwood & Sons, 1908.

Winship, A. E. "The Mission of School Music." *Journal of Education* 84 (21 September 1916): 257–60.

Winslow, Agnes Hollister. *An Appreciation and History of Music.* Camden, NJ: Victor Talking Machine Co., 1928.

Wood, Mabel Travis. "Becoming Familiar with Great Music." *Radio Broadcast* 2 (March 1923): 406.

Yoo, Lilit, Stephan Moore, David Sullivan, and Ichiro Fujinaga. "The Effect of Vibrato on Response Time in Determining the Pitch Relationship of Violin Tones." *Proceedings of the International Conference on Music Perception and Cognition,* 1998, 477–81.

Yorke, Dane. "The Rise and Fall of the Phonograph." *American Mercury* 27 (September 1932): 1–12.

Zak, Albin. *The Poetics of Rock: Cutting Tracks, Making Records.* Berkeley and Los Angeles: University of California Press, 2001.

Zpoc. www.zpoc.com/index.php.

RECORDINGS

Bach, J. S. Adagio from Sonata in G Minor, BWV 1001. Jascha Heifetz, violin. *The Heifetz Collection,* vol. 3. BMG Classics compact disc 09026-61734-2.

———. Adagio from Sonata in G Minor, BWV 1001. Joseph Joachim, violin. *Great Virtuosi of the Golden Age, Volume 1.* Pearl compact disc GEMM CD 9101.

———. Adagio from Sonata in G Minor, BWV 1001. Joseph Szigeti, violin. *Joseph Szigeti: A Golden Treasury of His Best English Columbia 78s.* Music & Arts compact disc CD 813.

———. Concerto in D Minor for Two Violins. Jascha Heifetz, violins. *The Heifetz Collection,* vol. 6. BMG/RCA Victor compact disc 61778.

———. *The Well-Tempered Clavier.* Glenn Gould, piano. Sony compact disc 52600.

Beatles. "Strawberry Fields Forever." *Magical Mystery Tour.* Capitol compact disc CDP 48062.

————. "Strawberry Fields Forever." Take 7. *The Beatles Anthology*, vol. 2. Capitol compact disc CDP 7243 8 34448 2 3.

Beiderbecke, Bix. "Goosepimples." *Bix Beiderbecke, 1927–1930*. Classics compact disc 788.

Brahms, Johannes. Hungarian Dance No. 1. Violin-piano arr. Joseph Joachim. Jascha Heifetz, violin. *The Heifetz Collection: The Acoustic Recordings, 1917–1924*. BMG compact disc 0942-2-RG.

————. Hungarian Dance No. 1. Violin-piano arr. Joseph Joachim. Joseph Joachim, violin. *Great Virtuosi of the Golden Age, Volume I*. Pearl compact disc GEMM CD 9101.

————. Hungarian Dance No. 1. Violin-piano arr. Joseph Joachim. Toscha Seidel, violin. *The Auer Legacy, Volume Two*. Appian compact disc CDAPR 7016.

Brown, James. "Funky Drummer, Part 1 and 2." *Star Time*. Polydor compact disc 849 108.

Chopin, Frédéric. Nocturne in E-flat, Op. 9, No. 2. Violin-piano arr. Pablo de Sarasate. Jascha Heifetz, violin. *The Heifetz Collection: The Acoustic Recordings, 1917–1924*. BMG compact disc 0942-2-RG.

————. Nocturne in E-flat, Op. 9, No. 2. Violin-piano arr. Pablo de Sarasate. Mischa Elman, violin. Biddulph compact disc LAB 035.

Clapton, Eric. "Blues Power." *Eric Clapton*. Polydor compact disc 825 093.

————. "Blues Power." *Just One Night*. Polydor compact disc 800 093-2.

————. "Cocaine." *Just One Night*. Polydor compact disc 800 093-2.

————. "Cocaine." *Slowhand*. Polydor compact disc 823 276.

Cole, Natalie. "Unforgettable." *Unforgettable, with Love*. Elektra compact disc 61049.

Early Klezmer Music, 1908–1927. Arhoolie compact disc 7034.

Ellington, Duke. "Diminuendo in Blue and Crescendo in Blue." *Ellington at Newport 1956*. Columbia compact disc CK-40587.

————. "Diminuendo in Blue and Crescendo in Blue." *Smithsonian Collection of Classic Jazz*. Smithsonian Collection of Recordings compact disc RD 033-3.

————. *Early Ellington: The Complete Brunswick and Vocalion Recordings of Duke Ellington, 1926–1931*. Decca compact disc GRD-3-640.

Fatboy Slim. "Praise You." *You've Come a Long Way, Baby*. Skint compact disc BRASSIC11CD.

Great Virtuosi of the Golden Age, Volume II. Pearl compact disc GEMM CD 9102.

Hendrix, Jimi. "Crosstown Traffic." *Electric Ladyland*. MCA compact disc 11600.

————. "Hey Joe." *Are You Experienced?* Reprise compact disc 6261-2.

————. "Hey Joe." *Live at Winterland*. Rykodisc compact disc RCD 20038.

————. "Killing Floor." *Live at Winterland*. Rykodisc compact disc RCD 20038.

————. "Killing Floor." *Radio One*. Rykodisc compact disc RCD 20078.

I'm Making You a Record: Home and Amateur Recordings on Wax Cylinder, 1902–1920. Phonozoic compact disc 001.

Jan Kubelik: The Acoustic Recordings (1902–1913). Biddulph compact disc LAB 033-34.

Joel, Billy. "The Entertainer." *Streetlife Serenade*. Columbia compact disc 69382.

Kreisler, Fritz. *Liebesleid*. Fritz Kreisler, violin. *The Kreisler Collection: The Complete Acoustic HMV Recordings*. Biddulph compact disc LAB 009-10.

Lansky, Paul. *Notjustmoreidlechatter. More Than Idle Chatter*. Bridge compact disc BCD 9050.

Led Zeppelin. "Whole Lotta Love." *Led Zeppelin II*. Atlantic compact disc 11612.

Maud Powell. Biddulph compact disc LAB 094.

Oliver, Joe "King." "Dippermouth Blues." *Smithsonian Collection of Classic Jazz*. Smithsonian Collection of Recordings compact disc RD 033-3.

Original Dixieland Jazz Band. *The Original Dixieland Jazz Band, 1917–1921*. Timeless compact disc CBC 1-009.

Pearl Jam. "Spin the Black Circle." *Vitalogy*. Epic compact disc EK 66900.

Public Enemy. "Fight the Power." *Fear of a Black Planet*. Def Jam compact disc 314 523 446-2.

Radiohead. "Creep." *Pablo Honey*. Capitol compact disc 81409.

Sarasate, Pablo de. *Zigeunerweisen*. Jascha Heifetz, violin. RCA compact disc 7709-2-RG.

————. *Zigeunerweisen*. Pablo de Sarasate, violin. *Great Virtuosi of the Golden Age, Volume I*. Pearl compact disc GEMM CD 9101.

————. *Zigeunerweisen*. Zino Francescatti, violin. *Zino Francescatti: The Complete HMV Recordings*. Biddulph compact disc LAB 030.

Schaeffer, Pierre. *Pierre Schaeffer: L'Oeuvre musicale*. INA-GRM compact disc 1006-9.

Showbiz & A.G. "Diggin' in the Crates." *Showbiz & A.G.* Polygram compact disc 828309.

Stravinsky, Igor. *Serenade in A*. Igor Stravinsky, pianist. Sony Classical compact disc SM2K 46297.

X-Ecutioners. *X-pressions*. Asphodel compact disc 0977.

Vieuxtemps, Henri. *Rondino*. Eugène Ysaÿe, violin. *Eugène Ysaÿe, Violinist and Conductor: The Complete Violin Recordings*. Sony compact disc MHK 62337.

Yarbrough, Camille. "Take Yo' Praise." *The Iron Pot Cooker*. Vanguard compact disc 79356-2.

Battle Sounds. www.battlesounds.com videocassette, 1997.

DJ QBert's Complete Do-It-Yourself, Vol. 1: *Skratching.* Thud-Rumble DVD, DIY001-DVD, n.d.

Scratch. Palm DVD 3046-2, 2002.

Shure Turntablism 101. Shure videocassette, TT101, 2000.

The Simpsons, episode CABF12, "New Kids on the Blecch," originally broadcast 25 February 2001.

Turntable Wizardry Stage 1. Up Above videocassette, no label number, n.d.

CD TRACKS AND PERMISSIONS

1. A. H. Mendenhall, Phonographic Letter, n.d. (early 1900s). Released on *I'm Making You a Record: Home and Amateur Recordings on Wax Cylinder, 1902–1920,* Phonozoic compact disc 001, phonozoic.com. Used by permission of Patrick Feaster.

2. Joe "King" Oliver, "Dippermouth Blues," 1923. Fantasy Jazz Records. Used by permission.

3. Joseph Joachim, violin, performing Johannes Brahms, Hungarian Dance no. 1 (arr. Joachim), 1903. Released on *Great Virtuosi of the Golden Age, Volume I,* Pearl compact disc GEMM CD 9101. Used by permission.

4. Jascha Heifetz, violin, performing Johannes Brahms, Hungarian Dance no. 1 (arr. Joachim), 1920. Released on HMV 78-rpm disc DA 245.

5. Toscha Seidel, violin, performing Johannes Brahms, Hungarian Dance no. 1 (arr. Joachim), 1940. Released on *The Auer Legacy, Volume Two,* Appian compact disc CDAPR 7016. Used by permission.

6. Mischa Elman, violin, performing Frédéric Chopin, Nocturne in E-flat, op. 9, no. 2 (arr. Pablo de Sarasate), 1910. Released on *Mischa Elman,* Biddulph compact disc LAB 035. Used by permission.

7. Jascha Heifetz, violin, performing Frédéric Chopin, Nocturne in E-flat, op. 9, no. 2 (arr. Pablo de Sarasate), 1918. Released on *Jascha Heifetz: The Early Victor Recordings,* Biddulph compact disc LAB 015. Used by permission.

8. Paul Hindemith, *Originalwerk für Schallplatte:* Instrumental *Trickaufnahme,* 1930 [excerpt]. Previously unpublished. Used by permission of Dr. Martin Elste and the Staatliches Institut für Musikforschung PK, Berlin.

9. I.Emerge, "Hardcore Scratching," 2003. Previously unpublished. Used by permission of Michael Weinstein.

10. Paul Lansky, *Notjustmoreidlechatter,* 1988. Released on *More Than Idle Chatter,* Bridge compact disc BCD 9050. Used by permission of Bridge

Records, Inc., New Rochelle, New York, www.bridgerecords.com. (p) and (c) 1994, Bridge Records, Inc.

11.   Fatboy Slim, "Praise You," 1998. Released on *You've Come a Long Way, Baby,* Skint compact disc BRASSIC11CD. Used by permission.

12.   Camille Yarbrough, "Take Yo' Praise," 1975. Released on *The Iron Pot Cooker,* Vanguard compact disc 79356-2. Used by permission.

13.   Public Enemy, "Fight the Power," 1990. Released on *Fear of a Black Planet,* Def Jam compact disc 314 523 446-2. Written by Carlton Ridenhour, Hank Shocklee, Keith Shocklee, and Eric Sadler. © 1990 Terrordome Music Publishing, LLC, as administered by Reach Global Songs (BMI) and Songs of Universal, Inc. Used by permission. All rights reserved.

Conducting (and conductors), and sound recording, 15, 22, 59, 106, 109

Cook, Norman (aka Fatboy Slim): "Praise You," 138, 145–51, 156

Copeland, Keith, 79

Copland, Aaron, 29

Copyright, 150, 157, 162, 163, 175–82, 184, 233n48. *See also* Digital sampling; Fair use; File-sharing

"Cornet Chop Suey" (Louis Armstrong), 75

Crawford, Richard, 59, 76

"Creep" (Radiohead), 43

"The Creeper" (Duke Ellington), 75

"Creole Rhapsody" (Duke Ellington), 76

Crespin, Régine, 23

Crooning, 40, 202n101

Crosby, Bing, 40

Crossfader, 118, 125, 128–29

"Crosstown Traffic" (Jimi Hendrix), 43

Cutting, contests, 132, 133–34

Dammert, Hansjörg, 107–8, 112

Dancing, and sound recording, 15, 74, 117

Davidson, Jane, 95–96

De Treville, Yvonne, 38

Dexta, DJ, 123

DiFranco, Ani, 13

"Digging in the crates," 11, 118, 135

"Diggin' in the Crates" (song, Showbiz and A.G.), 11

Digital recording, 41, 43–44

Digital sampling, 46, 137–57, 189; copyright and, 150, 157; defined, 138–39; ethics and, 149–51; gender and, 148–49; as musical borrowing, 139–41; as performative quotation, 140–41, 152–155; as politi-cal statement, 153–54; and race, 149–50; as transformative, 156–57

Digital sound processing (DSP), 43–44

Dillmann, Alexander, 104, 105

"Diminuendo and Crescendo in Blue" (Duke Ellington), 75, 76, 77

"Dippermouth Blues" (King Oliver), 79–80

Disc inscription, 104–7, 111–12

Discs. *See* Records

Dissing, in DJ battles, 124–25

DJ (disc jockey), 11, 30–31, 113, 114–27, 131–36, 152, 154, 191, 223n2, 224n7

DJ battle, 114–36, 225n28; "biting" in, 126; boasting in, 124; demo-graphics, 122–23; dissing in, 124–25; equipment, 117–21; gender in, 123, 131, 134–36; messages in, 123–25, 127, 128, 130; originality in, 126–27; origins, 121–22; race in, 122–23, 127; routines, 123–31; rules, 122; as safe space, 115, 131–32; and self-expression, 131; use of analog vs. digital equipment in, 120–21. *See also* Beat juggling; DJ; Scratching; Scratch sentence; Turntablism

DMC (Dance Music Community), 121, 123

Dodds, Baby, 74, 79–80, 81, 230n28

Dodds, Johnny, 82

Dopey, DJ, 123–24

Downloading, 158–59, 161–87, 231n15, 233n43. *See also* File-sharing; MP3

Dozens, The, 132–34

Drake, Nick: "Cello Song," 167

Dramatics: "Whatcha See Is Whatcha Get," 152

Drucker, Eugene, 22

Hungarian Dance no. 1 (Johannes Brahms), 88, 89, 90

"I Am Stretched on Your Grave" (Sinéad O'Connor), 137
Idea-expression dichotomy, 156–57
I.Emerge, 127–31, 225–26n29; "Hardcore Scratching," 127–31
Illustrated Song Machine, 19
Imaginary Landscape No. 1 (John Cage), 45, 113
Improvisation, and sound recording, 75–81, 127, 212–13n15
India, sound recording in, 12–13, 14, 23
Indian music, 12, 23, 33
Indy, Vincent d', 35
Internet, 13, 124, 158–87, 195n16
Invisibility. *See* Recorded music, traits
Invisibl Skratch Piklz, 224n8
ITF (International Turntablist Federation), 122, 127
It's Gonna Rain (Steve Reich), 30

Jackson, Janet, "Someone to Call My Lover," 158–59
Jakub, Beth, 5, 21
Java, recorded music in, 13–14
Jazz, 15, 39, 50, 67, 72–84, 133–34, 209n75, 211n1, 212n8, 214n27; and DJ battle, 133–34; and improvisation, 75–81; and limitations of early recording equipment, 81–84; and portability of recordings, 73–74; and repeatability of recordings, 77–81; study of, 77–79, 213–14n24; and time limitation of 78s, 74–77; and visual aspect of performance, 78–79, 214n27
Jefferson, Thomas, 163
Jiránek, Josef, 40
Joachim, Joseph, 86, 87–88, 216n17

Joel, Billy: "The Entertainer," 36, 234n56

Katz, Anna, 4, 29
Kaufman, Louis, 93, 94
Kazaa, 162, 170, 176
Kenney, William Howland, 206n29
Khan, Maujuddin, 23
"Killing Floor" (Jimi Hendrix), 36
Klezmer, 39
Kool Herc, 116, 223n4
Kramer, Jonathan, 29–30
Kreisler, Fritz, 34–35, 88–89, 92, 97; *Caprice viennois*, 34–35; *Liebesleid*, 89
Křenek, Ernst, 107, 111
Kubelik, Jan, 89
Kunst, Jaap, 2
Kuttin' Kandi, 123

Lansky, Paul: *Notjustmoreidlechatter*, 138, 141–45, 156
Led Zeppelin: "Whole Lotta Love," 43
Lehmann, Lotte, 38
Lennon, John, 40, 41
Leoncavallo, Ruggero, 35
Leppert, Richard, 19
Lessig, Lawrence, 163, 178, 180
Lewis, Sinclair: *Babbitt*, 69; *Main Street*, 203–4n1
Liebesleid (Fritz Kreisler), 89
Lip-synching, 21, 27
Listening (and listeners), and sound recording, 8–12, 15, 16–20, 21–22, 25–26, 31–32, 51–67, 73–74, 165–75; and affordability, 11–12, 52, 54, 55, 164, 169; and breakfast, 16–17; and invisibility, 18–22; and jazz, 50, 73–74; and phonograph conducting, 15, 59; and portability, 15, 55–56, 164; and repeatability, 25–26, 53; retrospective listening, 28,

198n61; solitary listening, 17–18; and tangibility, 10–12, 170–72; and temporality, 31–32, 199n72
Liszt, Franz, 95
Live performance: visual aspect of, 19–22, 78–79, 95, 96, 97, 126, 214n27; vs. recorded music, 4, 5, 9, 14, 22–25, 33, 36, 46–47, 68–71, 74, 76, 143, 189–90
Livingston, Theodore (aka Grand Wizard Theodore), 116–17
Loops and looping, 30–31, 42, 46, 116, 130, 137, 139, 147, 151, 152–54, 156, 176
LP (Long-playing record), 11, 12–13, 21, 30, 31, 34, 35, 50, 51, 77, 119, 120, 121, 146, 171–72
Lyon, Raymond, 109, 113
"Lyrics of Fury" (Eric B. and Rakim), 137

Magee, Jeffrey, 75
Magnetic tape, 30, 41–43, 46, 101, 112, 191. *See also* Cassette tape
Maholy-Nagy, László, 105–7
Main Street (Sinclair Lewis), 203–4n1
Manipulability. *See* Recorded music, traits
Manuel, Peter, 12–13
Marclay, Christian, 45
Marsalis, Branford, 151
Martin, George, 41
Marx, Karl, 10
Marx, Leo, 3
Marx, Richard, 43
Maxwell, Jimmy, 73, 77
MC battles, 225n28
McGurk Effect, 20–21, 96
McLuhan, Marshall, 191
McPartland, Jimmy, 77
McPhee, Colin, 16
Mead, Andrew, 32

Mechanical music, 111–12
Memorex, 2
Men, and sound recording. *See* Gender, and sound recording
Menuhin, Yehudi, 24, 34
Michael, George: "Waiting for That Day," 137
Microphone, 23, 37, 40–41, 81–83, 93–94. *See also* Electrical recording
Milhaud, Darius, 15, 108, 112
Miller, Christine, 56
Milli Vanilli, 21, 27
Minimalism, 30
Minneapolis Phonograph Society, 59
Mixer, 115, 117–20, 125
Mixmaster Mike, 224n8
Miyakawa, Felicia, 225n25
"Mood Indigo" (Duke Ellington), 83
M.O.P.: "Ante Up," 126–27
Morgan, Al, 74
Morpheus, 176
Morris, Joan, 28
Motion Pictures Expert Group, 160
MP3, 5, 12, 158, 160–62, 164–66, 169, 170, 172–75, 180, 183–86, 191, 229n5; explained, 160–61; and peer-to-peer networks, 161; vs. traditional recording media, 163–64, 168–69, 170–72, 178
Munchkins (from *Wizard of Oz*), 102
Murphy, Eddie, 128
Music appreciation, 61–67, 68, 71
Music education, 61–67; in colleges and universities, 65–67; in rural American schools, 62–64
Music memory contest, 64–65
MusicNet, 184
Music Store, Apple, 184, 187

Musique concrète, 45–46, 113, 191
Mutter, Anne-Sophie, 27

Napster, 161–62, 168, 174, 175–76
Neue Musik Berlin 1930, 100, 103, 110
Notjustmoreidlechatter (Paul Lansky), 138, 141–45, 156

O'Connor, Sinéad: "I Am Stretched on Your Grave," 137
Oliver, King: "Dippermouth Blues," 79–80
Opera, 16, 19–20, 21, 30, 32, 50, 51, 52, 57, 70, 108, 174
Original Dixieland Jazz Band (ODJB), 72, 73, 77, 81, 211n1
Ory, Kid, 134
Overdubbing, 42, 100–101

"Papa's Got a Brand New Bag" (James Brown), 153
Parker, Charlie, 78
Patti, Adelina, 28
Pearl Jam, 11, 27; "Spin the Black Circle," 11
Peer-to-peer (P2P) networks, 161–62, 167, 169, 170, 172–73, 175, 183, 186; explained, 161; and MP3, 161
Perceptual coding, 160
Performative quotation, 140–41, 152–56
Performing (and performers), and sound recording, 13–14, 20–21, 22–24, 26–29, 32–34, 41–42, 72–84, 85–98, 114–36; and invisibility, 20–21, 22–24, 94–97, 214n27; and jazz, 72–84; and manipulability, 41–42, 115, 118, 125–31; and receptivity, 37–41, 93–94; with recorded music, 70–71, 107, 108; and repeatability, 26–29, 77–81,

94–95; and retrospective listening, 28, 198n61; and tangibility, 13–14, 120; and temporality, 32–34, 74–77
Perlman, Itzhak, 20
Pfeiffer, John, 189, 235n2
Philip, Robert, 2
Phonograph, 8–10, 19, 26, 31, 118, 194n1; as dictation device, 71; as furniture, 54; in home, 54–61; in school, 61–67; terminology, 194n1, 224n9. *See also* Turntable
Phonograph concerto, 107–8
Phonograph duet, 101, 109
Phonograph effect, 3–7, 9, 14, 27, 31, 32, 35, 79–80, 83, 85, 115, 121, 136, 146, 156, 163, 166, 189; defined, 3
Piano Phase (Steve Reich), 30
Picó, 15
Pierné, Gabriel, 35
Pines of Rome (Ottorino Respighi), 108
Pitch correction, digital, 43–44
Player piano, 64, 100, 111, 208n65
Pogacnik, Miha, 27
Porcello, Thomas, 25
Portability. *See* Recorded music, traits
Powell, Maud, 33, 92, 218n33
"Praise You" (Fatboy Slim), 145–51, 156
Pratt, Waldo Selden, 66
Pressplay, 184
Prince: "Gett Off," 123
Projecting phonograph, 19
Public Enemy: "Fight the Power," 151–57, 169, 228n23
"Pump Me Up" (Trouble Funk), 151, 154, 157

QBert, DJ, 118, 119, 134
Quantization, rhythm, 43

○○○

COMPOSITOR   BookMatters, Berkeley

DESIGNER   Victoria Kuskowski

TEXT   11/14 Adobe Garamond

DISPLAY   Akzidenz Grotesk

PRINTER AND BINDER   Sheridan Books, Inc.

○○○